# Journal of the

# Virginia Writers Club

"Spring 2021"

Virginia Writers Club © 2021
P.O. Box 586
Moneta, VA 24121

Editors John A. Nicolay, Marco Faust, & Jim Reynolds

"Spring 2021"

Reach us at VWCJournal@gmail.com

https://www.virginiawritersclub.org/chapters

Chapters

| | |
|---|---|
| Appalachian Authors Guild | Northern Virginia |
| Blue Ridge Writers | Richmond Writers Club |
| Chesapeake Bay Writers | Riverside Writers |
| Hampton Roads | Valley Writers Club |
| Hanover Writers Club | Write by the Rails |

Cover design by J. Nicolay, "Rosslyn, VA"

$7.50

The Virginia Writers Club

*Fostering the art, craft, business, and advocacy of the literary arts throughout the Commonwealth*

## Note from the President

For over one-hundred years, the Virginia Writers Club (VWC) has been providing support and guidance to Virginian writers. Since, that century mark in 2018, the Club has sought ways to add benefits to its writers. This journal offers one of the greatest opportunities and benefits to members.

    As in all things new, there is a learning curve and trial and error. This publication program is a milestone, an opportunity for all members of VWC, whether in a chapter or not, to see their works in print.

    Along with member submissions, the journal is offering a feature, Ask Janell, in which VWC member Janell Robisch answers your questions about writing, publishing, and marketing your works.

    On behalf of VWC, I want to thank John, James, Marco, and Janell as well as the board members and chapter leaders who have supported the journal. Participants should be proud.

    Your club has much to offer. From a writer's profile on the VWC website, a private Facebook group to connect with fellow members, announcement submission forms for sharing publication releases and news on the website, Golden Nib, including the new non-chapter member submission option, scholarship, and the annual symposium, there are many opportunities You help make VWC a vibrant community even during a pandemic.

*Leslie Truex, President*

# Note from the Editors

Adventures portend opportunities, and the unanticipated. Communication, as everyone is apt to say, remains the key to success. One of these, to repeat what I say often, "Check your parachute before you jump off the cliff." Check.

We discovered our communication channel needs to be trim, and focused. We also believe that local chapters play an instrumental role in any VWC program, including this one. This partnership, we discovered, is better served if the journal editors are the first stop for submission, and then we bundle submissions for the local chapter to review, fine tune.

Fortunately, the experience of our editorial team runs deep, and we are collaborative. But everything takes time. Publications run on a schedule. The next journal comes around in July. We encourage members to submit in April-mid May. In time members of the VWC will get the hang of submitting for both the April and July editions early in the year. The editors can then draft both editions and members can focus on the Golden Nib.

This year the Golden Nib will request chapters (and unaffiliated members) to submit their top three placements in the three genres to this journal, and the 1st place winner in the three genres to the Golden Nib coordinator. Publication provides sunshine on the work of our members who may not place 1st to earn recognition through publication. The Golden & Teen Nib prints in November, but the contest has an end of August submission deadline.

John Nicolay, Marco Faust, & Jim Renolds
**Reach us at VWCjournal@gmail.com**

# CONTENTS

## Fiction

## Poetry

# Nonfiction

## Ask Janell

*In this column, experienced publishing professional Janell E. Robisch answers your questions about writing, editing, publishing, interior book design, and book cover design.*

Hello, Virginia Writers!

Welcome to *Ask Janell.* I can't wait to get started with this column. I'm hoping it will be helpful to all the different writers out there who are members of the Virginia Writers Club.

Since we haven't had time to gather questions from the actual membership yet, I'm going to start by answering some common questions that the editors of the journal have given me, and I hope these answers will be helpful to you.

In the meantime, please send your questions to me at janell.robisch@gmail.com with the subject "Ask Janell Column," and I will try to answer as many as I can in future columns.

In this first column, I'm going to start with a very common topic, one with which I'm pretty familiar: self-publishing. Self-publishing is a very common option in today's marketplace not only for fiction writers but also for nonfiction writers and poets.

One of the biggest reasons for this is that self-publishing is open to everyone. Anyone with the right knowledge and/or support can self-publish their work. There are no gatekeepers to pass and no agents or editors to hold you back.

This doesn't mean that everyone can succeed at self-publishing, whatever your definition of success might be.

But let's get more specific. On to our first question:

Self-publishing seems easy, but what are the next steps? How do I get started with self-publishing?

First, self-publishing, like traditional publishing, is far from easy, but it has its advantages, including the opportunity for more income, more author control, and a quicker schedule.

Here is a general breakdown of the steps included in self-publishing. Keep in mind that each one of these steps includes many more nested steps I'd be happy to cover in more depth later, but for brevity's sake, I'm including only the general phases:

First Draft Composition
Editing & Revision: May include any or all of the following steps
Review by alpha readers or a critique group or partner after first draft composition*

- Self-editing
- Review by beta readers after self-editing*
- Developmental editing*
- Copyediting/line editing
- Proofreading (after formatting).
- Formatting (interior book design)
- Cover Design
- Book Description & Metadata Composition
- Publishing
- Launch and Continued Marketing

The steps with asterisks are optional; your need for them will depend on your skill and experience levels and personal preferences.

Self-publishing is a highly customizable process and depending on your skill and comfort level with each step of the process, you can do it all yourself or hire out some or all of it, even the writing (through ghostwriting). Having worked in the publishing industry since the early 1990s and having specialized in working with indie authors since 2015, I do most of the work of self-publishing myself, but even I get someone else to do the copyediting for my books.

I will say that as far as book sales to unfamiliar readers go, your most important elements are an excellent, genre-appropriate book cover and a gripping book description, so you might want to focus your money there if you have a very limited budget.

See you next time! In the meantime, please send me your questions on writing, editing, publishing, interior book design, and book cover design.

Resources

1. "15 Steps to Self-Publish Your Book"
(https://www.helpingwritersbecomeauthors.com/steps-to-self-publish-your-book/), K. M. Weiland, Helping Writers Become Authors

2. "5 Important Steps Before You Self-Publish"
(https://www.thecreativepenn.com/before-you-self-publish/),
Joanna Penn, The Creative Penn

3. "My First Draft Is Done! What's Next? A Manuscript Guide for Indie Authors" (https://speculationsediting.com/archives/first-draft-whats-next/), Janell E. Robisch, Speculations Editing

4. "Opinion: What Makes Readers Buy Books"
(https://selfpublishingadvice.org/opinion-what-makes-readers-buy-books), Maggie Lynch, Alliance of Independent Authors

Do you have a question that you'd like to see answered in a future column? Email it to Janell at janell.robisch@gmail.com with the subject line "Ask Janell Column."

# FICTION

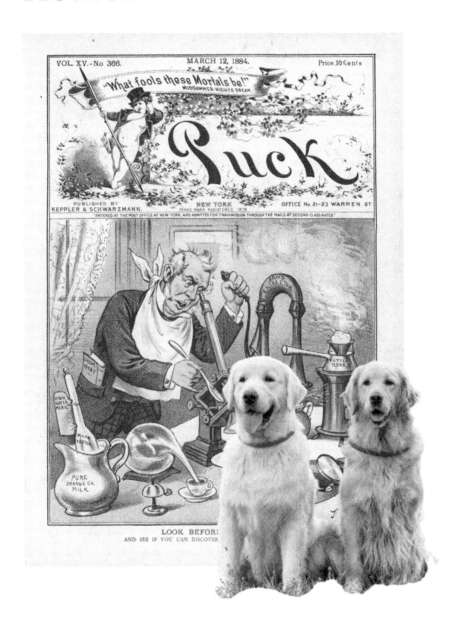

# A PREACHER CAME
by Stephe Seton as told by Bert Seton, *Blue Ridge Writers*

My father grew up in a community fixed to a ridge not far from
the Virginia stretch of the Appalachian Trail. His people were best
described as nonsensical stubborn rock lichens who transformed
themselves into a part of that landscape. I never counted them.
Numbers shifted. About the only time they assembled in one
place would be the Sunday service, and that time would be
celebrated with a picnic whether a preacher showed or not. The
food drew them. Church time was the ante paid.

This church was no more than scrap lumber fixed to
posts, a tin roof, and a small pot-belly stove to burn off the chill. It
smoked fierce. My father said it was intentional to keep the time
in that firetrap to a minimum. It did not have pews exactly, more
split logs with branch legs and troublesome splinters. Most people
carried a cushion of some sort just to stay wounds. Kids endured
them. Services were always marked by some kid hollering, only to
be quieted by an adult with a slap across the head or foot to the

rear.

These days nothing much remains of the eight to ten shelters along a two-mile stretch. My last trip up the rutted mountain fire road was near on ten years ago. I hazard that by the mid-sixties, edging the seventies, the last of those people died or drifted. As a boy I did not see the end, but then we never do at that age.

At sixteen my father determined I would spend two-three, maybe four weeks serving his mother's wood pile and weeding her garden. She cooked with wood in a large cast iron stove. The stove was fired through the day and recharged each morning of the year. It did not take much wood to keep coals. She understood how to pace the timber.

Someone brought cut logs to the village. About the only work around that paid cash was timbering, and with that, the jacks got to keep the tops of the cut trees. They took chainsaws to the logs fashioned rounds, finally loaded them into a four-wheel pickup truck to haul to the ridge. From there the wood moved place to place. Some of the men would split it first to lighten the loads on makeshift wagons.

My summer investment transformed me from a skinny boy inclined to avoid such chores at my parents' home to a muscular boy fit to take on the worst of the school bullies. On the ridge I knew three or so boys near my age, 13 to 17—in that range. Each boy stood right for his age, drank whiskey, smoked if they could, teased girls for favors, and carried on the usual teenager bravado. Girls seemed scarce as their fathers kept a tight watch until they were of marrying age, to local reckoning, about sixteen. I knew all about this as I was scarcely there a week when Mr. Trudweller's girls Mattie, sixteen, so, and Sarah, about twelve, hatched a plan to call me kept. I found the episode foolish entertainment although I tell you, as a sixteen-year-old boy, both girls drew my attention. Anyway. That's another story.

As said, my prison term would be two, three, maybe four weeks, nothing early for good behavior as if I had options to behave otherwise. My grandmother Elsie was never in the mood to monitor me and didn't. She fed me whatever and I bunked in the loft with mosquitoes, black flies and mice. My day settled on splitting the logs, stacking them, breaking for lunch, then the afternoon off. Weeding stole a few hours a week, but not so much as Grandmother invested herself into her patch as well.

"Ripe enough to bury" as they said, I took a makeshift bath on Saturday. Folks around the ridge did not have plumbing inside their log or board houses. Each family owned a large tin tub used for laundry and bathing. Grandmother had a makeshift privacy arrangement where she wrapped a sheet around three trees, but I didn't bother with this. No one ever came around. She was not the sort to pay attention to a naked boy. Cold water justified short stays standing in that tub near a stream. Grandmother might take the chill off with a pail of boiling water. Mostly not. She made her own lye soap from rendered lard. Anyone who has experienced this harsh detergent knows it takes a layer of skin in the scrub. Once a week to bathe allowed the skin to grow back.

By Sunday morning everyone smelled of soap, no more. By Tuesday adults kept their distance from each other. Kids relished their coming of age, like coon dogs on a scent.

My father's father died a year back. I helped bury my Grandfather Seton. I mean, I worked the cemetery hole to accommodate him. My father was called on to say a few words at the time, then the old man took up residence with groundhogs, or whistle pigs as they called them. Such things did not occupy the thoughts of mountain people. Just how life was, and death brought with it escape.

It was on Monday of my second week that my afternoon took me and another local boy near my age off to the woods to hunt down morel mushrooms and ginseng, which could be sold. Joel Tinker stood a few inches over of my height. He was skinny, wore ill-fitting clothes—sizes too large. He cinched his faded, torn jeans with a length of rope as a belt. Still, he tugged at them constantly to keep them at his waist. Often, they fell to the ground giving good inspection to his baggy boxer shorts years past good purpose. I found his appearance amusing, said as much.

He would toss me to the ground to wrestle my jeans down, then to gawk at the boxers I wore, clean and white. No more. I would fill my hands with his blond mop of hair until he squawked, relented only to take me on again as I scooped the soft earth for the ginseng root.

4

I offered, "Sarah Trudweller tells it. You were seen messing with her sister down at the creek near their place." I moved to another likely root.

He worked ground not more than a foot from my hands. "That so?"

"So. A little truth to it?"

"Depends." I pulled the root and brushed off the dirt before placing it in a rucksack. "Her telling or yours?"

He thought about this, visualizing. "Not so close to count. More to nonsense. Mattie's a tease."

I nodded. "That she is. Sarah, too."

"Sarah worth waitin' for? She's prettier, think? Not near of age."

"By reckoning around here, not so far off. Three years, so. You're what? Fifteen?"

"Fifteen plus." He sat down on the dark mulch covering the forest floor and pulled his Zig Zag rolling papers, his Ramback Gold tobacco out of a small cloth sack he carried to that purpose. He was adept at rolling, and offered me the first of his efforts, which I accepted.

With my kitchen friction match ready to ignite I waited for him to prepare a second smoke. When he placed the shaft to his mouth, I lit his, then mine. We puffed to amuse ourselves with curls of smoke for a few minutes.

I pushed the idle topic. "Sarah is a friendly thing. Cute as they come."

He laughed. "Seems like I was past apprizin' their charms. So Sarah got a look at Mattie, me."

"Details didn't land. Sarah seemed to think her father got wind of it. I doubt it. You're still single."

"I tend to stay off that burden. Get myself work with the forest people." It was the only work these men heard of. "You?"

"My thoughts on those girls didn't move past an hour. Mr. Trudweller was hell bent on raising me up as a Christian fit to marry one or the other, maybe both. It was all very funny. He came at me with his old Bible, but the sot tripped, and the good book took flight. He screamed to heaven. "

"Sounds like him. Too much corn, not moderatin' at all. Your grandfather made the best liquor in these parts. Miss that."

Curious I asked, "Who has a still these days?"

"I heard Fosie Charles got your grandfather's still and runs it. He drinks half what he makes and pours the other into the gullets of the old buzzards these parts. You want some? Not near as sweet as Grandfather Seton's batch. That's true."

"If you can lay on some, sure. Tonight?"

"Tonight. At the church past sunset. I'll set a fire, so you know."

He stood, dropped his pants to urinate. I watched him play this way then tossed the butt of my cigarette into his water. Amused, he drowned what ember remained.

By end of the afternoon, we had gathered near twenty-five dollars of the root and enough mushrooms to brighten game stew. One of the men would sell the ginseng and carve off a portion for himself. As I think back, it was Mr. Foster, long dead now with most of them of his time. He purchased a sack of tobacco and several Zig Zags wrappers. Joel and I split these. There was enough left over such I passed some money to my Grandmother as did Joel to his people. That was how money was handled, and Foster knew this to be the case.

That evening when the stew of whatever passed, tin dinnerware cleaned then laid out on a wall-mounted running board near the trestle table, the same my grandfather claimed as his last stand. Grandmother may have grunted. Sunset was her settling time. It was too dark in the house to do much of anything. She might read her Bible a verse, so but quickly drifted off. Her room was a quarter of the house, half the back. Simple accommodations. The bed, now forty some years old held fast despite the mice in residence. She would haul the feather mattress to the yard in spring, open it up, wash the feathers, let them dry, stuff them back and stitch the canvas back together. Year after year she plied the ritual.

I stole away to rendezvous with Joel at the church. The shack rested minutes down the path from Grandmother's place.

Smoke curled off the church chimney. I found Joel inside, stoking the small fire sufficient to ward off the slight chill of the evening. A kerosene lamp stood watch.

We greeted. We fashioned smokes before Joel reached into his sack to extract the pint jar of whiskey. He offered me first pass. I sniffed it, tasted it. As I recollect my grandfather's run set the standard against which all others dared compare. I knew to take it easy, let it rest. Not water in the sense of throwing it back. My father taught me to moderate, although I am sure he was not referring to alcohol.

Some time passed. We concocted stories about the girls we knew or wished we knew. Our season was nigh. Biology being what it is, hidden impulses enslaved us boys, ambitions restrained only by adult watchful eyes.

We drained the jar. I cannot speak for Joel aside from his incessant gibberish and giggling. Much the same said of me, truth of it.

Joel stoked the fire with the end of a stick, feeding it enough to keep it alive. I leaned back against the wall rolling another. The door to the shack opened. Both of us startled.

A voice boomed, "This be a church? Who's praying in God's house?"

It was sufficiently dark such that neither of us could make out the man in the threshold. We stood in the shadows.

I answered the call, "Who are you?"

The man crept toward us, "Pastor Jerald Weams on a call."

*Call?* That made no sense. The man now stood before us. He was tall, thin, dressed in black, heavily bearded. He reminded me of that Russian~Rasputin. I didn't have much to offer. "You traveling these hills at night? How far you travelin'?"

Joel was too much in the grain to move much beyond where he stood. He said nothing.

Weams warmed his hands at the stove. I could not age him precisely for his hairy mask. Say thirty. He spoke to the heat, "Might reside in this church. Any food here abouts?"

I shook my head. "Folks are settled for the night. I suppose you can rest here. Not for me to say one side to the other."

"The Lord provides. You Christian boys?"

"Close enough."

"Your salvation rests on your answer, boy. What's your name?"

"Bertram Seton. This'n Joel."

7

"You boys up here to pray?"

"Might say."

"What's this place called?"

"The church? Most folks refer to it as the meetin' house. No regular minister. Folks like you travel through time to time. Mostly someone around here will read some verse, speak to it, witness."

"So. Wherever three are gathered. How many people live these parts?"

I didn't know exactly. "Varies with the weather. Say twenty. Some summer here. Hard life."

"Good life for believers. The Lord provides, true and certain. I'll bring the message. You'll see. These people have money? For a passing of the plate?"

"You bring a plate? Passing around here involves food. These people couldn't collect twenty dollars to save their souls, certain on that. You might get a meal."

"Where do you live?"

The man struck me as creepy, odd. Not reassuring. He continued to rub his hands. "Near. With my grandmother for the time."

"Near, eh. Then I can stay with your folks to rest. Have a revival. Bless the dead. Anyone need marrying?"

I laughed.

He tightened, "That funny to you?"

"No prospects today. I can't speak to you resting at my grandmother's. You manage the night. Daylight provides more opportunities for conversation."

He walked the room which was the sum of the place. Wind cut through the loose boards. He stalled at a bench, tested it with a hand, then pulled it to the little stove. Joel slid down the wall to settle near the stove. He held his knees as a kind of pillow for his head.

"What's wrong with your friend? What are you boys doing in this church?"

Liquor fortified me, "Not entirely sure you have any claim to us or this building."

Joel stirred. "No claim." He struggled to shape the circumstances.

"Don't test a man of God. Jesus got himself tempted in that wilderness. He sent Satan on his way. That story teach you?"

I didn't want to get into it. "My friend and I are leaving. Morning comes, you'll find your way."

I braced Joel to a shoulder. We left to park the night at my grandmother's place.

He was able to climb into the loft where he fell onto my bed oblivious of location, or how he got there. I did my best to leverage myself next to him. Five pounds more to either of us, we would settle the floor. I would spell out the preacher to my grandmother in the morning, or maybe afternoon considering the damage the alcohol inflicted to my not so intact brain.

Mid-morning came. Joel arose first. I could smell ham cooking.

He said, "Come off this branch. I got to pee."

I stretched, turned off to find my shoes. Joel took the ladder to the main room.

I heard him, "Mornin' Grandmother Seton. Smells good."

As I descended, I saw that she was looking to me. "You boys take to some water and soap 'fore you sit the table."

Joel waited for me just off the porch.

"You boys don't take to risin' for the day." It was that rough minister sitting in a ladder back on the porch. He held a black book.

"No offense pastor but how is it you find yourself sittin' on my grandmother's porch?"

He glowered, "Best bind your tongue. You might feel a touch of the rod. Your grandmother... ." He glanced to the door as if it was transparent and he could wave at the old woman.

Joel and I took to the back of the log house at the edge of the trees to pee, then to the tub to wash. The cold water snapped me clear.

When we returned to the house, Weams sat to the head of the trestle table. Grandmother placed a plate of biscuits on the table next to a second plate of fried ham slices. Her ham tended to tough, fit to cobble a shoe. A bowl of red eye gravy steamed. She poured Joel and me coffee. Weams waved her off with "The good Lord has provided a feast. Food sufficient."

9

I reached for a biscuit. Weams squinted to inspect my behavior. "Let us thank the Lord for this magnificent meal." *Magnificent?*

He launched into a recitation wavering between repentance and gratitude. He drummed on ten minutes until Grandmother coughed and placed "Amen" in his lap. He appeared to be taken aback as Joel and I watched him. Joel grabbed my leg to jostle me into laughter.

Weams snagged three biscuits which he broke apart to accept the greasy gravy, nothing more than pan drippings. His fork lifted several slices of the ham to the plate. "Mighty good Grandmother."

Grandmother stood to the side, as the custom in these hills required the cook to wait until those at the table had eaten. She said to the man, his course beard taking a share of crumbs, "How's that you found your way to us?"

He looked toward her. "Like Paul, I travel to those in need of the word. How many folks here?"

With a look of surprise, as if she never took the time to count them, she lost herself in reckoning. He went back to the biscuits to clear the plate. She followed the question, "Varies some. Twenty, say with children. The men work the timber such that they move and camp with the crews.

Might not see some for weeks to pass." She looked at the empty plates. *Might he lick the grease?* "You thinkin' I should batch up more biscuits?"

He lifted the splotched blue enamelware serving plate, "I'm set. The boys et their fill? What are you boys, somewhere fourteen on?" He didn't expect an answer. "These boys found themselves in the church last night. You suppose they prayed or some other mischief? Not good to leave boys to their devices. They tend to spoil themselves. That's how they are. You boys messin' with each other?"

I had no notion to his text.

Grandmother took little interest. Idly she repeated, "Messin'? What's your drift there, parson?"

"Noticing. These boys are alone in that church, not lookin' any steady. They slept tight together. Takes them in the wrong direction. That's sayin'. Be mindful, Grandmother. The

flesh is weak. Satan works on children so. Get's them to actin'
ways Hell welcomes. We all need to be watchin'. The day of
judgment is near to hand. You boys messin'? The Lord knows.
He's got an eye to you, sure." He went on for a few more minutes.
Joel cast side glances to me, to Grandmother, while the same,
avoiding Weams. I watched the character pick at his beard.
*Messin'? What was he talking about?*

Joel broke the cadence, "I got to get home. Thank you for
the breakfast, such, good." He took me by the arm. "Pace with
me."

Joel's log home stood close on a quarter mile across the
ridge. His father would be logging. His two sisters, both just
annoying girls about seven to eight, so, occupied his mother.

As we walked, taking time to roll two cigarettes and light
them, he said, "We got some time. You want to try this messin'?"
He laughed hard.

"What was that crazy minister talkin' on? You understand
his intent?"

He blew a cloud of smoke to the front and walked into it.
"Naw. Must be somethin' terrible as he carried on so. I sure ain't
messin' around him no matter. Can't think he would ever stop
his yamerin'. You think he is stayin' at your grandmother's?"

I shuddered to the thought of it. Sharing my mattress
with that filthy man? I said, "I'll stay with you until he's off.
Grandmother won't mind any. I can still work her firewood. Your
mother be good with that?"

"I reckon so. You put up with my sisters she'll reward you
high. I can say that. You spell her those girls."

I tossed the butt to the ground and peed on it. He
followed suit.

Later that afternoon I took to splitting the wood. Weams
was not there. My grandmother brought a bowl of biscuits
drenched with honey she had gathered that winter from wild
hives. I asked her if Weams was staying.

"Seems he has no options. You share your bed."

"No offense, Grandmother. I'll stay with Joel. I can't
share a bed with Pastor. He sets me to unease."

She nodded. "Eats like no meal will come again." She
watched me finish the biscuits. "He tells me he'll do the service

come Sunday then move along."

"Sunday?" I counted days. "Joel will take me. What did he mean by messin'?"

"That you boys would get naked."

"Naked? So? I seen Joel naked many times."

"Never you mind his words, then. Some folks anticipate the worst and find it no matter what it looks like. Understand?"

Not really. Later in life, yes to be true I did understand. My father said, "Some people need a peg for their hats."

ℰꙨ

Saturday came. I bathed at Joel's. His sisters hung around as we did, giggling, dancing. When their time came, we left them. Mrs. Tinker washed our clothes that morning. We both wore cutoffs not fit for traveling beyond the periphery of the house. By the afternoon, our clothes would dry.

We spent the time at an artesian spring, smoking, chattering about girls, reliving our thoughts on Mattie and Sarah, embellishing our memories to test each other's credulity. In time we both stretched out on the grass to sleep.

Weams woke us with the toe of his boot, "You boys down here messin'?"

Joel had his limit, "Say we were. What's any of this to you?"

A swift kick of the boot to Joel's side. He cursed with the reward of a second kick and a damnation pledge. I stood, then pushed Weams such he lost his footing and stumbled into the narrow stream, no more than two feet wide, water not seeming to move. Weams twisted to catch himself, to no avail. Bewildered, he settled in the water. "You earned a thrashing, certain." Weams would be no match for us. We were stronger and faster.

I cautioned Joel, "Best to leave him be."

Joel pointed a menacing finger to Weams, "Stay your distance. You'll see your ass in the valley you touch me or my friend again." Boys used the ass-in-the-valley threat often as that place every boy understood. The ultimate dare to knock a kid so fiercely the boy would roll to the valley.

To clear any doubts, I added, "I don't know your way.

You've got no place here."

Joel and I left. When he was out of sight, we stepped off the trail. Joel said, "Let's mess with a smoke."

⌘

I heard Mr. Tinker come in late and talk without discernable words to his wife. Mrs. Tinker cooked up a kettle of dried beans, potatoes, wild herbs, sweetened with a slice of fat for the church social. By now everyone likely knew about the itinerant preacher. I imagine most of them saw it as a carnival sideshow, like the bearded lady or the eight-foot giant or the two headed snake resting in a jar of moonshine.

By seven Sunday morning I went to my Grandmother's. Weams parked on the porch, appearing to study the text. He raised an eyebrow as I approached. Neither of us offered a word.

Grandmother would not make Sunday breakfast anticipating the feast to come. A plate of fried rabbit sat to the side. Church fare. I pulled a handful of crackers from a tin to slather with butter and mountain blueberry jam. She kept the butter on the running board until it soured, then it went to some other purpose.

She asked after the Tinkers. I told her they seemed the same. "She washed your clothes, I see."

"More to serve Joel, I imagine."

She offered the rare smile. "'spect this is so. The boy could use some mending. Pastor tells me to mind your soul. Your soul in trouble?"

I swallowed my cracker. "Not so much as noted. You have thoughts on this man?"

She glanced toward the door, then whispered, "His time to move, all I can say."

⌘

Before heading inside to take seats to be had near family, women sat their covered food on trestle tables placed that morning. Everyone had long ago staked their place, and each knew not to stray to the sitting bench. A scowling Weams stood at the front.

13

Children settled, gossip subsided, eyes turned to the *source de notre apprehension.*

He spoke, deep, sonorous, "This day we glorify God. You sinners come to repent. To open yourselves to the mercies of a God determined you off to Hell. Repent of your sins..." He drummed his dark, foreboding view on our worthiness to see God in his glory. Satan looked promising thirty minutes in.

Joel sat next to me as I did not come enough to own any bench real estate. I whispered, "I'm thinkin' hell can't be that bad."

He leaned in, "Can we mess around?"

"Can't see a reason not to."

Weams barked at us, made mention of us messin' around, then back to his retelling of the entire gospel, *Mark* to *John.* He read from the text interminably if only to keep the silence of his voice at bay, self-patronizing, attached to rhythm. Occasionally someone would slip out to tend the lunch, make sure no racoons without religion arrived.

An hour down, Weams called the congregation to follow him to the river to be cleansed of their sins and redeemed in the blood—or water as the case may be. The nearest river as I recalled ran to the bottom of a gorge at the edge of the church property. No child could easily find a way to the river's shore, and while you could peer over the edge to witness the thread of water, to step into that water required a circuitous, rambling trip down the mountain, then another hour to find it by road. I summer fished it many times giving up dawn to settle the day at dusk.

Exactly what Weams intended, aside from messing with us, remained for speculation. Perhaps seeing the river sufficed. He broke into song, "As I went down in the river to pray, studying about that good old way and who shall wear the starry crown? Good Lord show me the way!"

Everyone knew this spiritual, so when Weams got down the list of kin who would join in the caravan to the river all present joined in, lesser or more. He raised a hand to quiet the eighteen, so, gathered.

"Join me in the waters of life. Who among you surrenders to the Lord?" He turned to pick up a bucket of water, the river's metaphor, but his grasp was shorter than his reach. He tumbled forward, over the edge, down into the ravine some thousand feet give or take, mind you, not a straight shot, but close enough.

I expected him to fly up. Perhaps he did as well. All stood motionless for a moment. Kind of a magician's trick I suppose. That he should walk around a near tree and say, "Ta da!"

A couple of the men leaned over the edge. One said, "You see him? Down couple hundred feet I'd say. You?"

The other nodded, "Give or take, close. He sure ain't going anywhere. You remember the time old man Johnson took that step? Took us three days to find him, cinch him to a mule."

*Mule? What mule?*

Everyone took turns peering into the abyss. At some of this round robin spectating, my grandmother said, "Not wasting a good meal. Let's take the time."

That was how it ended. Pastor Weams was not of our people. Not to make more of it than any death might be regarded, no thought pushed more than palaver for a day to three. Everyone wanted Grandmother's reminiscing about the short time he sheltered and ate three times his portion. The women clucked their tongues, nodded their heads. I could have filled in blank spaces with the down to the stream face-off, Joel and I drinking corn in the church, messing around whatever. I took a pass. It just didn't seem to scale my Grandmother's retelling.

Before the week came around, everyone returned to routines. I peered down into that harrowing pit a couple times. I laid eyes on a Weams' broken speck on the rocks below. Joel and I sat on that precipice, our legs dangling, although truth known, we could have stepped off as scrub trees and rocks provided some insurance. We rolled papers and smoked. No corn this time.

By the third day the Weams' speck disappeared. No more to it.

To this day I think about that strange pastor and what he intended with his admonishments. Messin'? I think I have that figured out.

*Bert & Joel*

# FAMILY INHERITANCE
by Pamela K. Kinney, *Richmond Chapter*

"Sam Danvers, where were you last night?"
I looked at my wife, Tessa.

No way could I tell her the truth about where I'd been all last night. First, because she would think I'm lying, before she realized I believed what I'd said, that I was nuts. Until the second full moon tonight.

Few women can say they're married to a weresheep.

She stepped closer. "What's going on, Sam? Ever since your father passed away last month, you've not been acting like yourself. I suspect you've been keeping a secret."

"Only an old man's rambling about being sorry for keeping me at arm's length for years. He just poured his," my voice broke, at almost saying the "W," word, and amended, "*love* to me." I added, "What did you think he said to me? That I'm the proprietor of a family curse?" I tried to laugh but couldn't.

"No, of course, not." She kissed me, and I relaxed into it, loving her.

Maybe I could tell her. I hoped she wouldn't be horrified to discover what I became at the full moon. It's not like I shifted into a monstrous wolf.

*No, just a mutton shifter. Tell her that any kids we have will inherit becoming weresheep at your death. If nothing else, she can sheer you in the spring and be able to knit booties and little sweaters for the potential lambs.*

I couldn't tell her. Maybe after this full moon ended.

Tired after my first night of the sheep, I crawled into bed after showering and slept for a couple of hours. After I awoke and dressed, I got on my computer in the home office to search for any information about weresheep.

Besides the famous werewolf, I found people turned into tigers, lions, leopards, jaguars, bears, and foxes. Even

17

tales of curses or people magicked into dragons, dogs, cats, frogs, but not one sheep story.

I leaned back in the chair, remembering the talk between my father and me. He left my mother on my sixth birthday, and we ever saw him again. For all I knew, he was dead. Then I received a call from the nursing home in the next town over. He was dying, and he wanted to talk to me. I didn't want to go, but Tessa said I should.

I found a man who'd always figured significantly in my memories now nothing more than a shrunken old man.

"Hello, son," he said in a cracked voice. "Take a seat."

I remained standing. "Okay, old man say what you need to tell me. Personally, I don't care a flying fig for any excuses you might give me why you left Mom and me, or where you were all these years."

Tears filled his eyes. "I'm passing on to you what my father passed on to me just before you turned six."

"What? You're passing on money, stocks, bonds, some family piece of jewelry?"

"No, once I die, you inherit becoming a weresheep."

*He's bonkers.* "Yes, you are giving me something- bullshit. I'm not buying into your crap. Weresheep. Why not werewolf? That sounds scarier."

He struggled to sit up, failing. "Do you think I wanted this curse? Your grandfather spouted to me about some he-witch cursing an ancestor of ours when he was caught cheating at cards. Our idiot many greats grand pappy said his boss made him do it. The witch told him since he had the herd mentality, he deserved becoming a member of the barnyard."

Father began a round of coughing that turned into choking. He fought to breathe.

I bolted to the door. "Nurse!"

Just as one ran into the room and to his side, he died. A white, wispy cloud left him and slipped into me through my nostrils, my mouth, my ears, and other unmentionable openings. I could feel it inside me, and I cried out, brushing past the doctor who'd stepped inside, and kept going until I reached my car in the parking lot. Feeling numb and sitting behind the wheel, something overcame me, and I opened my mouth.

"Baaaaaa."

Did I just cry out like a sheep? It's not true. Father was looney. I'm not a weresheep, and neither was he.

Later, I met with Father's lawyer to settle his affairs and find out what he'd left me in his will. He hadn't much, a watch, ten dollars, a few bits of clothing in his closet and chest of drawers, a broken TV set, and furniture. I sent all but the money to the local thrift store. But I couldn't get rid of the family curse by donating it to the thrift store. That would remain with me until I had a child to inherit the curse when I died.

I gritted my teeth. No way should any child of mine go through this. I needed to tell Tessa. Maybe she would agree to not having kids. Again, she might leave me thinking I was crazy, or believe me and run for the hills.

I made dinner to soften the blow of what I would tell Tessa and almost grabbed two lamb chops in the freezer to defrost when I understood if I ate one of those that would make me a cannibal. Instead, I made meatloaf, baked potatoes, and candied carrots. Tessa didn't say a word as she ate. I waited until she finished. I couldn't eat.

When she'd finished, I said, "Tessa."

"Yes?"

"Honey, I'm a weresheep."

She laughed, but when I didn't laugh with her, she stared at me. "You're serious, aren't you?"

I nodded. "That's why my father had me come to the nursing home, that I would take the mantle of sheep shifter from him at his passing."

"Weresheep?"

She didn't belittle me or call me crazy. To be honest, she sounded like she believed me.

Before I could go into my spiel about not having kids, she

said, "I thought I smelled something different about you when we first met." She leaned back in her chair. "My kind have been eating humans for centuries. But I love lamb better than human meat." Hunger gleamed in her eyes, and I watched in shock as her pearly whites grew longer and sharper until they crowded her mouth.

My heart spiraled into overdrive, and I bolted upright, my chair crashing to the floor. Tessa rose to her feet too, and her shoes cracked apart, large, hairy feet springing free. She giggled as her lovely, painted, manicured nails lengthened into terrifying, sharp claws, still colored hot pink.

"I smell your fear, sheep husband. I'll hold off the complete metamorphosis until you shift. I want to hunt the sheep, not the man. Can't wait to taste your lamb chops."

Unable to stop the change, I metamorphosed into the ram and bolted out of the house and into our backyard. Even with my horns and hooves, I found myself no match for my wolfish wife when she completed her full shift. She leaped upon me before I made it around the corner of our house and sank her fangs into my throat, cutting off my bleating.

# DEAR JOHN, I'VE FALLEN FOR A DOG
by Jane Harrington, *Valley Chapter*

*Excerpt from the upcoming novel In Circling Flight (Brighthorse Books) with permission from the author and publisher.*

It's Sirius. That's what I named him. I got him on the midsummer morning when that star first rises in the pitch dark before dawn, marking the time of the dog days. Always thought that idiom was about heat so pervasive that it made dogs lie around for days, but when we came out here to the Blue Ridge, I learned it was really about the year's first sighting of Sirius the dog star—the brightest in Canis Major, the brightest next to the sun. It seems you just find out the reasons for things in the country. I don't know why.

Set on seeing the rising, I got up at five o'clock that day. Hadn't missed it in the nine years since we moved here, always spying it just when the *Farmers Almanac* said I would, a pinpoint of a thing, sort of orange at first and pushing itself out of one of those mountains like a tiny spark from a volcano. Easy to pick out, that dog star, following as it does the hunter Orion, in a straight line with the three stars of his belt—all I could ever see of that constellation growing up, the rooftops and streetlights in the way. But there's more of that hunting god up there, and a weapon or two, all so clear in the night sky hanging over these hills. Remember when we were still camping, the house not yet under roof? The shadow from the tent was so crisp, a black box on the field. I shook you awake, said, "Johnny, is there an athletic complex or parking lot next to us?" And you shot right up, worried, I guess, that that might be true, that the city lights had followed us somehow and were glaring at us as we slept. But then you laughed—that laugh that used to find a bit of humor in just about anything that had a way of skipping around inside me—and you pointed to the full moon, shining like the sun, only in gray scale. "I can see the berries on the autumn olive," I whispered. "At *night.*"

Not so for Sirius's emergence this year. The mist was so

thick I couldn't see anything in the sky, or a persimmon tree in the field, or even the lights on that cell tower put up on Chestnut Hill last year. So I went out to the SPCA shelter, later when they opened, and got my dog star. He's big, with silky fur, all black but for a fine blaze down his neck like a stream of milk, pure and white, forever dripping from his mouth. He's a good boy. Well, in dog years, older than a boy. Maybe in his thirties. Which makes him the perfect replacement for you, so there's no need for you to be here anymore.

When I was asked by the man at the shelter, I told him that, yes, I had a fence. You'd say, *That s a lie, Leda,* and I'd say, *No, I m just being precise. We have a fence around the goat yard, don t we?* I said that to Sirius on the way home, in fact, his taking your part of the conversation in my mind. "If he'd asked if I had a fence around the property that could keep a dog from running off, I would have told him no." Sirius was sitting in the passenger seat, freed from that cage where I'd first seen him with his head between his paws and a faraway look in his caramel-colored eyes. He'd lived in the shelter for some months and was probably getting near to the day he'd be euthanized. But he didn't know that, and I sure would not tell him. I kept up talking about other things, because I think it calmed him to hear my voice. "If he'd just made himself clear from the start so I could understand what he was all about," I said to Sirius, "I'd have told him where that fence was." From the time I pulled out of the parking lot, he'd been yipping forlornly, and I didn't like the sound of that. It was terrible, familiar. I knew he was missing someone. Maybe someone from the shelter, but more likely that old person who'd given him up when she moved away to live with her daughter. You see, I asked about his background. I didn't want a dog that seemed perfectly fine now, but was holding some form of trauma inside him that was waiting to spring out when it was too late. After, I was already in love.

He's not going to run off. I knew that from the first night I had him, when I was out on the porch, sipping my iced coffee. Not sure why I do that, because it keeps me up and working things out in my head half the night. But the taste is wonderful. Never really enjoyed that wine you were making in the spring, just drank it with you because it was nice to do that, to talk on the porch and watch the sunset. "To the perfect red," you would say, toasting whatever you'd concocted. "This isn't it yet, but I'm going to make the perfect red." That cabernet from those grapes you bought up along the CCC road built during the Great Depression had come the closest, you thought. It tasted okay, I guess, but it was kind of thick. The word *viscous* came to mind, but I didn't say that because I figured it might seem an insulting choice of an adjective and then you would stop talking for the rest of the evening. The word stuck in my head, I suppose, because it popped right out that afternoon I was clipping hooves in the goat yard. There's still a bloodstain on the pine slat from where I grabbed the top rail and leapt over. I'd nicked my fingertip with the clipper when I heard the sound. You'd think the hard rains would have washed that away by now.

Sirius, though—I was telling you about that first evening he was here. He was sitting tall and pretty at the edge of the porch, looking out to the tree line, and he spotted a buck and shot out after him, his hackles raised. I jumped up, scared and blaming myself for not keeping him on a leash so soon after bringing him home, and I have to admit I yelled out, "Come back, John!" It was his first night, remember, and I wasn't yet used to calling him by name. I don't make that mistake anymore. I want you to know that. Anyway, I didn't even need to give him chase because once that deer had disappeared into the neighbor's woods, Sirius came prancing back, all proud-like, and he sat again at his post at the corner of the porch, looking out, scanning. Protecting me, protecting this place. You see, he's not running off.

I don't think there's any hunting dog in him. He used to fear the shooting that goes on out in those woods. First time he heard one of those rifle blasts, he scurried into a corner of the living room, tail between his legs. So I brought him up next to me on the couch, our Target special that arrived here by UPS on the very day we moved into the house, and I hugged him to make him feel better. He licked my face for a long time. He likes the taste of salt. Now every time we hear those gunshots, he comes to find me and sit with me wherever I am. Could just be all about the salty treat, but it still feels like a loyal act on Sirius's part.

He looks after the goats, too, patrolling the fence lines. I don't let him inside their yard, because I'm afraid he'd just try to chase the poor things off, and, well, there's really nowhere for them to go. He used to bark incessantly at them, but I'm training him not to, using the command "Leave it!" that I read about in Cesar Millan's dog-whispering book. It works pretty well most of the time, like when I want to shoo him away from the step in front of your workshop, but out at the goat yard I have practically yell it if I want him to calm down. Most of the time, that is. A couple of months ago there was a turn of the weather, and big yellow poplar leaves, speckled with brown, were drifting down from the little copse of trees inside the fence. They were watching the leaves, the goats, then eating them where they landed. I expected Sirius to get all worked up, figuring he'd want to get in there to see what those things falling from the sky were, to catch them before they hit the earth. But he was as mesmerized by the scene as I was, as the goats were, like we were all witnessing a miracle. Manna from heaven, for the Israelites left out in the wilderness.

Sirius goes on long walks around the farms and fields with me, always staying near enough to turn and see me from wherever he gets to exploring. And it's uncanny, but no matter what kind of convoluted circuit I come up with to hike, he always knows when we're heading back home. I can tell, because he picks up the very next stick he can find and bounces along with it, head high. He wants me to throw it once we get up to the house, and then he runs after it as fast as any dog I've seen. Every few days or so, I gather up what he collects. I won't be needing to search for much kindling this year. See what a help he is? I've already made a pile over there by your workshop, next to that enormous stack of wood you split last spring.

Seemed like you'd never stop hacking away at those logs, getting another truckload each time, you'd finish up with one batch. "Shoot, Johnny, how much wood do we need for one winter?" I'd asked you. But you just shrugged, so I passed it off as maybe a bodybuilding thing or a release of anxiety, because I didn't know then that you were set on leaving, that you would be gone from here before summer's first fireflies resurrected themselves from their grassy tombs. You wouldn't be aware of this, but your woodpile is now adorned with a piece of that metal sculpture you put on the roof of your workshop. The top of it blew off in a freak windstorm in July that tore across the fields, snapped tall trees in its path right in half—a "derecho," that weatherman who wears a bow tie called it, some kind of weather system that had never ventured up from the southern hemisphere before. The clattering on the workshop roof was so loud and sudden that my heart almost stopped. I think that's when I first got the idea to go to the SPCA.

Doesn't look like a phoenix to me anymore, that sculpture. Not even one with its head blown off. Just looks like a welded-together scrap pile from the dismantling of an old still which, of course, it is. I really thought your moonshine-making was impressive, as if we were stepping back into a time when those squiggly tubes and burping liquids were common contraband in the hollows around here. Had a few good field parties, didn't we? Invited those fiddlers, and we started learning to play that old-time music ourselves, to be a part of keeping that Appalachian tradition from dying out. But maybe that whole direction of looking—to the past—was part of the problem. Got your head wrenched the wrong way. And no amount of log-splitting or metal welding or woodcrafts or any of your other pursuits were going to yank it back where it needed to be. Especially not the search for "the perfect red," one of your last quests in that workshop of tools and benches and drawers still filled up with the many ways you tried to get things right.

"You're projecting, Leda," you said when I insisted that sculpture was a phoenix. And I asked you if you'd ever heard of a thing called artistic genius, because regardless of your intention it looked incredibly like one, its bird head pointing straight up into the blue. I needed it to be a phoenix, John. That's the thing. You were just so distraught that day you took the still apart, repeating over and over how you were sure you were turning into him. "Did he make moonshine?" I asked you, and you thought I was trying to be funny at an inappropriate moment, but I wasn't. It just took some time to understand what you were telling me, those things that happened there and happened there in that apartment where you grew up. Took a while to sink in, is all to make sense of it. Then a lot of things made sense: like why you didn't want us to have children, like why you wanted us to live somewhere and somehow so completely the opposite of what you'd ever known. "Let's call it Way Out Farm," you'd suggested, "a double entendre, because it's way out of the city and this land is our way out of the grind." I had pointed out that it was actually a triple entendre, because weren't we "way out" people? In time, you proved a fourth meaning to be true.

As I kept telling you when you were taking your hammer to the still, you were merely erratic that night before. "Loved ones lie about it," you insisted, this seeming to be an area of particular expertise for you. Which put us in a box, it did. "Just because a person gets drunk once in a while, even blacks out, doesn't mean he's hurt anyone," I said to you. "And just because the face you are seeing in the mirror is getting more like his, well, that's simply the way physical traits are over time, that's heredity." And I suggested we be the undead and throw away the mirrors. But you accused me again of not taking things seriously. I surely was, John. I surely was. And I told you and told you, you were beautiful, and you didn't have a violent bone in your body. But even if you wanted to believe that, I imagine those little ones had already started twitching in your index finger.

Sirius likes to stand at the door of the house, looking out through the glass. He can see your wood stack from that spot. He doesn't seem interested in the fallen pieces of metal splayed over top of it but keeps his eyes on the field mice darting in and out of the crevices between the logs. When he whines, I let him out to chase them. He gets one every once in a while, and if he's hungry, he eats it. One time I glimpsed him cracking a skull in his jaw, and it had such an effect on me, I'm real careful to look away now. But I figure it's good having a mouser around a farm, seeing as he ran off all the feral cats, thinking them a danger to me, I guess. He digs for gophers and groundhogs, too, with little success. If I took him out regularly at night when they were more active, he'd probably fare a lot better, but I've been jittery about walking in the dark since you've been gone.

Had to be outside late last night, though. Sirius was

pacing in front of the door and just wouldn't stop, like he needed to go. I was up anyway, full of coffee and trying to work things out in my head, so I figured I'd take him out, just in front. Didn't need a flashlight because it was one of those full moon nights, or near so. While I waited for him to poke around, I scanned the sky for the dog star. The whole constellation of Canis Major had climbed up over the mountains by the time we were out, so I connected the dots in my mind to make up the triangular head and stick body and tail of the big dog. "See there, Sirius, your star is just about where his rabies tag should hang," I said. And then I saw the big bear. And I don't mean Ursa Major. I mean, a real bear. It was on all fours, sniffing around the step of your workshop, and Sirius was looking right at it, his muscles as taut and ready as I'd ever seen them.

"A bear is set on destroying you. It's useless trying to chase it off, and screaming or running away won't work either," you'd said on a walk we took in the woods one night. "Play dead in order to survive." Frightening, that. Rang in my head every time we took a night walk from then on, and rang in my head last night with Sirius, and even rang in my head that afternoon I'd been clipping the goats 'hooves. I knew, of course, that there had been no bear in your workshop that day, and that you weren't playing anything. But I suppose you hold tight to any little scrap of what you so desperately don't want to lose. I'd already deluded myself into thinking that that skinny stream that had seeped from floor to step in the time it took me to race over was from a broken bottle of the viscous cabernet. Even while I knew it wasn't. Even while I knew it was your perfect red. Still a fine dark blaze, forever dripping on the pale granite. About all that's left of you.

Caffeine and adrenaline must be one potent combination, because lightning fast, I grabbed Sirius by the collar just before he sprang. Keeping my eyes steady on the bear, who was rising on his back legs by then, I yelled, "Leave it! Leave it! Leave it!" and I pulled Sirius against his will, all eighty-some pounds of him, and we fell through the door and into the house before the bear got heading in our direction. I lay there on the floor, my heart thumping as hard as it had that day you left me, the pain so strong I thought my sternum would break. I held

Sirius as close as I could for a long time. He was making the funniest sounds, his mouth moving in an odd sort of way, like he was trying to talk to me. Trying to calm me. To stop my awful yipping.

No, I didn't follow any of your advice regarding the bear. Admit, survival did not exactly turn out to be one of your areas of expertise. If I hadn't done what I did, my companion would be gone for trying to keep me safe. I didn't want that, John. I never wanted that. Don't worry yourself, though. I will keep to the house at night. I've started making wood fires already, even though the solstice—your usual date for toasting the first fire—is just nowhere. The bursts of sparks from the logs, not fully seasoned yet, made Sirius anxious initially. His eyes would dart here, then there, as if tracking meteors. But now he just stretches out and sleeps, or watches lazily, his head between his paws. He doesn't much get that sad, faraway look in his caramel-colored eyes anymore. Perhaps he's forgotten about the one who left him behind at the SPCA. Or maybe he's just forgiven her. I kneel next to him sometimes on the hearth, his shadow pooled strangely around him from the bright flames lapping the sooty walls of the firebox. I rest my cheek against his side for as long as it takes to feel a pulse or a dream shudder, any sign that he is alive. Then I drop a new log on the fire before the lights of dying embers go out.

The *Farmers' Almanac* is predicting a mild winter. And while that is good news from a practical standpoint, Sirius not likely much with a shovel, I wish for snow. The kind that comes quietly in the night, filling you up in your sleep so you know it's out there before you even open your eyes. The kind that washes out everything, the way the sun erases the stars at dawn. "Silent snow, secret snow," you'd whisper when we'd wake to that world, alluding to your favorite short story while we kept each other warm and gazed through the pane to the persimmon and autumn olive covered in white, like ghosts caught in mid-dance in the field.

# NIRVANA
by G. W. Wayne, *Blue Ridge Writers*

Bud walked from bedroom to the kitchen and back. Repeatedly. Isolated in his small rancher in the woods on Saturday as the unpredicted ice storm had delicately lathered branches with paralyzing, lacy froth.

The weather gurus had forecast a cold rain.

First, a simple glint on limbs in the dull light of the gray storm had appeared. Then a thickening embrace swelled to bend twigs, branches and eventually limbs. Bud had backed from his dining-room window as the glaze had grown.

Could his roof hold a tree's direct hit? If not, whom would he contact first? His insurance agent? A roofer? The fire department?

Hours spent pacing.

Stops for a cup of coffee. A nibble on one of Angie's gingerbread men.

Another coffee.

The soft patter of the freezing precip abated. The trees about his home were holding. Even the one he and Angie, his dear friend, had remarked looked ripe for a fall. An old, tall one on his neighbor's property. Right at its periphery. Angie said it was a pin oak. She could tell by its bark.

Bud doubted that. It looked too tall for a pin oak. Too scraggly. Not spread out like it should. But he wasn't going to argue with Angie. He had met her just last year at church. He loved her. She brightened his life just as he had despaired of emptiness after abrupt widowerhood.

They had texted during the storm. Sparingly. Conserve batteries. She was safe. That was good.

Evening came. Close to the winter solstice, light failed quickly and by five thirty Bud's dining-room window walled up black matte silence. He relaxed. Made dinner. A bowl of homemade chili over rice. Decaf green tea. Ice cream.

A sudden crack interrupted Bud's first spoonful of salted cherry vanilla whirl. Whistling rush. Tumbling of branches shattering. He flinched. Stood motionless.

Then Bud realized he had felt no impact onto his house

from the delayed treefall. Still, it might have caused some damage to his roof? Or gutters? Or nearby shed? Or maybe the picnic table where he and Angie had sat enjoying one of her veggie lasagnas only two weeks ago on an anomalously warm December day in Fluvanna?

Bud weighed waiting until morning to assess the matter. When he could see clearly. When much of the ice might be melted. The temperature was forecast to rise to several degrees above freezing overnight.

But if he waited, and he had roof damage, that might mean water leaking in.

If he looked now, he could call a roofer. Get at least a tarp put on, despite the late hour. Mitigate the peril. At his age, he would not risk clambering on a slick roof.

I'm pretty well off, Bud consoled himself. But I want money for Angie and me to take a nice, long excursion post-Covid. Not to replaster ceilings. He and his loving friend had imagined meandering about the Greek isles between bites of that eggplant-noodle-based dinner she had brought him those several weeks back. Delicious. The food and the hoped-for adventure.

Angie. What a smile.

He had to look, although it would be dangerous. Not even starlight above. He could not neglect his property. He had to know just what had happened. Exit out my back porch, thought Bud. The railing is sturdy. The planks up against the house aren't frozen. Safest way to start.

It did not take Bud long to exhale and feel tension leave his shoulders while he held onto the slats and leaned over the eastern end of his back porch, shining his flashlight onto the long trunk of the fallen tree. It was that suspicious, leaning old monster he and Angie had observed. It had come close to his home, landing about ten feet away. There was a mess of thick, finger limbs splayed about his patio. The trunk lay whole across his backyard. It had missed his shed. Grazed his picnic table. Everything looked okay.

Back inside, Bud called his landscaper. Yes, Jonas assured him. He could saw it up and haul it off. On Monday. That was fine with Bud. Jonas had already taken down a few problem trees for him. One after a microburst last year. Bud liked that Jonas cut up the wood and donated it to locals for firewood. There were a number of poor in Fluvanna. His gardener also employed his cousins and a brother. That also sat well with him.

As Bud relaxed in bed later, he reasoned the expense he would voluntarily bear... it was his neighbor Gideon's tree, after all... might be balanced by a friendlier relationship between them. That would be welcome.

Bud reflected on Gideon. Such a scowler. Bud only knew his name because he would occasionally take some misdelivered mail from his box and walk it up to the man's front porch, ring his doorbell, and hand it to him.

Never a smile from the recluse, just a quick grunt and a swipe at the proffered envelope. Often just junk mail. "Hi, neighbor," Bud would say.

Gideon would look at Bud crossly, then close the door.

The last time, Bud noticed Gideon had installed one of those doorbells with a camera in it. "Just leave it on the porch chair," he had said gruffly through the door.

Bud had leaned close to the device, smiled, and said, "Sure, here you go. Have a good day." As he did so, he noticed a small sign in the window next to the door.

Bud had sighed, shaken his head, and wandered slowly back to his front yard to trim a few cracked and bent stalks from his hibernating butterfly bush. The swallowtails had been abundant last summer.

Turning his head back and forth on his pillow later as he closed his mind to his sullen neighbor, Bud floated briefly in that dark, weightless drift from consciousness to slumber.

Several times that night, he dreamt of Angie.

࿇

By morning, much of the glaze on the trees about Bud's half-acre had melted away. The grass and macadam were wet, but walkable. He waited until after breakfast, so as not to wake his neighbor, then ambled across the sodden yard and up to Gideon's door. Rang the bell. Stood in front of it so its camera could reveal who the caller was.

Bud shivered. It was damp. Windy. His fleece pullover wasn't giving him much shelter. The temperature belied the feel of the weather

. No one answered.

What an odd man, Bud thought as he returned to his home, passing the "Trump 2020" sign still stuck tilted in the wet earth. The election was six weeks past. He had dutifully removed his "Biden - Harris" sign the morning after the contest.

Bud worried a little. What if Gideon was ill? He never had any visitors, at least no cars ever sat parked in Gideon's driveway except the man's rusty F-150. He tried to recall if he had seen any lights on in the next-door house as he had walked up to it.

Angie and he had discussed Gideon occasionally in autumn while sipping a crisp Sauvignon Blanc on the patio. No answers had been forthcoming from her on how to get the man to warm up to Bud. "Some people just get twisted up in an infinity of fear," she had said. "Be patient. And, expect nothing."

Bud wasn't sure why she seemed so negative, but let it drop.

Maybe if I leave a note between the doorknob and the jamb, Bud reasoned. I can make sure I set it so I can see it from my front porch. If it's still there after a day or two, maybe I'll call the police for a welfare check.

Bud tried to remember just how long it had been since he had last dropped off some errant missive to Gideon.

Decided it must have been at least several weeks. Could not recall if he had seen the pickup in the driveway repositioned.

Not good, he decided.

ॐ

*Good morning, neighbor,*

*Perhaps you didn't hear it, but a tree from your yard fell into mine last night. I'd just like to let you know I'm taking care of it. I'll have my landscaper over tomorrow to cut it up and haul it off. Maybe we could share some coffee while it happens.*

*Take care, Bud Seele*

Bud folded the note in half and tucked it into the pocket of his hoodie he had chosen for his return trip to Gideon. He adjusted the skullie he wore underneath the heavier jacket's cover to protect his ears. No point in catching cold, he had reasoned while ditching his pullover for the warmer outerwear.

Maybe I should bring him over a few of those gingerbread men, Bud thought. Tasty. But no, that would require a plate to carry them. He'd need his hands to balance himself if he slipped any. Wouldn't want those sweet little treats to wind up wasted in soggy grass.

Bud trudged back to the silent house. He wedged the note carefully into the crack between Gideon's solid wooden door and its post. The knob rattled a brief complaint as he did so.

The door opened. "Hey, neigh..."

Bud heard a sudden-sharp crack. Felt brief, intense pain.

Lying on Gideon's porch floor, Bud looked up and saw for one last instant the corner of that sign: *Protec...*

Bud floated briefly in dark, weightless drift.

# THE TALE OF LADY EVANGELINE
by K. A. Kenny, *Blue Ridge Writers*

It was colder than she'd expected, one of those March nights when winter regains its sway, and Lady Evangeline feared she might be lost. Her handmaidens had told her of the wise old woman—known in whispered circles for helping troubled women. But alone in the dark wood, Evangeline despaired of ever finding the rustic cottage.

A gusting wind lashed bare branches over the face of the moon and shifted long shadows on the forest floor. Evangeline pulled her thin scarf close around her head and tucked a wave of raven hair back from her eyes. When she looked up again there the cottage stood, crafted in the trunk of a gnarled tree.

Ridges of moonlight and darkness gave the cottage the appearance of a troll's face— the twisted doorway, a disfigured mouth; two misaligned windows, the squinting, wrinkled eyes; and the broken stump of a branch for a nose.

The sight gave Lady Evangeline a start and filled her with

foreboding. Lifting her white linen gown clear of the mud and turning to leave, she caught her foot on a knotted tree root that seemed to reach up like a back-broken snake.

"Milady," called a frail, high-pitched voice. One of the squinting cottage eyes glinted as a candle was lit. "Have you come to pay an old woman a visit? Please come in."

The bent figure that came to the doorway grinned a broken, four-toothed smile. Her balding, brown-splotched pate reminded Evangeline of the skull Father Joska kept on his scribing desk. The crone beseeched her so earnestly to come that Evangeline felt too ashamed to refuse. So, lifting her gown high in her long white hands to clear the roots, she followed the woman inside.

The musty, one-room cottage had an ash-filled stone hearth with glowing embers, a slatted bed with a deerskin blanket, and a rough-hewn wooden table with two rickety chairs. Peg-mounted shelves above the table held ceramic jars, glass bottles and flasks, and dust-covered books. A straw broom stood in one corner and earthen flagons in the others. The only light came from the full moon in the window, candles on the table and windowsills, and hearth embers.

The woman shooed a black cat from one of the chairs. The cat hissed and clawed, leaping away only when threatened with a broom. "Fester hasn't seen many high-born ladies," she explained, offering the chair to Evangeline. Though her words were pleasant, the old woman's cracked voice and the curve of her thin smile sent chills up Evangeline's back.

"I am Matta Crowley," said the crone, lifting a kettle from the hearth. "I know," Evangeline said firmly.

"Some toadwort tea?" When Evangeline's thin brows shot up, the woman added, "Toadwort is native to this forest, it makes a fine herbal tea." Evangeline nodded, and Matta Crowley filled two brown-stained, wooden cups.

"How nice you are to visit me. I was told you might come by. Tell me, my Lady, what might an old woman do for a beautiful young princess?"

"My handmaidens said you might be able to help me. I—"

Evangeline suddenly burst into tears. She covered her eyes with a white, lace- trimmed kerchief clutched in her delicate, milk-white hands. When she tried to continue, her words broke into sobs, shakes, and sniffing.

"A broken heart is it?" Tiny curls crept into the corners of a lipless, slit-like mouth.

Evangeline nodded, dropping her gaze and her folded hands to her lap. After two long breaths, she pulled erect. "I think I shall never love again. Never. I'm only sixteen, and this has never happened to me." She pushed her long hair behind a shoulder with a trembling hand.

Matta Crowley slid one eye to Evangeline's untouched teacup then sipped from her own. "Warm tea will help you feel better, dear child," said the high, cracking voice.

Evangeline buried her face in her quivering hands, sobbing tears flowing freely. The crone touched a jagged, yellow claw to Evangeline's arm and stroked her black, flowing hair. "Now, now, my dear, I know it hurts. Tell me what favor you wish from me?"

"I want to never feel this pain again. I hurt so much, so very, very much. And I know..." Evangeline stopped to swallow. "I know it will never ever end."

"There, there, my sweet one. Sixteen is a very tender age, and there is much I can do with you. But are you sure this is what you want, for your pain to go away? Here, my child, drink some tea." She nudged the teacup closer.

Evangeline picked it up, but, seeing her hands moist with tears, returned it to the table and touched the lace-trimmed kerchief to her hands, fingers, and eyes. When she finally reached for the cup and drank, a dark smile widened on Matta Crowley's face.

"Can you truly take my pain away?" Evangeline asked, her delicate hands twisting her kerchief.

The old woman's eyes glowed like coals in their dark, hollow sockets. "Is it just the pain you want removed or the memory also? Or perhaps something more?" Her thin mouth drew into a gap-toothed sneer.

Evangeline took a gasping breath. "I...I must keep the memory, so...so I remember never do this again. But, yes, oh yes, I want the pain to go away." She brushed a tear from her downcast cheek then returned her hand to her lap. "This morning Sir Reginald told me he had to return to his betrothed in Andalusia. *His betrothed?* How...how could he do this? All summer he told me he loved me. He said I was the only one." She stared beyond the crone now, and her mouth tightened. "I had many suitors. Many handsome men wanted me. But I chose Sir Reginald...and he ruined me. He asked me for my favors, and I granted them, favors I promised my mother I would never give to anyone until I married—"

"Yes, dear child, I understand. I was young once and beautiful, and men loved and desired me." She sighed and closed her eyes wistfully then laughed. "But I made the mistake of loving one back."

Evangeline tried to imagine the sunken, dung-colored figure as a young woman.

Matta Crowley continued. "I was given the choice to be loved and to enjoy that love but never to love in return."

Evangeline's eyes took on a new glow. "Oh, that is a choice I would willingly make.

What must I do?"

The old woman lifted a small black bottle from the shelf above. Cradling the bottle in her clawed fingers, she removed the stopper.

"One drop upon your tongue will make you eternally young and beautiful to all desirable men, and you will forget the pain of having ever loved." A crooked smile tightened across her broken teeth.

"Eternally young and beautiful?" Evangeline squinched her face in disbelief.   "Only to desirable young men,"

Crowley said. "Others will see you as you truly are. Every young man who gazes upon you will burn for you. Having once seen you, he will give his heart instantly and completely. He will want you and no other, and having given his heart, he will be incapable of ever loving another."

"And I will feel nothing?"

"You will feel as he does, but only for a single night, and only with your loins and your lips—never with your heart, for there is where the pain lies. You will share his flaming passion, but come morning, he will only disgust you. And that disgust will take away all your pain."

"But can I never love again...truly love?"

"Dear child, have you not tasted true love? You said you

never wanted it again."

Evangeline pressed her delicate, white hands to her face and nodded. "Yes, the cost is too high."

"My Lady," a deep voice boomed. "Excuse me, my beloved, I see you are busy, perhaps another time."

Evangeline was startled to see her father's knight standing in the dark doorway, his hands clasped before his sky-blue tunic as if in prayer. Sir Geoffrey had pursued her last year, but she had already chosen Reginald. How had he followed her...and on such a night? How dare he after she'd rejected him, and after she'd caught him in her handmaid's chamber.

Before Evangeline could protest, Geoffrey rushed past her to kneel at the foot of the old crone. "My Lady, you are the fairest, most desirable woman I have ever known." Evangeline stared in utter confusion. "Please let me hear one kind word from your lips. My dearest one, I curse myself for whatever I did to lose your favor."

Matta Crowley rested her ragged hand on the knight's bowed head and stroked his dark, candle-lit curls. "If you wish to please me, Sir Geoffrey, some venison would be welcome or a wild pig for the roasting spit. Would you do that for your beloved?"

"I will hunt for you, fair lady. And when I return, I will prepare the meat for you." With that, he left without giving Evangeline a second glance.

The old woman laced her clawed fingers above the table and peered over them. "You see how the magic works, dear child. If you visit your Sir Reginald once again, his passion will ignite more fiercely than ever. You may enjoy him as you wish, then be rid of him. As your passion cools to contempt, his will grow to eternal torment."

"And he will feel what he made me feel." Evangeline huffed a laugh, rested her chin on her raised, delicately folded hands, and looked across at Matta Crowley. "My handmaidens said you were a witch, but I didn't believe them."

The old woman lifted the kettle to offer the lady more tea. "Yes, I am a witch, and so shall you be, my child. So, shall you be."

# LIKE SOPHIA LOREN
by Denise Moreault Israel, *Virginia Writers Club*

She looks like Sophia Loren. A soft, voluptuous, dark-haired beauty, so lovely. No one diverted their eyes. And she was of Italian descent. Without knowing Sophia, it is hard to know if the resemblance ended with the physical.

Oddly, Lorena is her given name. It really is. I met her at a professional meeting. She turned away from the work arena since the birth of her daughter six years before. It seemed we were both hungry for professional contacts.

Gravitating to Lorena is easy. She has a wondrous, captivating smile. Her hair is black and silken. It is the sort you want to touch. I don't think she needs any makeup. Her skin is a Mediterranean olive and the rosy glow emanates from her cheeks. I do not know who talked first, but we fell into animated conversation so quickly that when the seminar ended, we were still talking in the hall.

Our friendship posed challenges. I could not quite figure out what caused our warm to cool companionship. If you eavesdrop on our conversations, you will think we had everything in common. Yet we remained on the runway, idling but never taking off. It is only in reflection many years later that I can guess at some forces at work.

Lorena's house is in a neighborhood of old Victorians, some of them in better shape than others. Lorena's house has a gothic feel in its dark cedar shingles and pointed dormers. It could use a face-lift but won't get one. Lorena and Len don't believe in it. I think they will let the house age with them.

Lorena and Len put their money into their children's

Denise Moreault Israel *Virginia Writers Club*          Like Sophia Loren

private school education. Len worries about the future and keeps a tight grip on the finances.

Lorena relayed how they came to buy that house. They hadn't looked at any other. I was amazed at this revelation. This was a house that did not have curb appeal. Len took her to see the house a month before their wedding. He simply said, "Could you live here?"

Lorena said, "With you I could live anywhere."

Lorena came from upstate New York. Len met her at a presentation his business sponsored for psychologists about a new book his company was about to publish. At the time she was newly divorced with a young son. Len freely announces when asked about how they met she was the most beautiful woman he had ever laid eyes on. That he was almost afraid to speak to her. That her eyes grew bright when she smiled at him. It amazed him she agreed to see him and then continued dating him. He doesn't divulge that he learned that her former husband had abused both her and her son. That as a result the marriage became a package deal, and he wanted that guy out of his family forever.

These are facts he told me privately after Lorena and I had become good friends. "Don't tell Lorena I told you. But she needs a close friend who she can confide in and who knows her story. These people who she socializes with from the neighborhood are gossips. You never know when they will turn on you."

ॐ

It is one of our Fridays together. We are in Lorena's kitchen having tea and muffins Inga baked that morning. Suddenly her son, Conor, bursts into the kitchen and begins demanding that Lorena give him $20 due him for a job he finished or Len. He is belligerent and at one point I am fearful he will strike her.

Conor yells, "I want my money now. It's mine. I need it!" He is right in Lorena's face.

As calmly as she can, Lorena says, "I don't have any cash right now. I'll get some this afternoon. Come back at three."

He yells again, "I know you have cash. I'll go upstairs to your drawer. "

Lorena says again, trying to be calm, "Conor, Dad is home, so you'd better not do anything you will regret." Conor pauses and glares at her with his fists clenched. After thirty seconds, Lorena takes her wallet from her hidden purse and gives him the money. Conor grabs it from her hand and leaves. He leaves, slamming the door. She turns to me and says, "I don't want Len involved in every scene I have with Conor. It gets too ugly."

Then Lorena launches into a first-time description of her trials with Conor. But this scene forced it.

"Conor's behavior has always been difficult to manage. Len has done his best to get close to him. We have also had Conor see child therapists. Nothing seemed to help. He is disrespectful to me. This drives Len crazy and he loses his temper. When this happens, Conor storms off and sleeps at a friend's house. Lately we have been hearing from the friend's parents that they have both gone missing overnight and suspect drugs."

Biting my lip, I ask, "What does the therapist say."

"The psychologist says we need to start family therapy to work out issues of authority and security. He also thinks that Conor may have some underlying psychiatric conditions. He's not sure but wants an evaluation."

Her eyes tear-up.

I thought Lorena and I would become closer following her confidences. It was several months and lots of telephone tag before we could set another date. By that time, my sense of intimacy dissolved.

"You look great. How have things been going?" I ask.

"We are great! Inga has just won a writing contest and I have a new job possibility!"

"Really! That's wonderful. Tell me about it."

"It's the director of a psychology evaluation unit at a hospital for children with special needs. It's what I was trained to do but didn't know if a position would ever become available in this area. Ever since marrying Len and moving here, I knew I might give up career opportunities."

I respond, "Isn't that fantastic! You'd be perfect for that position." The conversation continued in that vein and depth.

Following a knock on the door, an attractive thin, blond

41

woman in a tennis skirt strides in. She is about five foot-two. Her arms are waving in the air. "Hi Lorena. Oh! Sorry, I didn't know you had company."

She does not make eye contact with me.

"That's okay," says Lorena. "Ellen, this is Heidi, my neighbor."

"Pleased to meet you Heidi."

Heidi does not acknowledge me and as she flops into a chair. She talks directly to Lorena about their girls' school politics. I am completely taken aback by her rudeness.

"We have got to take this teacher singling out students in front of the class when they have not done well on an assignment. It is inappropriate. Will you join me at the meeting with the principal?"

Lorena in a soft voice says, "Don't you think we should go directly to the teacher first?"

Heidi gesticulates. "No, I don't like this teacher. She has been sharp to my daughter before. I think we need a major intervention. Are you with me?"

The color rises in Lorena's face, but she says, "Sure, Heidi. I'll go with you."

After a few minutes, I can't stand it anymore. I say, "Lorena, I really have to go. Nice meeting you, Heidi."

Several weeks later, Lorena calls me sounding harried. I suggest we meet at an intimate coffee shop in my neighborhood. I sense she is feeling fragile and needs to get away from familiar surroundings.

I see her pleasant, somewhat plump silhouette ambling down the sidewalk. She seems uncertain, but I wave. She waves back.

As soon as we are seated, her words come out in a torrent, "The job I was hired for is the one Heidi's brother thought he was a shoo-in for!"

"What!"

"Yes. I didn't know he worked there when I took the job. She apparently didn't know that I had taken a job in his department."

"Wow! That pits you against each other, I guess?"

"Now I don't know what to do. Stay there or resign? The

problem is there just **aren't** many jobs like this one in this town. The other problem is that I am not a fighter. I get easily manipulated."

I change topics. "What has Conor's therapist suggested you do when Conor bullies you?"

"He says to make the rules, stand my ground, and not waiver. Not easy. He can be rough. I suppose I would have to excuse myself when the agency deals with Coner. A conflict of confidentiality rules."

"I guess that's possible. Do you think I should stick it out to see?"

"What do you have to lose?" I'm irritated that she draws me into her drama.

&

Lorena calls me for an impromptu dinner at her house. This is a first. She has only met my husband, Alan, once in passing, but knows he is a classically trained musician. They are having their neighbors over. Neither she nor Len know much about classical music I gather.

We are dining alfresco. The temperatures are perfect. The insects seem to sleep. The slate patio area is flaking and uneven. The old wrought iron furniture rusts. We settled in.

Len takes a few strides to meet us as we arrive. He is a tall, lanky man with the cocked stance of someone not comfortable with his extreme height. His face is long with an angular jaw and his smile starts cool, turns arrogant. His forelock of dirty blond hair falls over his left eye. It is difficult to feel at ease around him.

Len says, "I assume you are Alan. Alan Steyn, is it? Alan, this is Paul and Lydia Wyman. And Paul and Lydia, this is Ellen. Please, all sit. *I'll* serve some wine. Pass the cheese plate while I finish roasting the Cornish game hens. Lorena, will you get the waters?" Len is formal, stiff, officious.

Paul is wearing a surgical brace collar. I ask, "Paul, did you have surgery?"

Paul is a short, squat man. He's got black hair that won't be tamed and puffy eyes that don't meet you full on.

"No. Support. It's work related. I have continuous pain. Strained muscles. I have physical therapy. I wear the collar to

43

immobilize the muscles as much as possible."

He is clearly uncomfortable.

Lorena joins us and asks, "How difficult is it to be away from home for months at a time?"

Paul says, "Actually I'm hating it. I've come to the point of disliking my partners. I spend my personal time reading and sleeping. I'm not sure how long I can keep on with this lifestyle, but I'm not sure I have a choice. Living is just too expensive."

Alan asks, "Are you enjoying the accolades?"

He smiles. "I do enjoy the applause and the positive newspaper reviews. Maybe that's what keeps me going."

Lydia, a fading blonde with heavy make-up, affirms. "Of course, that's what keeps you going. You love the music."

Len serves the hens and rice. The salad bowl circles the guests. The wine glasses are refilled.

I think about Lydia. How does she handle her husband's absence for most of their marriage? She has a young daughter in Inga's class at the private school. I guess the touring pays for this and her fancy neighborhood.

Everyone compliments Len on his culinary skills. Len clearly enjoys being the center of attention. The women ask him about his recipes and techniques with the roasting and flavorings. The conversation runs dry.

Alan abhors silence and turns to Paul. "I was interested to hear you don't get bored with playing the same pieces over and over. That is exactly why I did not pursue a career in performing."

This launches a feisty debate over all the pieces that are in the touring string repertoire and what he finds to interest him. This excludes the rest of the guests who separate into groups by sex ignoring Len. By the end of the evening, the mood chills.

&

I am surprised to hear from Len two weeks later. We are asked to join Lorena and Len at a Lebanese restaurant. I suspect Len wants a confrontation with Alan.

When we arrive, Len gets up from the table and ushers us in, almost as if he owns the place. He and Lorena already have

44

drinks. He is drinking scotch. Lorena has a glass of white wine. I say I'll have the same and Alan says he'll have a beer. The restaurant emotes of incense-like smells, the above the grilling of lamb.

Len says he is part Lebanese on his mother's side. He wants to order for us. The restaurant plays traditional Lebanese music in the background. Len has downed two more scotch drinks. He starts a third. He is getting loud and cocky. I'm getting anxious. Lorena is more subdued than usual.

Len looks for a conversational hook. "Alan, how do you like what you do professionally?

Alan slips into his rehearsed response. "I tried a variety of career paths and didn't like them. I'm a Renaissance man of sorts."

Len sits his scotch on the table. "You mean you often failed?"

Alan laughs. "That's one way of putting it. I like what I do. I get to use my science and law background to do specialized searches. I also get to be my own boss. Like you."

Len tries another tack. "I thought Jews were ambitious. What happened to you?"

I gasp.

Alan looks at him and says, "I guess you assume I'm a Jew from my last name. My father was not a Jew."

Len looks deflated. He had wanted to bring this man down and it didn't work. Lorena has that strained look in her eyes. She tightly intertwines her fingers.

Len grimaces. "You are right, sir, and I do like being my boss. I guess we have a lot in common." He snaps his fingers in the air. The waiter appears.

His words slur. "Another round of drinks for the gentlemen. A dessert wine for the ladies."

Alan's mother is Jewish.

Lorena and I capture the conversation for the rest of the meal. Finally, staff clear dishes, serve final coffees, and take the checks.

When we leave, we follow each other to our cars. The night is clear and crisp. Alan gets in the car and leans in to unlock my side. As I open the door, I hear Len whispering to Lorena.

"I don't think these are the kind of people we should socialize with."

Lorena pulls him close. "Shh. They'll hear you."

I carefully get into the car, but don't slam the door shut until they have slammed their doors. I tell Alan to drive off quickly.

Lorena and I have met at her house for tea. I can't even remember who started the custom and by now I don't care anymore. After telling me about her and Len's decision to send Conor to a boarding school, she says, "Also, I wanted to thank you for supporting me, with my professional life. Things finally came to a head. Heidi's brother-in-law, George, transferred to another department. He and I had several run-ins over who was in charge. I just kept telling him I was making the decisions. I guess he couldn't take a woman telling him what to do."

The saddest part of all this is that Heidi takes George's side. She has been quite stand-offish. Some other mothers take their cues from her. I commiserate with her. Privately, I reflect on all the bullies that have crossed Lorena's path.

ಐ

A few months later and it's November. I haven't heard from Lorena, though I have left a couple of messages. I focus my attention on other friendships.

As I sort through the mail, I examined a square envelope with a return address of "Nathaniel Court". How strange. I open it eagerly. It is an invitation to Lorena's fiftieth birthday party hosted by Len. It will be a dinner party of Lorena's women friends. I RSVP promptly to Len's work phone. Then I think about choosing a gift suitable for such a special birthday.

I reject most ideas as they occur to me. They are just too conventional. I want something that has spoken to me as a mature woman. It touches the artist in me. I decide on the trilogy, *Kristin Lavransdattar* by Sigrid Undset. It won the Nobel Prize for Literature in 1927.

I can't think that Kristin's and Lorena's lives are at all similar. There is something long-suffering about both. I've wrapped the books with care. I tend to agonize over details. The design of the paper, a ribbon, a bow or not? Then what to wear. It will be obviously dressy casual.

In Lorena's neighborhood, women have a certain way of signaling their tribe. The brand of their shoes, jeans, jewelry. I'm not in the know. Lorena has her own style. It is a sort of New York matron with a heavy twist of California. Whatever that means. I don't know how she pulls it together.

&

When I walk in, Len greets me at the door and takes the gift. I see Lorena seated in the chair nearest the fireplace, wearing a Navajo-style shawl and large sliver and turquoise pin on her shoulder that I learn is a gift from Len. She is stunning as she beams at the gaggle of about a dozen women. I take the only seat available near the back of the room next to a woman I don't know. There is something familiar about her. I scan the room. I am surprised to see Heidi and next to her, Lydia. I don't know anyone else. All eyes turn towards Lorena.

Len signals for Lorena to walk into the dining room. I can hear her delightful squeals when she sees the spread before her. The table is beautifully set. I learn our feast represents Lorena's favorite Italian dishes: veal marsala, risotto, and roasted asparagus. There is also a lovely antipasto salad.

Len serves the wine. Then the drum of women's voices begins.

I turn to the woman seated next to me. She too seems not to know anyone. She is tall, thin, and quite beautiful. Her long hair is a shiny black. Her eyes are black as well. She is olive complected with red lips and high cheekbones. She is wearing a white, long-sleeved blouse with pleating down the front. A tan, three-quarter length skirt is set off at the waist by a wide, dark brown, soft leather belt. She is wearing cowboy boots.

"Hi, I'm Ellen. You look familiar. Have we met?"

She says, "Not likely. This is the first time I've been here. I'm Lorena's younger sister, Gina. Len flew me out in for the party."

"How wonderful that you could be here! Do you and Lorena get together often?"

47

"No. We don't have very much in common. I'm just a country girl and she is the city girl. She has the fancy education, and I haven't finished college." Her eyes focus on her tightly folded hands.

I am nonplussed. This seemed out of character for Lorena

We continue talking about her life in Wisconsin on her family dairy farm. It sounds rugged and challenging. I catch Lorena's eyes looking at the two of us. I wonder what she is thinking.

I go to speak to Lydia when she is not sitting with Heidi. She seems genuinely pleased to see me and we fall into conversation about the rigors of Paul's schedule and the stress it puts on her to parent alone. I gather she doesn't often have a sympathetic ear.

It is time for the opening of the gifts. Lorena displays an attractive bowl of blown glass. The guests "Oo." Next a set of monogrammed finger towels in a pale shade of green. Lorena's favorite color. Her sister gives her an album of family photographs. Lorena looks surprised and appreciative. Then she opens my gift. She examines the books closely and smiles. She has no inkling of what they are about. She looks up at me and nods. Someone in the group shouts, "I loved those!" I am grateful for the reprieve.

Gina turns to me and says, "Are you a close friend of Lorena's?"

I nod. "Friends."

"I can usually tell. There are those in her inner circle and those who want to be. That's what it was like in high school. I was always in her shadow Younger sister. Classmates used me to get closer to her. Boys did too. I was the annoying younger sister."

I laughed, "Isn't that the way with sisters. I have younger sisters. We were rivals."

Gina narrows her eyes. "It couldn't have been as bad."

Lorena circulates between guests, thanking them. When she reaches Gina and I, she sits down in a chair facing us. This is the first time in the evening that she has spoken to me.

"I see the two of you have met. No introductions needed. I'm happy Gina found someone to talk to."

"Yes. Gina and I have been talking about her life in

Wisconsin. It's interesting."

"No doubt. Surely that can't be all?" Lorena says a bit snidely.

"No. That's not all," says Gina. "I was telling Ellen about our high school years."

"Really! Surely, that's a bit off limits," says Lorena sharply.

"I'm not sure why! I was there too! It's mine to tell as well."

Lorena looks to me, "Sisters."

Gina abruptly and stands, towering over Lorena. "Well, I guess sisters carry their grudges!" She spins, leaving the room.

Lorena clinches her teeth. She then meets my eyes, regains her composure. "I apologize. Gina and I dance over on a variety of issues.

She takes my hand and leads me to the fireplace where there is another chair. Len, who had been watching, brings us each a fresh glass of wine.

&#x283;

I haven't seen Lorena since the party. It's been two months.

I call her to make a lunch date. We pick a place in her neighborhood across from Inga's school so she can pick her up. The school uses shortened days on Fridays. Lorena takes a half day on Fridays from work.

The holidays are over, and it is a bitter, wintry day at the end of January. My cell phone rings at ten just as I'm finishing an errand. It's Lorena saying something has suddenly come up and could she take a raincheck? She is terribly sorry. She will call me next week to reschedule. Of course, I'm disappointed.

At noon I find myself in Lorena's neighborhood. My favorite meat market is nearby. I've been shopping here for ten years. With one exception, the staff are a surly lot. My connection, a pleasant man with a noticeable hair lip, greets me cheerfully.

Afterwards I sit in my car getting my bank deposit in order. I look up as two women bundled up for the cold stand in front of the same restaurant that Lorena and I had chosen. Do I recognize them? Wait, Heidi and Lydia. Another woman hurries up to meet them. Her face is covered. That waddling gait.

Lorena's gait. So, this was Lorena's sudden event that bumped me out of the equation. I take it in.

I think back to what Gina had said. I dab my eyes.

I am so shallow and vain.

*Len signals for Lorena to walk into the dining room. I can hear her delightful squeals... . The table is beautifully set.*

# NEUROPHILE
by Marco Faust, *Hanover Writers Club*
Illustrated by Dave Powell


Prologue 2071 AD
Ken wheeled smoothly into the dim early morning light of the
hallway from his 12th-floor apartment, the door gently sliding
shut behind him. Another day had begun at the Jasper Transition
Center. The black tiles sparkled from their overnight cleaning,
and the scent of cleaning fluid still hung heavily in the air, but he
and the other neurophiles could not smell it.

Gracefully, he glided toward the lounge, anticipating an
assembly of early morning risers. He was delighted to see Sandy,
the newest neurophile on the floor, 15 meters ahead, slowly
making her way there as well.

Ten years a neurophile, he could safely move much faster
than she. Neurophiles less than two years old could never operate
their ground drives at full speed. At three months (neurophiles
report their age from the time they transitioned), Sandy was still
only allowed the lowest speed on almost everything, and Ken
quickly overtook her.

"Good morning, Sandy," he said cheerfully while still 3
meters behind her. Recently transitioned neurophiles were often
hard of hearing, as they didn't fully understand the mechanics of
adjusting their volume control, and he didn't want to startle her.

Without turning or seeing him, she recognized his voice
and responded slowly, "Good morning, Ken," trying to sound just
as cheerful—but failing miserably. Showing emotion with her voice
was one of the hardest things to learn. It was almost exactly the
opposite of a natural body where hiding emotions had seemed to
be the real challenge.

"Oh, that was much better," Ken lied enthusiastically.
"You're getting it," he said to encourage her.

"Oh, well, thank you," she said again in a plodding and
bland sort of way. She had a long way to go.

Ken slowed to her speed to continue the conversation.
"And how is Miss Sandy today?" he asked.

"Oh, so, so," she said and then added, "Insomnia..." She

left it at that, knowing that Ken understood.

"I don't get why they don't fix that sooner for people. I mean, everyone goes through the same thing. They need to get serotonin up to a higher level, but they raise it so cautiously. I don't understand."

"They told me," she began slowly, "that Sarah toner is dangerous for us." She had intended to say serotonin, but the speech module got it wrong because she had not concentrated enough on the words. Both she and the speech module would get better.

Ken knew she had intended to say the correct word and felt sympathetic. He remembered... "Yeah, they tell everyone that," Ken said with resignation. "Eventually, everyone is up to 800 nanograms per milliliter, and insomnia ends. That's higher than normal for the human brain, and they can't figure out why. I hope they fix that soon," he said, and then added, "unfortunately, that doesn't help you."

Sandy was not sure what to think of Ken, as he seemed odd. He was unattached, and she often got the sense that he was hitting on her, and lots of floor residents, as he seemed to be flirtatious with all the neurophile women.

"After Albert transitioned," she began as they continued to plod down the hall, "he came home in about 3 months, but his chemistry was still messed up. So, he was often up all night." She wanted to say how much better it was to be at Jasper with people that empathized with her and knew exactly what she was going through, but she skipped it because of her painfully slow speech.

Her transition team kept saying that getting used to her new body was a process that took time. Everything she had learned as a child had been thrown away along with her natural body. Literally, every movement had to be relearned and coordinated again. Fortunately, the neurophile unit was exceptionally easy to control. Transition specialists came by every day to manage her progress.

"How is Albert?" Ken asked. "Is he still around? Haven't seen him for a week." He almost sounded hopeful.

Ken wanted to ask her why they had not come to Jasper after Albert's transition, but that risked getting into his own depressing history. Ken was indeed interested in companionship and perhaps even romance. That Sandy was married did not really matter to him, although it would undoubtedly have been a problem for her. One thing he liked about Sandy was that he was absolutely sure that she had been a woman. Ken knew this because Sandy and Albert had visited Jasper before her transition, and Ken was a member of the group that gave prospective tenants tours. The thing he feared most about companionship, romance, and especially sex, was the possibility of getting involved with someone who had been a man before conversion. Not everyone maintained their original gender identity through the transition.

He never mentioned it, but his significantly younger wife had moved into Jasper with him following his transition. But suddenly, after eight months, she had left in disgust with the neurophile concept. At age 72 and undoubtedly many years from needing it, she had vowed to never become one. And she had no intention of spending her remaining years among neurophiles, she had told him.

Eventually, when faced with life or death, she would realize the necessity of it, but years of her absence had extinguished any positive feelings he had toward her. They each had children from previous marriages, but with no children together, he had not seen her since the day she moved out. Only a few email messages had been exchanged, mostly over financial matters. Upon completing his transition, he had stayed on at Jasper (an option for all residents) as an unofficial and experienced neurophile to mentor newbies as they adapted to their new lives.

"Albert's getting by," she answered, and then added, "problems with the kids," succinctly summarizing Albert's angst. Implicit was that Albert, right then, was sound asleep in their apartment.

Ken performed the neurophile version of rolling his eyes by rotating his entire head a little. The neurophile transition kept the biological eyes, but not the surrounding muscles. "Huh, we all seem to have that problem," Ken said sympathetically. "I contend that there are only two kinds of children: Those that are problems, and those you never see. You're lucky if they are a problem," he said remorsefully. Like his wife, his children had decided they wanted nothing to do with their neurophile father.

Sandy tried to perform a remorseful chuckle, but it did not come out right and sounded more like an aborted sneeze. "Hah!! We have the worst of both: We never see them, and they're always a problem—they want money."

They were reaching the lounge area, so Sandy slowed even more to make sure she did not run into anything or anyone. The salutations "Good morning, Sandy. Good morning, Ken" were heard multiple times as their presence was noted. They responded in kind, although Sandy wasn't sure of everyone's names yet, so she usually left that off.  Including Sandy and Ken, there were now seven neurophiles present, all relatively new, except Ken. The lounge was little more than a wide spot in the hallway, in the middle of the 12th floor. There wasn't room in it for all of them, so the group spilled out into the hall itself.

Suddenly the building shook, and an enormous bang was heard. Ken froze, his well-honed control as a neurophile allowing him to remain motionless without even thinking about it. But Sandy and the others immediately twitched nervously, a motion typical of new neurophiles when frightened, who still needed to concentrate hard to remain motionless. "It's an earthquake," someone speculatively shouted, but everyone quickly realized that it wasn't.

Except for the twitching, silence pervaded the floor for 20 or 30 seconds, and everyone eased a bit. But suddenly, a bloodcurdling scream rent the air. This time the sounds clearly came from just down the hall on their floor, the direction Sandy and Ken had just come from. Everyone turned toward it, but there was nothing to see. Then the floor shook again, as when enormous masses collide violently.

A general silence again fell over them, and after a brief pause, a few murmured. But then some nondescript noises came from the same vicinity, and everyone strained to determine what they were hearing. They were finally rewarded with the sound of squealing ground drive wheels. It was the first noise that had clearly originated from a neurophile, and it suddenly dawned on them that someone probably needed help.

Immediately, it was apparent that Ken would take the lead. Although unprecedented, he assumed that there must be a reasonable, relatively benign explanation. As the most experienced neurophile, it made sense that he be the one to investigate.

Cautiously he whirred down the hall while light banging sounds were occasionally heard. It quickly became apparent they were coming from apartment 1212, John and Judy Tremaine's residence—both neurophiles, the oldest neurophiles on the floor. They had long been friends and lived just opposite Ken.

The banging noise had stopped as he paused at the closed door. Turning up the sensitivity on his electronic ears to maximum yielded nothing. He glanced down the hall at Sandy and the others as they watched anxiously. Ken performed a neurophile's version of a shrug by raising both arms, palms up. Then he pushed the doorbell twice in rapid succession.

The only noises he heard came from the other neurophiles in the lounge.

"Is everything OK in there," he hollered. "John, Judy, is everything all right?" Ken heard nothing, so he inserted his rubberized index finger in the door release and cautiously tried to open the door. Fully expecting it to be locked, he was momentarily pleased as the door glided open.

Nothing could have prepared him for the devastation. Clutter and debris were scattered everywhere among the things typically found in the apartment of neurophiles. He could tell that many items were the fragments of a neurophile that had been entirely ripped apart. Most of the significant parts were present: a ground drive unit with its three wheels pointing helplessly towards the ceiling lay near a wall to his right; an arm lay near the windows opposite the door; and the bulk of the life support system protruded from the wall to his left, attesting to one of the loud crashes. Clearly, this neurophile was not capable of sustaining the life of its biological master.

"Oh shit!" he exclaimed. It was utterly unprecedented in his experience. He had never seen or even heard of anything like this happening to neurophiles, but here it was. Further surveying the carnage, Ken recognized a badly smashed portion of a neurophile's exterior beside a pool of neurophile blood (a reddish fluid much thinner and lighter than normal human blood). Next to it, facing up, he spotted the head. "It's John," he realized, "but where's Judy?"

"Judy," he called out, but the stillness held. Cautiously,

he moved into the room about a meter and stopped.

What had happened? It had only been a minute or two since the squealing wheel sound and only five since the two loud noises: Could all this have happened that quickly? Looking around, he surmised some of what must have transpired. The loud crashes were evidenced by two heavily damaged sections of the plaster walls, one with the life support system embedded—the other on the opposite side of the room. One of the two loud noises had been responsible for the ground drive's detachment, so from what he remembered of the chronology, the squealing ground drive wheels had probably not been John's.

Ken found it difficult to wrap his head around this. He had never heard of a neurophile committing a violent act—ever. Neurophiles only came from society's upper crust, not the people who commit atrocious violent acts of any kind. Could another neurophile have done this? Judy, perhaps?

Just then, a loud, whirring noise filled the room. It was like the sound of a ground drive unit, but enormously louder and defective. Ken suddenly realized that John's fate could be his own, and he began to leave.

As he rotated to face the door, he glimpsed the likely assailant. Another neurophile, both arms flailing wildly, was rapidly headed toward him, having emerged from an obscured portion of the room. Was that Judy? It was hard to tell. There was hardly anything recognizable about the unit, as nearly every square centimeter of exterior metal was missing or severely damaged. The face panel dangled to one side, so he didn't see it clearly, and he wasn't about to stop to look more carefully.

Ken engaged the drive to the highest possible speed. He bolted through the door and immediately turned to his right upon getting into the hall. He could no longer see it, but the sound told him that the deranged neurophile was getting awfully close.

The wall to Ken's immediate right exploded toward him, violently shaking the building yet again. The metal door frame, torn from the wall, narrowly missed him as it clattered to the floor. Thick white dust enveloped Ken and obscured the onlooker's view of him. Ken was ferociously thrown against the opposite wall of the hallway, and his body rotated enough to see the expanded opening from the apartment.

As the dust settled, allowing the lounge crowd to see, the deranged and severely damaged neurophile slowly emerged. Its arms continued their frantic, erratic movements in all directions. It crawled slowly into full sight, and the ground drive wheels made a hideous grinding noise. At first, it seemed headed down the hall away from Ken, and he momentarily felt safe from the thrashing arms. But the deranged neurophile suddenly rotated and headed straight toward him.

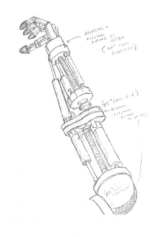

Neurophile Arm
Illustrated by Dave Powell

Ken had been stunned by the initial explosion and the subsequent collision with the opposite wall. Recovering, he noted that the deranged unit was still over 3 meters away and moving at a glacial speed, so there was apparently ample time to get away from those dangerous flailing arms. But there was no reason to delay, so he promptly ordered his ground drive unit to full speed, to distance himself quickly.

Ken suddenly discovered that something was terribly wrong, as his attempts to move failed. From their vantage point down the hall, the horrified onlookers could see that Ken's drive wheels were sitting at a strange angle, the support bearings apparently having been sheared away from the ground drive chassis by the violent impacts. Ken desperately tried every order he could think of to move, but nothing worked.

Slowly but steadily, the berserk neurophile continued to approach, its flailing arms getting closer with each swing. A horrible outcome seemed inevitable, and doing anything about it, impossible.

"Help me!" Ken pleaded desperately, knowing full well that no one could do anything.

A swing grazed his chest, and Ken realized he had to do

something else. Seeing the next swing approaching, he raised his left arm to block it. Heavy structural metal in their arms collided violently. The assailant's left forearm was severed at the elbow and continued its trajectory, grazing Ken's shoulder, before impaling in the wall. Ken's forearm had been struck, and although intact, control wires were crushed and severed, causing the arm to hang uselessly at his side.

The assailant then swung its right arm toward him. Because of the angle of its body, the swing missed, but only by inches. The left-arm swung again, but the missing forearm caused it to be well short of Ken.

Relentlessly, however, the assailant's roaring ground drive moved it closer. With yet another swing, the undamaged right arm finally reached the thin sheet metal of Ken's left side. The swings continued, but at first, the impacts produced nothing but scratches.

Blow after blow, the steel hand pierced ever deeper into Ken's life support region, eventually causing some high current wires to be severed, creating an intense electric arc flash. A sudden change in the swing's direction brought the hand squarely through Ken's neck area, cleanly severing the supports and the attachment hoses that kept his brain alive. Ken's head fell to the side, held only by several wires that had not been cut. Neurophile blood spurted under moderate pressure from the severed hoses and drained by gravity from his dangling head. Sparks again flew until a circuit breaker opened. All intended motion ceased, but the momentum of the eviscerating swing slammed him against the wall of his own apartment.

As if satisfied, the deranged neurophile turned toward the others. Suddenly the loud grinding noise disappeared as if something jammed in the gears had fallen out. More significantly, the ground drive instantly regained its more-than-full-speed abilities.

Those in the crowd that could see what was happening suddenly realized that their distance from the menace was inadequate, and they immediately searched frantically for cover. But where to go?

Despite its newfound speed, the attacker only made moderate progress toward them. It still moved erratically, frequently bouncing off the walls as it careened down the long hall. Its intact arm, meanwhile, continued to flail furiously, causing the hand to strike furniture and other items, and cutting deep grooves in the walls, producing copious amounts of debris and dust that flew in all directions.

The remaining neurophiles tried to find cover by retreating into the small lounge. But there just wasn't enough room for the six of them. Being slower than the rest, Sandy found herself at the back, in the middle of the hall. Rotating her head as far as it would go, she glimpsed the aggressor rapidly bearing down on her. Desperately, Sandy ordered her ground drive unit into reverse and lethargically moved away from the others. She hoped to cross the assailant's path before it arrived, as there was plenty of room on the side of the hall away from the packed lounge.

"Oh, my God!" exclaimed one of the neurophiles crowded into the lounge, "It's Judy." She had gotten an unobstructed view of the faceplate that still dangled below Judy's head.

Judy abruptly threw her drive wheels into reverse. Seconds later, she again shifted into full speed forward. The momentary reprieve, however, was just enough to allow most of Sandy's body to get out of her path. Judy's remaining arm continued to thrash about violently, and a sharp swing to her left caught Sandy just below the neck area. Sandy rotated abruptly and was propelled toward the wall opposite the lounge. Judy's direction also changed, causing her to crash into Ramone, another recent transition, bringing her to a sudden halt and momentarily pinning him between the berserk Judy and others in the crowd.

Judy shifted to reverse, again moving toward Sandy. The distance was enough to allow Judy to pick up significant momentum, despite being in reverse, which was supposed to be a languid speed.

Judy squarely struck Sandy's left side. The front drive wheels of the Neurophile do not pivot and provided reliable traction. Unfortunately, Sandy worked as intended and gripped the floor tightly, refusing to slide, causing Sandy's entire 200-kilogram assembly to topple over.

Neurophiles are not supposed to tip, but the designers had considered the possibility. In the event of a free fall to the ground, consciousness would be lost, but the supports attaching the head and the precious brain inside would hold, and essential life-sustaining flow of neurophile blood to the brain would be maintained. Sandy was far enough from the wall to allow significant speed to build up as she fell. Unfortunately, just before reaching the floor, her head slammed into a protruding building support pillar, collapsing the protection around the brain, crushing it, and killing her instantly. With the blood pump still operating, blood oozed copiously from the casing.

Judy briefly thrashed about near Sandy's broken body. Satisfied with Sandy's destruction, and much to the lounge dwellers' relief, she moved away. Later investigation concluded that all Judy's movements had resulted from random noise created by a degraded brain/body interface and not intentional actions on Judy's part. The report concluded that she had probably been dead inside the device for some time, but others disagreed.

Judy's wheels again squealed, moving her in the direction from which she had come. This time the randomness was gone, and she picked up sustained speed. Her remaining arm's erratic motions had also ceased, and she made rapid progress down the hall, away from the terrorized lounge dwellers. As she flew past, her arm caught Kenneth's shoulder in one last destructive gesture, causing his carcass to move briefly with her. After a few meters, Ken's body slammed against another column protruding from the wall, severing the wires that had previously dangled his head from his upright carcass. The head—his dead brain inside—went skittering across the finely polished floor.

Approaching the end of the hall and an inevitable collision with the wall, several observers reported hearing Judy yell, "I can't stop. I can't..."

The wall was no match for the 200-kilogram neurophile moving 30 kilometers per hour (an unattainable speed by normal neurophiles). The entire building trembled as heavy structural bricks yielded to her momentum. Her crushed remains and a hail of concrete block, bricks, and mortar fell 12 stories before smashing into a car, carefully covered with a sheet.

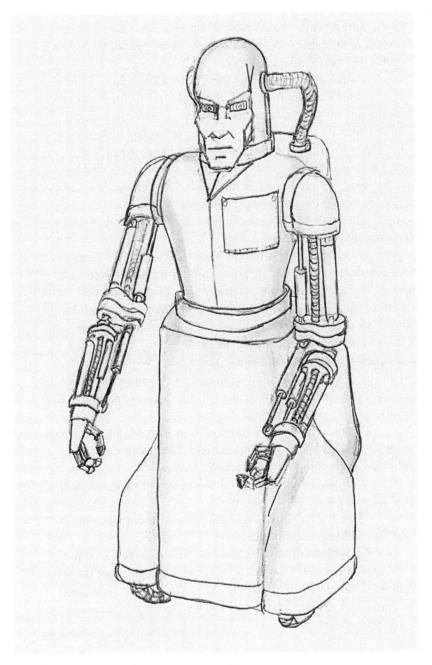

# A Train Going Somewhere
by John Cowgill, *Write by the Rails*

I love to ride a train. I have crossed Europe many times. One of the most memorable trips took me from Beijing to Moscow. It is a 5-6-day trip, 4,700 miles.

My Russian and English served me well on my adventure. It was around 9:00 pm on a bitterly cold winter night. It was very dark outside my train window. The light from my room was casting glimmers off the deep snow, a snow banked high along the rails. The train inched along. I had my private room with a separate bedroom. I was not sleepy. I just wanted to sit and look out the window despite not seeing much. I just enjoyed being on the train, noting my progress on a map of the run.

I heard two knocks at the door. I got up and answered. The conductor stood there.

"Good day." He lifted his hat to greet me. "We seem to have a little situation. We are going to be stopping soon to pick up a passenger, but we have no empty seats in the coach cars, and all the private rooms are filled except yours. We did not want to bother you, but the next train does not come until days from now. You can see that it is extremely cold outside, and this station is not a pleasant walk from a town without heat. We were wondering if you would be kind enough to allow this passenger to ride with you. I must note that she will ride a good distance as the next station is over a day away."

I enjoyed having this room all to myself. I could sleep in a bed with nobody keeping me up at night. No one in the room disturbed me. I enjoyed having a toilet to myself.

Without hesitation, "Yes. I will gladly let them ride with me."

"Thank you." The conductor tipped his hat. "I assure you. You will be compensated."

I closed the door and sat down. The train slowed down. The horn blew twice. The hydralic brakes screeched until the train came to a complete stop. I glanced through the window, seeing the usual dark sky with the train's lights reflecting on the snow below the windowsill.

"Knock! Knock! Knock!"

I went to the door.

"Sorry to bother you again." He tipped his hat again. "This lovely lady will ride with you."

I peeked behind him to see a beautiful woman wearing a distinctive white fuzzy hat with dark sunglasses.

The conductor injected, "I was just informed that she is deaf and mute."

She stepped into the room in her heavy black trench coat, holding her black snow boots in her right hand and her backpack in her left. I glanced down at her gray jeans and her bare feet with a few snow crystals between her toes. As I was about to ask her a question, I realized she could not respond. She sat down, putting her boots and backpack on the floor. Did she remove her boots so not to track snow into my cabin?

"Again, sorry for the inconvenience."

"I think I'll be fine," I replied.

"Have a pleasant journey." The conductor pulled the door shut.

She pulled off her hat, and her black hair flowed onto her shoulders, but she kept her sunglasses on. She smiled at me as I sat down next to her. I noticed a tattoo of four blue stars on the top of her foot, a small yellow smiley face on the top of her big toe. I pointed at her foot. She glanced down. She reached into her backpack and pulled out an old iPad. I sat back as she typed a message. Minutes later she handed the iPad to me, showing me what she had written.

She wrote that the four stars reminded her of her four friends that she made while as a prisoner bound to a kind of gulag in Siberia, although they are no longer called that. "The guards did not like the colors of our eyes and threatened us with beheading. We attempted to escape from the camp. In the confusion I slipped into the forests. My friends were not as fortunate."

She hid in the near forests, later returning to the camp, hoping to rescue them only to witness from her berth in the trees of their terrible deaths. They were the only true friends she ever had. She had this tattoo done on her foot to remind her of her friends. She often walks around barefoot even in the cold to punish herself. Guards often made them remove their boots to stave off escape.

Tears rolled down her face. I diverted my gaze, self-consciousness. Through the window, I looked to the falling snow. *Good time to wear boots.*

I typed asking her why she wears her sunglasses even though it is very dark. She typed her response. From the time of their capture, these guards beat them savagely. When she escaped, they sent out word to the local towns. She learned of a reward for her capture. While passing through one village, she found these sunglasses. She wanted a disguise. She broke into a clothing orchard and found clothes to wear. Strangers gave her a ride to a town, took pity. One family protected her for many months. She got clean, got better clothes and the tattoo on her foot. When she could get a ticket on this train, she did with the hope to get far away to Moscow. She did not know.

I motioned to remove her sunglasses. She hesitated, but I motioned again. She eased the sunglasses from her face. She glanced toward me. Looking at her bright green eyes. I typed a message saying, "You have beautiful eyes."
Tears flowed. She was crying.

I typed, "I am your friend."

She quickly gave me a tentative hug and a kiss on my cheek, then turned to the winter landscape.

I enjoyed her unanticipated companionship. We chatted over the days until she disembarked. I think often of this woman. Where has life taken her?

# JOHN'S TIME ON EARTH
by Stanley B. Trice, *Virginia Writers Club*

*A part of this story is true. I wrote this story to tell the black man's side of things, but I never sent the story out to be published. I let critics, who lurked out there to deter me. I think it is more important to tell what happened. Even if it is a white man writing this.*

As a child, John remembered the house he grew up in and the bathroom outside where he made friends with the black snake curled in the corner. The snake was as dark as his skin, and he wondered if it came from Africa like his ancestors. He was safe with the snake away from the fists of his father and the curses of his mother.

In his first few years of life, John heard his parents talk about Communism, Korea, and H bomb terrors. When he started school, Korea was forgotten, people were interested in rockets, and he found safety under a school desk. Instead of learning by sitting in the seat, he waited under it for the desk to fall on him. Like everyone else, he had a bond with paranoia and fear.

During these early years, John wondered if white folk would be killed when the bomb dropped or just black folk. Since the whites were just as scared of the bomb as he was, John figured the bomb did not care about skin color.

In school, John understood how white people needed hate because they fear of people different from them. He sometimes felt sorry for them with all that fear. He had no such need or fear. Deep southern prejudices, strong since a civil war John refused to learn about, seemed like a waste of time to him. He needed to eat after his father died and his mother didn't care anymore.

Instead of high school, John made money at a grain mill. He was paid less than the white men, but he had a job and would not go hungry. After a few months of hard working, the foreman approached John in front of the crew.

"I'm goin' to beat the hell outta you, boy." A look of fire spilled from the foreman's dark eyes. John learned that the other workmen had fed the foreman lies. John could not help doing a better job than men who would not stay sober.

John towered over the short, balding man who had a gut flowing over his belt line. "I didn't do nothin', Mist'r Foreman."

"There's a river not far from here where I go fishin' when I can. I'm fishin' for an answer here and now with you. You been messin' up like the others said?"

"Mist'r Foreman, I don't mess up nothin'. I like it here workin' for you."

The white man looked up into the dark nostrils of the black man before him. They both felt the eyes of the others in the shadows.

"Don't you let me see you mess up, ever. You hear me, boy?"

"Yes, sir."

The foreman stepped even closer to John and felt the man's hot breath. The foreman whispered, "You the best I got here. Watch yourself and just keep working. Hear? And my wife made too much fried chicken and cornbread yesterday. On your way home, stop by my mailbox and look inside. She knows when you come by."

He spun around fast for a small guy and before John could ask what he should watch out for. Angry eyes funneled out of the shadows. Everyone went back to work and sweated together as their smells became one.

John kept to himself listening to the white men at the mill arguing about an Asian war where white and black men were sent to die. John kept his draft card wrapped in the rag he used to wash out his toilet. The rag was his good luck charm that kept his draft number out of the top selection; he figured. But he made sure to tell the white mill men how someone could call his name any time so he might die instead of a white man.

John learned that when grain no longer grew, picking up trash was consistent work. White people wasted a lot. One day he waited outside a '65 high school graduation that he would have been at if he had stayed in school. While picking up stray, foodless paper, John listened carefully to a white woman speaking on stage. She introduced herself as Debbie as if it meant something.

"It's time for change," she demanded of her audience.

John watched her long brown hair flip in the breeze. White folk confused him sometimes. What needed changing? They had everything but time and age. Someone cried out that her mind had holes in it.

"At least I have a mind, mister." She got the laughter she wanted.

The white man called her some ugly words and stomped away from the crowd. When passing John, the man mumbled something at John, who took his trash stick and tripped him into a trash can. The white man wanted more to get away from the laughter than confront John, who was bigger. Debbie was the only person who saw the incident.

She stood on the narrow stage with fists on her hips and in front of a mike placed taller than she. Her stance was just wide enough to let people know she was serious about what she was saying. When she finished challenging the crowd to do something, Debbie strolled off the stage toward John and clasped his dirty hands. "You and I are going to be a team. We're taking on the establishment," she said.

She kept talking. John listened as he picked up trash. Finally, he figured he should say something. "Yeah, we can be a good team 'against the white 'stablishment who run everythin'." |

"Hey, as a woman they're not letting me live right, either. We're a pair, you and I. They hate us together."

"I don't hate them. They have accidents with their mouth, sometimes. That's all."

"They are an accident. Look at my parents and how white they are with me. They never understand where I'm coming from. You just wait and see. Just you and I will make a good pair."

Over the next six months, Debbie filled the emptiness in John and he went where she took him. When her parents found out, they had nothing more to do with their daughter. John and Debby married before anyone could stop it.

A white Baptist minister did the wedding. He complained the whole time about how his knees hurt with all his praying. He wanted the cruelty in the world to stop and people to understand each other. John thought the preacher should try standing up to pray.

John's Aunt and Uncle came along. So did Debbie's two

best girlfriends who left when they found out there was no liquor in the church reception. Since only the minister's wife brought food, the ceremony had a short abruptness to it that left John little time to understand bedroom procedures.

The next day, he went to work and Debbie changed John's house to suit the two of them. Soon, that change was for three.

They survived for a year and a half. In that time, they had a garden that died and a baby Alice who lived. They existed in a barely furnished shack that hung between what Debbie grew up in and what John had grown accustomed to living with.

All along, Debbie had a strength that kept them above the bad talk around town. She heard it at the laundromat, and he heard it at the grain mill. Nobody wanted a bunch of half-baked children wandering around, the Talk said. The Talk frustrated John because it hurt Debbie and he could not find an end to it.

Debbie told John to ignore the talk, but he wanted to fight and protect his daughter, who would be neither black nor white. Before Alice was six months old, the car accident changed things.

It was a hot August day when John got back home from the funeral, carrying Alice against the muscles of his right arm. A heavy rain that morning made the humidity come through the thin plaster walls of his tenant house. It dampened the ragged curtains and torn couch. More rain was coming.

In his left hand, he held a crushed red rose from his wife's casket. They were her favorite flower, but he could only afford two. The other went to the grave with her.

John was thankful that at least he got the same Baptist preacher who married them. It was only the three of them. As he got Alice's bottle ready on the stove, John re-read the police report summarizing his wife's car accident. Anger made him crumble the report in his hand and toss it on the floor.

"It's all lies," John kept his voice under control, although he wanted to cry out until someone listened. "There's too many people hatin' a black man marrin' some white woman and getting' a child," he told Alice in that torn house.

John looked out the kitchen's pane glass window as the rain came again. Pellets struck the red clay in his yard. Hardly any grass grew in the hard soil, and what grass he saw got pelted dead. "Dead like Debbie. She died by no accident. This I know," John said at the window.

He slammed his fist onto the countertop, causing a sharp noise that rattled the few dishes and glasses. Alice flinched. "I got to do somethin' about you. I couldn't protect your momma and I worry about protectin' you. You need better carin' than I can give," he said to his daughter.

John snuggled Alice gently to his chest and gave her the bottle. When she finished, he abandoned the crumbled flower on the table and carefully covered his daughter in a cotton blanket.

He walked outside, leaving the front door open, and put Alice across the front seat of the rusty Pontiac sedan. The car's gas gauge had less than a quarter of a tank, but the eleven dollars in his pocket had to go toward Alice.

"I'll figure something out later if I make it to later. Right now, I got to convince my Aunt to take care of you until I work things out."

As he packed what little he owned for Alice in the car, John wondered how he could have been so stupid as to bring a child into this world. "Debbie could talk me into anything 'cause she had a bigger plan for us to survive. Now, your momma's gone and I don't know what that plan was."

A rage built in his head and his frustration shook repeatedly through his mind as he drove slowly down the narrow, dirt road. A fast rain spilled across the car and road. It brought on more humidity and made John sweat even more. He could imagine Debbie scolding him to calm down. "But things have changed. I ain't got happy anymore."

Despite the car's low gas, John thought he could make it to his Aunt's place two counties over. And maybe he might have made it if the carburetor did not start acting up halfway over.

It could have been a crack in the distributor letting moisture into the points. In either case, the wetness got to it all. He had troubles with the old Pontiac and, as he nursed it along, he scolded himself for forgetting his toolbox. Finally, the car spat and heaved to a stop, leaving him and sitting in a hot humid car.

They were on the edge of a concrete bridge spanning high over a river gorge. Water poured from the mad sky and his Aunt's house was still thirteen miles away.

The unforgiving rain dampened any hope of restarting the car. Carefully, John covered his daughter and stepped out as hot pellets struck his bare head and unprotected face. He wasn't sure where he was going, but staying wouldn't help.

He marched with long steps until almost halfway across the long bridge. That was when he saw a white Ford Fairlane approach from the other way, with three young white men inside.

John knew them. There would be a fight if they stopped. He got furious about what they would do to his daughter. He walked slower, keeping his head down across Alice to hide her. He tried to come up with a plan in case the Fairlane stopped. He could not think straight. The car began slowing.

I can run fast, he thought. I bet I can run a lot faster than them. He knew he would outrun them if he thought of what they would do to Alice.

As the car drew closer, the tires grew quicker and faster. Suddenly, the car sped past him as the three white men yelled ugly words against his blackness. John breathed again, realizing they did not see that he carried a baby or recognized him. At least the rain was good for something.

He stood there muttering to Alice, "How can I go on? I'm messed up with the lies and the town talk. Now there is only me and you, darlin' and I got to give you up just to save you."

John hated the thought of being separated from his daughter. He looked down at her cradled safely in the fold of his muscular arms. "I didn't protect Debbie, so how am I going to protect you?" He looked up into the rain striking his face and watched as dark gray clouds passed swiftly overhead like dancing gravestones.

Looking over the edge of the bridge, John saw it was a long way down to the gorge. He looked into the deep chasm and thought that maybe God had put him in this place for a reason. "It was as if the world has nowhere for me to go but here," he said to the rain.

John leaned over the railing and saw a silver river twist between large, jagged rocks. He cried. The more he tried to stop, the more he felt like his whole inside was being wrenched out. His body shook like he had tremors. Alice made soft sounds and clutched at her dad's sleeve with tiny hands. He could not look at her face, but only felt the small tug. His tears flew out of his eyes as fast as the rain slapped his face and bare head.

There's a reason for everything, he believed. Yet, he could not think of a reason for what he was feeling. "What if this bridge was the last thing I walked on?"

John looked down at Alice. "You don't know the crossroads I'm feeling at right now," he whispered to her. "To keep walking or not. Who knows the road that hurts less."

He planted his right foot on the concrete base of the railing, trying to clear his head. He put his left foot high on the aluminum rail and pushed off.

Flying into the thick, wet air, John clenched his eyes shut to keep from seeing what was coming at him. All he felt for a few seconds was the violent rush of hot, wet wind pushing through his pants and loosening his shirt. Pellets of rain stung his bare skin where it could.

John thought he would have longer to think. He wanted to have some final piece of thought to keep him and Alice together as they passed into the other side. Yet, the fall was swift.

He did not let go of his daughter even after the first impact blew him sideways off a sharp rock, knocking the air out of his soon bleeding lungs. He did not let go until the forceful river separated them in its swift, cold current and carried them in a twisting way far from the bridge.

John knew a harsh darkness. It enveloped and stole him away, leaving him empty. He did not care and did not want to remember. He stopped thinking. Yet, a burden of guilt lowered over him like a cold, wet blanket.

There was no feeling or focus to his senses. John picked his way through shadows until finding himself in a room. He stood in front of a narrow window.

Sitting on the windowsill was the black snake of his childhood hissing at him. He wanted to go through that window, but he did not want to hurt the snake. Behind him, he heard a baby crying. John knew it was Alice.

"What protection did I give her by killing us both?"

With the snake hissing louder and Alice crying more, John spun around and ran toward his daughter's voice. He left the window and fell into the darkness that exploded around him.

John found himself with Alice on that long bridge with his right foot resting on the railing. He looked up at hearing a car approach from the direction he came from.

"Get in the car with that baby and outta the rain," yelled one man in the car.

John obediently climbed in the back behind the mill foreman who drove and the preacher who rode.

"I guess your car broke down," asked the preacher.

"Watcha doin' lookin' over the side of that bridge? You thinkin' of jumpin'? Not with that baby you ain't," said the foreman.

"I was headed for my Aunt's house up on Pork Mountain. You take me there?" Cold water dripped from John's face onto Alice, but she didn't cry. She only looked up at her dad's face and he thought she smiled.

The foreman and a preacher went up to that mountain and left John there. With all the rain, the foreman said for John to stay since the mill would be closed for a few days. Later, the preacher brought him and Alice back to live in a new tenant house.

"It's close to some good black people who'll watch Alice while you work," said the preacher. "And they got a good black church not far. Say hello to the preacher for me when you go on Sunday."

*Epilogue*

The mill closed years later, and the foreman drank himself to death. At the funeral, the preacher cried during his talk. John took Alice to the funeral, then to college two towns over. Not long after and before Alice became one of the greatest nurses the local hospital ever saw, John died in his sleep.

He went back to that narrow window with the blacksnake. This time, the snake slithered away. Debbie helped her husband through the window.

# WE NEED TO TALK
by Charles Tabb, *Hanover Writers Club*

Lois decided it was time she talked to Bill about what she wanted. Needed, really. She should matter, too.

Tonight was no different from any other night. They sat in their gray fabric chairs, the seats long ago molded to their bodies. This thought brought images of coffins, and she wondered if they, too, eventually reshaped themselves to fit their eternal occupants.

She watched Bill peering over his glasses at the TV and noticed his graying hair had thinned to wisps. His jowls sagged, and his stomach folded over his belt. She remembered running fingers through thick locks and feeling the muscles in his face when they kissed. She'd changed, too. Her svelte figure had been replaced by wide hips and thighs, and her graying hair hung in dull strands no matter what she tried.

Time was running out. It was now or never.

"Bill, honey, we need to talk. Could you turn off ESPN for a few minutes? The same thing will be on in another hour. Or just record it if it's that important. — No, you can't just mute it because then you'll just watch it without the sound. — Because we need to talk. — No, I don't want any ice cream. I want to talk. — Yes, it's *that* important. I was talking to Hunter the other day, and he agreed I should talk with you. — Yes, he called. He's doing fine. — Yes, he said he'd see you at the game this weekend. Honey, we really need to talk."

She braced herself for what she knew he'd say. "You know how we always used to talk about going on a tour of Europe? — I know it's expensive, but you know it's a dream I've had for, well, forever, it seems. — Wait. Where are you going? — No, sit down, please, and listen. I said I don't want any ice cream. — You can have some in a minute. We really need to talk about this first. — Because it's on my bucket list. There's this festival in Paris this summer where everyone dresses up in period costume. You know, like Marie Antoinette or Louis XIV, and it sounds like fun."

His question caught her by surprise. "My physical? — Yes, I... talked to my doctor about the results. — Yesterday. — I'm not talking about that now. I'm talking about going to Europe. — Not now. I'll tell you what he said later. I want to go to Europe."

She paused as her voice caught, and she looked at the floor, realizing what she'd always known. She pressed on nonetheless.

"I want to do that one thing. Just that one."

Looking back at him, she pleaded with her eyes, but as her father had warned, Bill was Bill. He'd do what he wanted. Her sigh sounded like a dying breath.

"Okay, fine. Never mind. You can turn your ESPN back on."

She hefted herself from the chair, resigned to the habit of her life as the TV blared again. "How about some ice cream?" she asked.

## CONVERSATIONS

by Stacy Clair, *Riverside Chapter*

I show up to Shelly and Mike's house, pizza in hand and *Cards Against Humanity* in the bookbag strapped on my shoulders. I stand at the doorway and take a deep breath. Exhaling with deliberate slowness, I knock on the large red door. I want to turn around and leave the moment I hear shoes on hardwood, shuffling towards the door to let me in. I should not have come. Mike is not one of my favorite people on an uneventful day. Let alone, with all the chaos and pain in the world right now. I fear, no, I know he'll run his mouth more than normal. I always try to be agreeable and quiet, but there are certain things I simply cannot ignore when ignorance is abundantly prominent. Shelly opens the door, a huge smile on her face, and takes the pizza from my hands.

"Mike's in the shower," she says. "He'll be out in a few minutes."

I hate that I'm instantly calmer knowing my enemy of opinions is not currently around and I can pretend, even if only for a limited time, that tonight will be a fun night shared with Shelly. Shelly is a sweet girl. She sees the good in everyone (which bodes well for me since I'm a sarcastic cynic who is hard to get close to.) She sees the supposed good in Mike as well. And I guess he's not all bad. He adores Shelly, so he's got that going for him. He's a decent cook, and he is a good handyman. They want kids, and I think he'll be a devoted dad, but I know he'll instill his one-sided opinions to his kids, and I hate that.

Shelly brings me out of my dreary thoughts as she comes to sit with me and hands me a glass of Malvasia wine. I thank her and take a sip. Light and sweet with a touch of bubbles. *Ahh...* I sigh in content.

"So, what's been new with you, Shayne?" Shelly asks as she drops to the couch beside me, gazing. She's so kind. So willing to give you one hundred percent of her attention. From down the hallway, I hear the bathroom door click as Mike retreats into their bedroom. I felt a cloud of gloom come over me, but internally shake it off. I fill Shelly in on my day.

Quarantine hasn't really changed my routine too much. Other than the occasional unplanned shopping trip, I haven't been too affected by the lockdown. Being a couch potato with no social life makes that pretty easy.

We continue to chit-chat for the next ten minutes until Mike comes out to join us. Shelly's face lights up when he walks into the room, and internally I gag a little. I know... I know it's childish of me. He's a nice enough guy on the surface. He treats my friend well, and he moved her right into his house without a second thought after her last relationship blew up. They started out as roommates, and then it just turned into something more. I'm happy for Shelly because she seems the most content she's been since I've known her. But the more I get to know him, the harder it is for me to see his redeeming qualities. With all the protesting, rioting and political uproar that's been going on since the death of George Floyd, I *know* Mike will bring up the topic. He likes to pick at me just to see how upset he can make me, then tell me I'm overreacting. Shelly tries, half-heartedly, to get him to stop, but he knows she thinks his jabs are harmless. She won't tell me, because she's trying to show support, but she thinks I overreact to his words.

"What up, Shay?" I hate when he calls me that. He's not my friend

"Hey, Mike." I say it with a fake smile plastered on my face.

We take a seat at the dining room table, start digging into pizza, and Mike deals our cards. For the first half hour we're sucked into food and inappropriate laughs. We take a break so Shelly can grab us some chocolate to munch on as we continue our game. I pick up my phone and check Twitter as I wait for her return.

"So, what do you think about the fucking idiots rioting and looting to show support for a drug addict thief? Even *you* can't put a positive spin on that dumb shit." Mike says as he gulps down his Mountain Dew straight from the can. *So, we're doing this.* I sigh and place my phone down and look across the table at him.

"I can't say I condone looting and rioting, but it got our attention, right? It got people talking." I wait for him to tear me down.

"Yeah, I'm paying attention. Paying attention to my tax dollars as they pay for overtime of all the cops that would rather be at home with their families than patrolling the streets for thugs." He smirks at me, waiting to see if I'll take the bait. He intentionally used the term "thugs," to see if I'll bring up a tweet Trump made regarding African Americans. I don't.

I say, frustrated, "Look, people are outraged. People are hurt. People are scared. People just want justice. People just want their freedom, day-to-day. African Americans can't seem to get the attention that's needed to stop the abuse of power."

He says, looking away - disgust on his face, "Abuse of power? What abuse? That man was a criminal."

"Yes," I affirm, "he was a criminal. No one says he wasn't. But he wasn't attacking anyone or running down kids or something. Jesus! He wrote a bad check! I'm not saying he shouldn't have been reprimanded, but,"

Mike cuts me off. "Reprimanded? What, like a fine? What about the business he was stealing from? You think they didn't deserve justice because they're big business? They're 'The Man?' Just because they might not be a black owned business, he can steal from them? That sounds like racism to me! And don't give me that bullshit about how black people can't be racist!" Mike spews, red-faced and angry, waiting for a fight.

"Ok, first off. I do not know who owns the business he was writing the check to. That's not the point. The point is," Mike cuts me off again.

"I'm sure the owners would disagree... Not the point... Not the point??? Who the fuck are you, or any of these other people, to take justice into their own hands? Where do you get off?" Mike takes a breath, and I used the opportunity to cut him off the same way he did to me.

"Look! This is bigger than George Floyd! What about Breonna Taylor?" Mike shoves himself back from the table and mutters angrily under his breath. "Wait. Let me finish, please. You started this conversation. The least you could do is hear what I have to say." Mike crosses his arms and then gives me a petulant raise of the eyebrows as if saying, 'well go ahead then.' I do my best to ignore his childishness and continue with a calmer tone.

"Breonna Taylor was gunned down by police with an

incorrect search warrant. She was sleeping in her fucking bed. Even if they had the correct address, did that give them the right to kill her?" Mike is giving me the silent treatment, so I continue.

"Ahmaud Aubrey was jogging down a neighborhood, and an ex-policeman took it upon himself to bring his son and another man to track Ahmaud and hunt him out in the open. They killed him because they thought he'd robbed a construction site. Even if he robbed a store, people rob stores every day, they rarely die."

Finally, Mike turns to look my way, arms still crossed, he says, "It's called a citizen's arrest. They were trying to detain him, and he became violent."

"Mike! You can't possibly back that -" I make sarcastic quotes with my fingers, logic up. "A citizen's arrest isn't an acceptable reason to kill another human being. It's also not an excuse for blatant racism. All he was doing was jogging." I am visibly upset.

"It wasn't his neighborhood. He never should have been there." Mike says, raising his eyebrow again to counter my argument.

I snap back. "So, what? You've never driven or walked down a neighborhood that wasn't yours? Of course you have. You know why you don't even think twice about doing it? 'cuz you're white?"

"Oh, here we go. Cry me a fucking river Shayne. You're fucking white too. You have the same doors opened for you as I do." He says condescendingly.

"First off, being a woman, no I don't. But that's an entirely different argument we can have later." I can feel my cheeks heat as Mike laughs at my statement.

"Look. What else do they want?" This time, I cut him off.
"They?!!" I yell.

"Yes, *they*. Fucking they. They are not racist Shayne. Stop jumping up my ass. They are referring to people. I don't care what color they are. Just people protesting. You're part of the 'the' I'm speaking of." He says this as an insult, but it's the first time I've smiled since this conversation started. He continues, exasperated at my response. "They got our monuments and statues removed. That shit is a part of history. You can't just remove it because you don't like how history was made. That's so selfish. I'm sorry it upsets you, but the Civil War wasn't about that. It was how our country became what it is today. And some people may not respect that, but I do!" Mike is sweating. I wonder, absentmindedly, if he might pass out.

"Part of the Civil War was about the right to own slaves. Not all of it but a portion was." I say. "I will not argue with you over the positives and negatives of war but, imagine if Germany kept all the Swastikas and Nazi-fare out on the streets to remind people of their -", I make my sarcastic air quotes again, "history."

"I'm not talking about Germany." Mike begins, but I cut him off.

"I know that, but the similarities are sickening! Nazis held people captive, there was police brutality based on race and the rest of the world turned a blind eye. People were tortured, murdered and blamed and it was all legal." I said.

"Yeah, and who saved them? The good ole United States. We're not so bad in your little scenario there, now are we?" Mike counters. "And now *your* governor wants to remove history because of violence. What kind of message is that sending about land of the free?"

"Ugh! I'm not saying America is all bad, Mike. Jesus! You can't be reasoned with! What I'm saying is, after the war was over and the Nazis were defeated and Hitler's piece-of-shit ass killed himself, imagine if every time the Jewish people walked down the street, or their kids or their grandkids or their friends or anyone who felt traumatized by the goings on in the concentration camps had to see the places where their ancestors were gassed alive? Or where their best friend's mom had her gold teeth ripped out of her mouth right before she was set on fire? Could a person, of such ancestry feel safe simply walking down the street with the yellow star of shame always pinned to their chest?" I stop and breath heavily, waiting for Mike's response.

"They kept Auschwitz up. People go there and take selfies and shit right on the same walkway others walked to die. Why is that ok?" Mike says back.

"They kept the concentration camp as a place for people to visit. If they put the statues and slave blocks in a museum, I think that's simply fine. It's ok to learn about history and see the awful acts mankind has partaken in. No one is trying to erase history, Mike. They just don't need a daily reminder of it." I exhale, calmer now. I think we might get somewhere.

Shelly, who had been watching from the doorway as our argument unfolded, comes to sit down and drops bite-sized candy bars in front us. "Okay, you two. Enough is enough. I just wish everyone would recognize that all lives matter and be done with it. No one race matters more than the other."

I sigh and look down at the candy in front of me. I unwrap one.

"Oh, what now?" Mike snaps. "Your best friend can't express the fact that her life matters because she's white?"

"Mike," Shelly begins, "I'm sure Shayne doesn't think that." She turns to look at me hopefully. She knows I care about her life. She's hoping I'll simply agree, and Mike will calm down.

I begin. "No one is saying all lives don't matter."

"Oh, yes they are," Mike starts.

"Back with the *they* stuff again, huh?" I seethe.

"Okay, you two. That's enough. I'm sorry I even brought it up. All lives matter. No lives matter. Whatever. Let's just play, okay?" Shelly says trying to calm us.

"No, I think I'd like to hear what your *white* friend thinks about Black Lives Matter and how she might relate with her *white* skin and her *white* girl hair. Tell us how your *white* privilege gives you the right to be offended on behalf of the black community." Mike is leaning towards me across the table now, shaking with fury.

I strive for temperate tones. "Look, I can only understand racism and fear based on my own experiences. But the fact of the matter is that I may not understand every point of view, but I can empathize, and I can be part of change. I *cannot* be offended when someone says Black Lives Matter. No one said, *only* black lives matter. Maybe if the hashtag said 'black lives matter too' or 'black lives matter also' people wouldn't get so bent out of shape about it. But I doubt it—judging by the look on your face, I'd say I'm right..." I sigh, then continue. "I can stop for a moment to be proactive instead of reactive. I can listen to stories and support change. I can be part of the positivity instead of the negativity. I'm not over here bashing all white people or all law enforcement. I'm not advocating for looting and tearing apart cities out of anger and grief. All I'm saying is I'm willing to stop and listen. And I'm willing to be part of the solution instead of the problem. That is what I can offer." I stop and wait for Mike to speak. He stares at the floor, still seething. I'm at a loss of what to say to calm him at this point and, honestly, I don't even want to. Let him be mad.

Mike spits at me. "So, you're fine with those *people*—you're fine with people removing history and trying to make us forget what our heritage stands for?"

"No one is trying to forget history. Those monuments and statues will be moved to a museum. It's unnecessary to see them every day. I enjoy seeing very disturbing museum artifacts, but not everyone wants to see that stuff. And honestly, even I don't want to see things like, let's say, The Body Exhibit every single day. I want to be in the right mindset to see and learn about such things." I say back.

"You shouldn't need to be in a *certain mindset* to see America's history. I'm done with you. I'm going to bed." Mike stands and kisses Shelly on the head, puts his plate in the sink and heads into the bedroom, shutting the door firmly behind him.

I look over at Shelly to gauge her reaction. She sighs and begins closing the pizza box and putting the cards back in their box. "I think game night is over," she whispers. She's upset.

"Shelly -" I say.

"Don't start, Shayne. I'm too tired. My best friend and my husband can't seem to get along for even an hour so we can all enjoy some pizza and laughs. Being caught between you two is exhausting for me. I think you should just go." She takes the pizza box to the fridge and puts both our plates into the sink. "Our half of the money for dinner is on the coffee table. Turn the lights out when you leave." And with that she walks out of the kitchen and into her bedroom, leaving me alone at the large dining room table.

I sit, stunned, for a moment. She's mad at me too. Not just at him. The Shelly I used to know would fight for human rights and equality across the board. I hate how quiet she's become since meeting Mike. The part of her that made us so close is lost. She's still a sweet person and I know she would never tell me I was wrong for standing up for what I think is right, but I'm also certain she'd tell Mike the same thing. She believes he has his convictions for a reason, and she's not in a place to change him. How do I argue with that?

I feel heavy as I stand and turn off the light. I leave their money, where it sits on the coffee table, and lock the door behind me as I walk out. Somewhere, in the back of my mind, in a deep dark place I can't bring to the surface yet; I know this is the last time I'll set foot in this house.

*Being caught between you two is exhausting for me. I think you should just go.*

## GROCERY CENTRAL
by Paula Weiss, Northern Virginia Chapter

An elderly lady, not very strong but not quite frail, and still pretty, stepped cautiously down the sidewalk carrying her reusable cloth shopping bags, which were required by law in the City and by thrift in Ploreville. The sidewalks of Ploreville—the Deplorable ghetto across the Potowmack River from the City—were notoriously pitted and treacherous, since the Social Credit authorities were uninterested in maintaining any infrastructure used by the reactionary ex-rebels. To the east, you could glimpse on the horizon the gleaming towers of the City of Anacosta, formerly Washington DC.

Her blonde hair had turned a salt and pepper gray with a few fair highlights. She wore a worn pink coat; when you were 79, you chilled easily, even on the pleasant June morning. In cash-strapped Ploreville, the clothing stores sold gently worn items discarded by Social Crediteers in the City. If you wanted to splurge, you could brave the carbon offsets that applied even to Plores, and buy something new.

Money had unexpectedly become scarce in Marjory Harris's household, or more precisely, in her daughter Emma's house, where she had moved after her son David had fled the Diversity Justice Republic for the still-free flyover US. As an Antifan commander, David had lavished cash and presents on his Deplorable family that usually were reserved only for high Social Crediteers. All that had vanished with him, although Marjory later found a large amount of cash stuffed in her usual hiding place, the laundry detergent box in the basement. Plores did not trust the government banks.

Marjory entered the Welcome bodega, as she did every Wednesday on weeks, beginning with an even-numbered date. In odd-numbered weeks, she came on Monday. "Welcome to Welcome's" said a large, neatly red-lettered sign on a whiteboard in the window.

"Good morning, Miz Harris," said Warren Welcome, the proprietor. Warren was a spare, medium-sized widower about ten years younger than Marjory, with close-cropped hair and a nut-brown complexion. In hardscrabble Ploreville, he had scraped together the money for the grocery himself decades ago and had made a go of it. You had to pay off various bureaucrats both in the City and in Ploreville, and you had to pay extra to the driver bringing you produce from the Economic Zones so that he would deliver to your store early in his Arlington run. Otherwise, you'd be stuck with wrinkled oranges and wilted lettuce. Doing business in Ploreville was about taking care of bureaucrats, truck drivers, and when you could, your loyal customers such as Mrs. Harris.

"Good morning, Mr. Welcome," she replied. As always, Marjory gravitated over to the produce. "Let's see what you have for me today."

Two rows of produce bins were ranged against the wall opposite the counter, seven bins on top and seven below. A long narrow shelf ran just above the top bins. Today, the top bins contained, in order, potatoes, onions, tomatoes, broccoli, cucumbers, eggplants, and small paper bags of blackberries, which were a luxury even though they were in season. On the small shelf above each relevant bin rested a single potato, two onions, a cucumber and two small bags of blackberries. Marjory thought regretfully of the abundance she and other Americans had enjoyed in her youth, before the civil war and the socialist DJR destroyed it all.

The store, like everything else in Ploreville, was shabby, but impeccably clean. Plores couldn't get loans from government banks, because their enterprises were not joint ventures with the state. Money stores were expensive, what with their high interest rates. Welcome kept the premises as clean as possible, enforced complete intolerance of mice and insects with a good tabby mouser who roamed the store, added a dash of color where he could, and planned on investing in a bright red awning, perhaps next year. Yet the casual patron might have wondered why Welcome, who in his constant tidying, seemed a controlling sort, would not have returned the stray produce back to their respective bins immediately after shoppers carelessly left the items on the shelf.

Marjory popped the potato, onions, cucumber and blackberries into her bag, selected a few dry good items, and then stood at the counter as she paid Welcome. A teenage boy came into the store from the back, grabbed several full paper bags, and went out to the bicycle to make deliveries. That was the son of Welcome's oldest son, who had attended Bethune Junior High with her David before the Antifans took David away.

"How's your sons?" she asked, politely. She sensed that Welcome seemed more anxious than usual. And what other problems could people their age have but children and grandchildren?

"Mostly the usual," said Welcome. He paused, wondering whether to confide in Marjory, but then couldn't resist. "I'm worried about Jeff. He says he wants to go Social Credit so he can go to college." Jeff was the youngest of the three Welcome sons.

"Oh no!" Marjory commiserated, her hand rising to her mouth.

The decision to "go Social Credit" was not a minor one. The government dangled it enticingly in front of the Black Plores, and to a lesser extent the Hispanics. A white Deplorable might apply, and after excruciating investigations and self-abasement as he acknowledged his racism, sexism, homophobia and transphobia, be granted Social Credit status, but the government distrusted them anyway and it needed a menial Plore workforce to serve elite Social Crediteers. But it remained a sore point with the leaders of the Diversity Justice Republic that so many blacks— more than the government would publicly admit—had fought on the side of the Red fascists during the civil war, and after the war most had steadfastly refused what they considered a poisoned Social Credit chalice.

Each Black Plore who could be lured into Social Credit allowed the government to burnish its credentials as the protector and defender of the oppressed Diverse Peoples, and each Black Plore who resisted the promise of more comfortable living and less freedom remained an affront to the government. For these reasons, the Black Plores enjoyed considerable prestige in Plorevilles up and down the East Coast, and when any slipped and fell into the hands of the security service, the dreaded Antifan Defense Forces, or ADF, they were punished all the more severely for their heresy.

But the temptation always existed. No Plore could attend college, a privilege reserved for Social Crediteers. The local high schools trained Plores for trades and service occupations such as bus drivers, florists, and drywall and floor installers. Thousands of Plores trudged into the City each day, on their buses and then through the great glass tunnel bridges to serve in menial City jobs, such as waitrons, sandwich makers, store clerks, and cleaning and road crews. A plumber or an electrician rose to the top of the heap, since while Social Crediteers usually considered themselves above menial labor, they still valued working toilets and lights. Each Plore household was required to dispatch at least one worker to the City in return for the small monthly stipend that kept many Plore families from outright destitution.

Two blocks away from Welcome's was a storefront labeled, "Social Credit Recruiting Office." It drew little traffic, partly because no Plore wished to be seen entering. Behind the dusty windows you could glimpse the shadows of uniformed officers waiting for a furtive visitor. Plore mothers darkly warned their children as they passed, "move quickly or the Blues will grab you!" and the children would cast fearful looks back at the windows.

If you were Jeff, 24 years old and repairing drywall in the City, but liking to read and envious of what he saw as the carefree Social Crediteers his age, it would be tempting to walk into that office and place yourself in the recruiters' hands. Otherwise, what was left to you? Forty, fifty more years of drywall? Maybe inheriting Dad's bodega and spending your days haggling with surly truck drivers? Jeff knew that the recruiters would gladly accept his application, although he was hazier about what would happen afterwards and became impatient when his father asked directly about whether Jeff could really trust the government to deliver on its promises.

"I don't blame him for wanting more education," said Welcome. "He reads some old paperbacks sometimes—not just the GVN," or the Great Virtual Network on which the government placed all approved reading and viewing. Unlike Social Crediteers, Plores were not forbidden from reading the yellowing stray paperbacks that still circulated legally around Ploreville, as long as they were not outright seditious. "But I don't think he realizes what he'd be giving up, or taking on."

Marjory nodded. As a Social Crediteer, Jeff would be

discouraged from visiting his family in Ploreville, and Plores were forbidden from visiting the City unless working there or on major holidays. Jeff would have to surrender his faith for pagan Mother Earth Diversity services and distance himself from his family. His political minders would monitor him constantly for signs of Plore backsliding, scrutiny that your blackness would not spare you.

But most ominously, the path only went one way—there was no way to change your mind and return to Ploreville. If you objected to your assigned job or housing, you would find yourself at ADF headquarters. If you worshipped as a Christian outside of the MED umbrella, you would be executed, black or not. Christian proselytizing, like firearms ownership, was a capital crime.

"I hope he gets some fancy restaurant meals out of it," Welcome tried to joke, but Marjory could tell he was despondent. Going Social Credit was a rejection of your parents and their values, preserved for you at great risk and sacrifice. The local Ploreville paper—under Social Crediteer control—would run a fawning story on the young Black Plore who had resolved to embrace Diversity, embarrassing Welcome before his neighbors and customers.

"Maybe he'll realize it's a bad deal before he does it," she said.

"Who could blame him?" Welcome said tersely, throwing his arm out, as if to say "given all this? What can I offer him?"

"This is why we are fighting to..." Marjory began, but discretion got the better of her, aided by Welcome's raised eyebrows. "Don't give up, ever."

"I hope you enjoy the food," Welcome said, dryly. "Don't eat it all in one meal."

As Marjory began to walk out the door, he called after her. "Be careful out there. We've started to see more ADF in the streets. I'm not sure they care too much about the Treaty these days."

"God bless you," she said, and left. It was a four block walk home past the shabby storefronts, but the sight of other passersby enjoying the warm sunshine cheered her. Children whooped and ran down the block, circling back to their mothers like birds to their nest.

Some passerby knew her by sight and reputation if not personally and greeted her respectfully. She was the mother of the legendary Plore who had become an Antifan against his will, protected the neighborhood, and then had amazingly defied the ADF to flee to the US and freedom.

At the corner, she glimpsed one block farther down the black uniforms of two ADF officers and decided to take a more roundabout route back to her house. They also knew who she was, and she did not want to risk any trouble. Until recently, you saw only Anacosta Mental Health Police patrolling the streets of Ploreville, so the appearance of ADF uniforms was a disturbing trend.

The ADF officers stood under yet another flagpole flying the DJR flag, a round green earth against a black Antifan background that angered every Plore over the age of thirty. She could see the hated flag fluttering in the breeze above them. She could not risk an encounter with the ADF on the day her knitting circle met. The participants donated all the completed hats and sweaters to charity, for which there was always need. But knitting was not the group's main function. Nor was reading the focus of the book club that met on the alternate weeks.

Marjory had originally hosted all the sessions until Emma realized what the club gatherings really were about. "Mom! You can't do this! We're already in their sights!" Marjory had asked, who would suspect a dozen nice older ladies of subversion?

"The Antifans, that's who!" Emma retorted. Finally, Marjory had reluctantly agreed that it was unwise to draw extra attention to their household. The participants rotated meeting places after that. Yet her daughters and their husbands would not stop Marjory.

"At least we can keep an eye on her," said Emma's husband Larry. "I'm kind of proud of her, you know. That's the right Plore spirit, the way we were before they beat us down." He was phlegmatic in defeat.

Regardless of where the ladies met, and today she herself was hosting, Marjory would relay the instructions for the week. The produce arrangement on the top shelf at Welcome's was a code. The first bin always represented Thursday, and the last Wednesday. One item atop a bin signaled which day clandestine

88

Plore travelers would arrive in Arlington en route to somewhere else, perhaps the bands starting to organize along the Florida-Alabama border. Or maybe a woman just wanted to see her dying mother in Anacosta or Philadelphia and couldn't get a permit to travel.

Two onions after the potato said, "two travelers on Thursday," and two bags of blackberries next to the cucumber said, "two travelers on Wednesday." Marjory was not entirely sure where Welcome got his information about travelers, but that was not her business, and a clandestine cell survived when it knew only the minimum it needed to know to operate.

A Plore family willing to give overnight shelter to a traveler would receive a paper delivery bag from Welcome's the afternoon before the traveler was expected to arrive, hidden in the back of a delivery truck from the adjoining Plore region to the north, Philadelphia-Wilmington Outer Suburban, or from Atlanta Outer Suburban to the south. Plores were banned from traveling outside their home region, but truck drivers were overwhelmingly Plore, and sympathetic to the cause. Sharing the housing burden minimized attention for the circle's participants. Even though Plores generally minded their own business, enough informants circulated in Ploreville to make caution advisable.

The next day or so, another truck or connections of the hostess with access to transportation and guides would convey the traveler to the next safehouse. Among themselves, they called it "the Plore Underground." The reference to "Underground" made it a knowledge crime, by daring to compare their enterprise with the network that hundreds of years ago had smuggled escaping slaves to freedom in the North.

The house was quiet when Marjory let herself in. Larry was driving his bus route along Columbia Pike like every Wednesday, the boys were in school, and Emma must be running her own errands before going into the City to clean offices. Next year the older boy would graduate and take a job in the City so his mother could stay home.

Two of the three cats came to greet her, rubbing along her legs. She helped herself to some of the blackberries and decided against sharing them with the knitting ladies. She laid out crackers and rolls, sliced some cheese, and placed a precious jar of strawberry preserves on the sideboard in the living room. Recalling that for at least two of the ladies, this might be their main meal of the day, she guiltily retrieved and rinsed those blackberries as well. She pulled her knitting project, a pink scarf, out of the sideboard where it had rested since the last meeting.

The ladies would not arrive for another half hour. She nibbled on the berries and crackers, while mentally composing the next illicit news bulletin, adding some unverified but generally reliable gossip that Welcome had shared with her.

Plores could read the official *Anacosta Post*, which they mocked, and watch the City's TV stations, with their condescending coverage of Ploreville backwardness. ("Eighteen-year-old girl marries second cousin," or "Hungry schoolchildren welcome burrito breakfast from City benefactors," for example). Plores had their own online newspaper, the *Suburban Record*, which listed high school drama performances and notified them of the steady rate increases for garbage collection, Wi-Fi, and bus fares, but never dared attack real issues of concern.

Marjory's news bulletin was typed or more rarely handwritten on no more than one sheet at a time. Copiers and printers were scarce in Ploreville, and all copies contained an encrypted coding that could be traced all too easily to the copiers' owners. Marjory was eager for an opportunity to access an off-grid copier or printer, but for now it was best to produce painstakingly each bulletin one by one. Like medieval monks, she thought ruefully. To protect herself and the family, not waste paper, and spare herself unneeded effort, she did not write until she had composed the bulletin copy in her mind—it was dangerous to leave seditious sheets lying around and the Treaty would not protect her if the ADF discovered them. She had a neat, distinctive cursive last taught in schools half a century earlier.

The knitters and the book club members would add other tidbits. Having been president of her Ohio high school's journalism club sixty years ago, Marjory insisted on including some indication of the reliability of the information, such as "reported by a high school student from a respectable family and corroborated by two eyewitnesses at Bethune Arlington that a classmate was beaten by a Social Credit history teacher for using the word racist epithet 'slave' instead of 'enslaved person.'"

The knitters and the readers would write more copies of the bulletins at home after all had memorized the contents for the week, safely ignorant about which of them had contributed each item. Then truckers would ingeniously smuggle them up and down the East Coast in the walls of their trucks. Sometimes bulletins from Plorevilles in Boston and Atlanta made their way back to Marjory and her circle, reassuring them that they were not alone.

Marjory stared into space as she organized her report, looking like just another dreamy if not senile, grandmother reminiscing about days past. She was determined to wrest some meaning out of five decades of suffering. The civil war had taken her husband and her youngest child. The Antifans had herded them from Ohio into the DJR and then to Anacosta and later taken her second youngest child to serve them. She was old enough to remember their comfortable prewar lives. Perhaps others were resigned to their serfdom, but counterintuitively, she had gained resolution with age.

"I may be an old lady," she always told herself firmly, "but I will be older tomorrow, so I should do whatever I can today."

The doorbell rang, and she let in the first knitter. Soon they would be sitting, upright and purposeful, in their circle, except for the one charged with keeping an eye on the street for black uniforms. Looking at her co-conspirators, Marjory always marveled at how fate had thwarted their ambitious plans to live and die in obscurity. Fate, in the form of civil war and the Diversity Justice Republic, had called on each of them to serve a cause greater than themselves. Who ever knew when one was young what would derail one's life? Or make their lives part of a greater tapestry of good?

# THE BONUS

by George Vercessi, *Virginia Writers Club*

Jared Wilson didn't have to step outside to know his front tire had finally gone flat. The old stake truck had been pulling to the left for the past two miles. He was hoping it would hold until reaching the milling town ahead, but it hadn't and now they were stuck on the mountain, the promised bonus for early delivery of his load fading with the late afternoon sun.

Wilson looked over at the child beside him and wondered if he hadn't made a mistake bringing her along. The small dog curled up in her lap met his gaze but didn't move, neither of them wanting to wake her.

Wilson climbed from the cab, shutting the door gently so as not to disturb his daughter, and shivered as he stepped onto the gravel road. His thin jacket served him well down in the desert, but it provided little protection up here in tall pine country.

He leaned against the radiator and quickly decided he had few options. Without a spare he could stay with the truck and hope someone would come along, which seemed unlikely since he had seen no one heading in either direction for the past hour, or he could hoof it into town. The road sign about a mile-and-a-half back read three miles to Indian Springs.

"Wake up, Maisy," he said, rocking her gently.

The child's eyes squinted open. "Are we there?" she said in a soft, dreamy voice.

"No, sweetheart. We got us a flat tire and need to walk a bit. You sit tight and I'll come round and get you," he said, scooping up the two remaining stale cheese sandwiches and stuffing them in his pocket.

Wilson walked around the cab and opened the door, being careful to support his daughter with one hand. "You gotta move over," he told the dog, easing him from her lap with the other. Then, wrapping Maisy in the frayed horse blanket covering her seat, he cradled her in his arms and stepped off the running board.

"Your turn, Sandy. Come on down now." The dog moved

to the edge of the seat, paused, and sniffed the mountain air. "Let's go, Sandy. It's okay," Wilson said.

If Wilson feared Sandy would run off, he needn't have. The dog inched to the side of the road, peered into the darkening forest and backed up against Wilson's leg.

"Nothing to fear so long as we stay together," he said. Then adjusting his grip of the child, he said, "Okay, let's go."

Maisy, still groggy, tightened an arm around his neck and nestled her head into his bony shoulder while Sandy trailed close behind.

They had gone about a half mile when a logger heading in their direction stopped and offered a lift. "That your rig, back there, friend?" he asked once they had settled in, Maisy on Wilson's lap, the dog on the floor between his legs.

He nodded. "Thought I'd make it to town before the tire gave out."

"No need to fret. Jake'll have you up and running in no time."

"That's good. I need to get to the lumber camp by morning."

"What're you hauling?"

"Generator. They promised a bonus if I deliver it by ten."

The driver nodded and pressed the pedal. At the edge of town, he pointed down the main street to a low-roofed building fronted by two gas pumps and a red neon window sign proclaiming *Eats*. "That'll be Jake's," he said. "I'll drop you there."

"Thanks mighty," Wilson said when he stepped down.

"Happy to oblige."

Jake's was a combination filling station, diner, general store, and post office.

Maisy's eyes popped open as the truck pulled away. Sliding down from her father's grasp, she looked around and asked, "We gonna eat?"

"In a minute, Pumpkin. First, we see about the truck."

The garage was dark. The only light came from the diner. They entered and stood together by the door, Sandy between them.

"Tell me where I can find Jake, ma'am?" he asked the

stout woman behind the counter.

"Ain't here," she said. "Probably back in an hour. Maybe sooner, maybe later. Hard to tell with Jake."

It was the *later* that troubled Wilson. If Jake returned within the hour and they got the wheel back here for the patch, he stood a good chance of making the deadline. Any later, and he'd likely lose the promised bonus. He looked up at the clock. It was nearly six thirty. "How long to the lumber camp?" he asked.

"Which one?"

"Armstrong's."

"Whatya figure, Sam, about nine hours?" she asked one of the two men at the counter.

"More like ten. Roads took a lickin' this past storm. Wouldn't want to go more than fifteen miles an hour in places. Twenty tops."

"Anyone else around who can help me with my truck?"

"What's the problem?" the woman asked.

"Flat tire."

She shook her head. " 'fraid not. Care for something while you wait?"

Wilson looked down at his daughter. Their last meal was several hours ago, each eating a cheese sandwich, leaving just the two he had stuffed in his pocket. "Maybe coffee, and milk for the girl."

"Take a seat and I'll bring 'em over."

"Where's your truck?" the other man asked.

"East about a mile and half."

He nodded. "Happens a lot on these half washed out roads. Lotsa folks don't often make it that far. But Jake'll have you up and running. Right, Sam?"

"Yep. Not much Jake can't fix."

The woman delivered the coffee and milk. "How 'bout the dog?" she asked. "Looks like he might like something to chew on."

"That's Sandy," Maisy said, rubbing the scrawny dog's ear. "Named him after Little Orphan Annie's dog."

"He's fine lookin'. Well behaved. I might have a bone in the back. If it's okay with your pa."

Wilson lowered his cup and smiled. "He'd like that, ma'am."

94

"I'll see what I can round up," she said and retreated to the kitchen. When she returned with a good-sized meat bone, Wilson and Maisy were finishing the last of their sandwiches.

"Care for anything else?" she asked.

"What'd I owe for the milk, coffee and bone?" Wilson asked. And when she said milk and coffee would be fifteen cents, no charge for the bone, he lowered his voice and, rubbing his stubble, asked, "How much for a slice of that there pie?"

The woman eyed his frayed jacket and worn shoes. "It's days-old."

"No it ain't," one of the men piped up, earning him an instant scowl.

"Is too. Pulled it out of the oven myself." Then turning to Wilson, "I'd feel guilty charging more than a nickel."

Wilson looked across the table. "You up for a piece of days-old pie, Maisy?"

The girl's face lit up. "Sure am."

"Well, then, we'll have a piece, ma'am."

She returned carrying two plates, setting one down before each of them.

"I apologize, ma'am," Wilson said, pushing his away. "I just meant the one for the girl."

"I know what you meant. Hers is on the house."

Wilson clearly didn't know what to make of the gesture, until prompted.

"Go on. Eat up. Can't be havin' stale pie hangin' around for the flies to get at."

"I suppose not," he said. "Thank you." If there was a fly around, he didn't see one.

"Where y'all from?" she asked.

"Other side of the flatlands. Old mining town of Lake Ridge. Don't know why they call it that. No sign of a lake within miles. Might've been at one time, but no one I know remembers it."

"How 'bout you? You ever seen a lake around those parts?" she asked Maisy, whose cheeks were stuffed with pie, while shooting Wilson a playful wink.

Maisy chewed some, took a sip of milk and swallowed.

"No ma'am. Just a dry riverbed through town that fills when it rains, but no lake."

"More coffee?" she asked. And when Wilson declined, she said, "No charge for refills." Before he could answer she retrieved the coffee pot and another glass of milk while the two men at the counter exchanged glances.

When they had finished, she cleared the table and slid in beside Maisy. "So tell me," she said, "how'd you get such a pretty name?"

The girl smiled. "Was my mama's."

"Ain't hers no more?"

The smile faded. "She passed."

The woman nodded. "And how is it you ain't back in Lake Ridge with your friends?"

"Twas my idea," Wilson said. "Her birthday being tomorrow, thought we might spend it together."

Maisy grinned. "I'll be getting a surprise when we get home. Right?"

"Sure enough," her father said.

"How old will you be tomorrow?" the woman asked.

Maisy raised herself in her seat, squared her thin shoulders, and replied, "Seven."

The woman had thought her younger, but wasn't surprised. Just about all the youngsters passing through were undersized for their age. It had been that way going on seven years since the crash.

Meanwhile, Wilson's gaze kept going between the clock and the street.

An older couple came in and took a booth beside Wilson's, and before long they were talking together. The couple said they knew of Lake Ridge, had passed through it several years ago coming west. They confirmed it wasn't much of a town, more of a waystation, to which Wilson agreed.

Unlike Wilson, who was growing noticeably anxious, Maisy came alive with the attention from the others. She had become quite a magpie, he thought, entertaining them with tales of the desert mining community and, with a little encouragement, an old miners' ditty she'd learned in school. Sandy, meanwhile, having gnawed the bone clean, was curled up at Maisy's feet.

As the hour neared seven, Wilson strode outside, searching the quiet street. When he returned, he approached the woman behind the counter and asked, "Any chance of contacting Jake?"

She smiled and said, "Ain't no telephone where Jake's at. But I reckon it shouldn't be long now."

Sure enough, less than ten minutes later headlights bounced across the window and they heard the door of a pickup truck. "That'll be Jake," the two men said in unison. Wilson jumped up, then paused when the door swung open. Seeing a woman, he turned toward the street, expecting Jake behind her.

"Jake, this here fella needs your help real bad," the man at the counter said with a wide grin while pointing to Wilson.

"Well, that's what we're here for," she said, and strolled over. She had a warm glow to her cheeks and an easy smile. She was taller and huskier than Wilson, with broad shoulders and a grip that encircled his when they shook hands. "Pleased to meet you. What's the problem?"

"Tire went out east about a mile and a half. I need to get back on the road as soon as possible."

"Gotta be at the Armstrong camp by ten in the morning," the man at the counter offered.

Jake gazed at the clock. "Doesn't give us much time. I'll throw some tools in the truck and we'll go have a looksee."

"Don't you want something?" asked the woman behind the counter. "You ain't ate since morning."

"Had a bite up at the Jones'," she replied. "Besides, you heard the fella, we don't have time to lollygag. Come on," she said to Wilson, motioning him to follow. "Oh, yeah," she said, turning back. "It's a girl. A tad over four pounds. Everyone's doin' fine."

As Jake headed out, Wilson looked back at Maisy and Sandy. "Would it be all right if they stayed put till we get the truck moving?" he asked the woman behind the counter.

She nodded. "You go right ahead."

Wilson thanked her and hurried outside, where Jake was tucking into a pair of bib overalls.

"I wasn't expecting a woman," he confessed as they drove out of town.

"Don't blame you. The name don't conjure up female

images," she said, before explaining, "Jake was my husband. I've been running things since he passed and didn't see any call to change the name. One day a stranger came around and asked if I was Jake. That tickled folks and they've been calling me that since."

"And you don't mind?"

She looked at him and smiled. "Heck no. He was a gentle soul. Went outta his way to help folks. I'm proud to carry it and to keep the business going just like he would."

"Looks like you got your hands full, what with the diner, post office, filling station and taxi service," Wilson said.

Jake laughed. "Taxi service? Where'd you get that notion?"

"When you mentioned the newborn back there, I guessed you drove the doctor out to the house."

Another laugh. "We don't have a doctor up here. Closest one's where you're headed, down at the lumber camp. I fill in as midwife."

When they reached Wilson's truck, Jake retrieved her jack, while Wilson shoved large rocks beneath the tires.

"We'll have this critter fixed in no time," she said, thumping the tire with her fist. After pulling it off, she looked it over and said, "You really shouldn't be riding on this."

Wilson nodded. "This job'll take care of that."

Together, they hoisted the tire into her truck, secured it and headed back.

Upon arriving at the garage, Wilson peered into the diner. Maisy and the others were playing some animated game that had the child in stiches and the others laughing with her. Friends back home had counseled against taking her across the mountains so soon after the long winter. Melting ice and snow tended to overflow creek beds, they warned, loosening rocks and boulders and washing out sections of road. Better she remained with them, they insisted. But he saw it differently. He couldn't leave the girl behind on her birthday, not this first birthday without her mother. She needed to be with him, he told them.

When Wilson joined Jake in the garage, she cautioned again against patching the tire. "There's one in back'll fit your rig. Ain't new, but it's got plenty more miles on it than this one."

"What'll it run?" he asked.

"You can have it for six dollars."

Wilson didn't have to look in his wallet to know he didn't have the six dollars, nor did he want Jake knowing it either. He'd have it tomorrow, though, plus more than enough for a whole new set of tires. That is, if he made it in time to get the bonus. Eyeing the tire as if considering her offer, he said, "I'll replace it on the way back."

"I'll stand you for it," she said. "You can pay after delivering your load."

"That's kind of you, ma'am, but I just as soon pay my own way."

Jake shook her head. There was no getting around a man's pride. She had seen it time and again since the crash. Able-bodied folks who'd just as soon do without than accept what they perceived as charity.

With the tire repaired and Wilson's truck idling out front, he entered the diner and found Maisy resting her head on the table, her eyes half closed.

"She got plum wore out," the woman behind the counter said with a chuckle. "One minute she's going full speed, next she's tuckered. You got one sweet child there, mister."

"I've been blessed," he said. "How much do I owe for everything?" Wilson asked.

"It's like I said, twenty cents. Fifteen for the coffee and milk and five for the pie."

"What about that?" he said, nodding at the half-eaten bowl of chili on the table.

"She hardly touched it."

"Still, right is right."

"That'd be ten cents, then."

Wilson dug into his pocket and, counting out thirty-five cents, set the coins on the counter. "That's for your kindness, ma'am," he said pushing the extra nickel toward her. He was about to retrieve his daughter and Sandy when he paused and turned. "Is it be possible to have a birthday cake for her on the return trip?" he whispered, adding, "I'll pay in advance." In the next instant, he was pulling a faded dollar bill from his wallet and placing it on the counter. "Will that do?"

99

"It'll more than do," the woman said, returning two quarters. "Fifty cents s'all."

Wilson scooped up the change. Then looking around, he said to the others, "It'd be real nice if you saw fit to join us."

"You bet," the couple replied. The men nodded.

"What's her preference, vanilla or chocolate?" asked Jake, who had come in and was by the door wiping her hands with a rag.

Wilson smiled. "She's partial to chocolate."

"We might even rustle up some balloons," she said.

"That'd be swell."

After settling Maisy in the cab and wrapping the blanket around her, and depositing Sandy on the seat beside her, Wilson went and thanked Jake for her help. "I won't say a word about the cake," he told her. "It'll be a surprise."

"We'll do it up right," she assured him.

Maisy's chocolate cake with seven candles was on the counter promptly at six, a full hour before they expected Wilson, who had telephoned from the camp earlier that morning saying he had delivered the generator shortly after eight o'clock without a hitch and anticipated being back in Indian Spring by seven that evening.

By ten o'clock Jake's coffee sat cold and untouched before her. The others had gone home. The ice cream was back in the freezer and the cake put away. The woman behind the counter gathered the balloons in silence, then took down the hand-lettered *Happy Birthday* poster.

The news reached them the following afternoon, when a logger rolled in and told them about the flatbed that missed a turn and went over the side sometime the previous day. He said it wasn't till after daybreak someone came along and spotted the twisted wreck, and a rescue crew was sent down.

"A man and a little girl," he said. "Both dead."

# A MOUNTAIN TREK
by Mary Elizabeth Ames, *Northern Virginia Chapter*

A group of Erwinians were on a field trip to the northeast outpost. The outpost was on the flanks of a high mountain range which lay to the north and extended to the northeast and the northwest. It was near to the northeast tip of Erwina territory, which almost touched the northwest tip of what had once been H'Aleth territory. This was the region most hotly contested by the Biogenics Corporation and the Cassius Foundation.

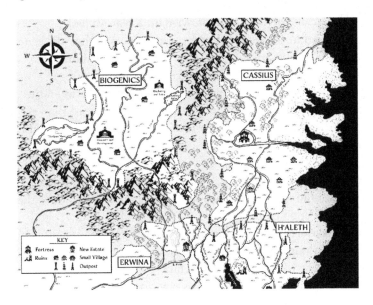

Master Xavier and Matron Kavarova led the group. They would serve as guides and provide security for the expedition. Both could transform into a large gray mountain wolf. Three young adults—Rachel, Evan, and Warren—served as scouts and proctors for four middle school students, Savannah, Erik, Henrik, and Ruwena, who were learning scouting skills. except Ruwena, all other members were *H. transformans*. They could transform at will into their respective alternate species, provided they had the full complement of genes for that species. Ruwena, a refugee from H'Aleth, was presumed to be an *H. sapiens* and, therefore, would not transform.

En route

The troupe would travel through montane forests and mountain passes, fording creeks, and traversing limestone caves to reach a forest glen where the northeast outpost was hidden. The students were warned that the mountain was restless from time to time. "There have been cave-ins, and some cavern chambers have collapsed," Master Xavier told the students. "One must listen to the mountain before deciding whether to shelter in a cave or traverse a cavern," he cautioned.

The students couldn't help but notice that Master Xavier and the scouts carried weapons. Madam Kavarova had transformed into a wolf. Her weaponry came with her alternate species. The expedition would take group near the borders contested by the Cassius Foundation and the Biogenics Corporation. Fortunately, most of the skirmishes between these two factions were taking place farther to the northeast than the expedition planned to go. Nevertheless, everyone would need to exercise caution—a key element of scouting.

As the group headed north by northeast, they traversed the dense hardwood forest on the lower slopes of the northern mountain range. As a precaution against potential invaders, there were no defined paths through the region. Master Xavier and Matron Kavarova knew the area very well as they had scouted and traveled through it many times in the past. So, the group threaded its way through the trees and vegetation without difficulty. The students were instructed to always pay close attention to their surroundings, both for safety and the ability to identify their surroundings in the future. This was their first real exercise in surveillance—and in finding their way back home again.

the nearest mountain peak was about 7,000 feet high. The trek would take the group up to about 1,500 feet by gradually winding up the slopes. Savannah was paired with Evan. Both of them could transform into gray wolves. Henrik, who could become a mountain goat, was paired with Rachel, who could transform into a lynx. Both alternate species were sure-footed in rocky terrain. Erik, who could transform into a raccoon, was paired with Warren, who could become a brown bear. The notion of a 20-pound raccoon being paired with a 700 pound bear was a source of considerable amusement. "I think it's great," remarked Erik. "I'll just climb onto Warren's back and ride the rest of the way."

"Think again," Warren countered.

Among the eight *H. transformans*, there would be plenty of sharp eyes, ears, and noses. This would prove essential as the troupe ascended higher on the mountain's slope. They would encounter more mist and low-lying clouds, limiting visibility.

Starting with the second evening and every other evening thereafter, the three *H. transformans* students would alternate between their native human form and their respective alternate species. In this manner, they would become acquainted with the terrain and learn how to traverse it, both as humans and as their alternate species. They would experience how it looks, smells, sounds, and feels from both perspectives. It was critical that they learn in both forms how the terrain should be when no invader was present. So, Erik did not get to climb onto Warren's back. He needed to learn about the territory from the perspective of a raccoon.

Long ago, when Ruwena first came to Erwina's main compound, she had learned her way around it by doing exactly the same thing that her classmates were now tasked to do. Only she did so as an owl. Late at night, she would watch from within the compound and for a short distance outside it (breaking a house rule). Alas, on this expedition, she could participate only in her human form. She had not yet revealed to anyone that she, too, was an *H. transformans*.

An Unexpected Encounter

The trip through the mountain terrain continued for three days and nights. As the group reached about fifteen hundred feet in altitude, they came to the entrance of a cave. The entrance led downward about five hundred feet until they reached an underground stream. They followed the stream in human form until they reached an enormous cavern.

The cavern was spotted with stalagmites and stalactites, pools of clear water that had been filtered through the limestone layer, and several types of minerals including iridescent and fluorescent crystalline formations. It was beautiful. The temperature was cool at an even fifty-five degrees Fahrenheit.

The students had never seen such a fabulous place. The exercise was still the same: learn their way around the cavern as humans and as their alternate species. There were many nooks and crannies in which they could get lost. Thus, the three *H. transformans* students, paired with their proctors, could explore the cavern under the watchful eye of Matron Kavarova. Ruwena tagged along with Savannah and Evan.

The trip through the mountain took almost a day before they ascended out of the series of caverns and narrow ravines they had traversed. It was here that Matron Kavarova encountered the scent of a hybrid animal. She immediately snapped a deep growl to Master Xavier. Her abrupt change and aggressive posture startled the students; however, Master Xavier knew exactly what it meant. Matron Kavarova had detected another being—a potentially dangerous one. As she sniffed the area and followed the scent, she drew Master Xavier's attention to its direction and path. It was perilously close to their own.

Master Xavier immediately turned to the others. "Move away now at a ninety-degree angle from our current path," he ordered, pointing in the opposite the location of the scent. "Students who have transformed will remain as their alternate species. Do not resume human form." He knew they would be better able to navigate the change in direction and have more agility to scramble up the rock formations. "Students in human form should not transform. We have no time to waste, so there is no time to transform safely," he added.

Master Xavier, Rachel, and Evan—all three in human form—made their weapons ready. The group traveled about 150 feet to one side until the footing was too poor. At that point, they were forced to resume their ascent. The climb was now much harder and more perilous. It required considerable effort and more time to climb over and around rock formations. It proved difficult for everyone. At least, the rocks provided additional cover for them as they moved upwards. Yet, it was not enough.

A large creature suddenly appeared and lunged at them. It looked like it was part wolf, part boar with the snout and horns of a boar and the body a wolf except for its short legs and hooves.

The animal was still too far away to reach anyone and, on poor footing, slid downward away from them. This did not stop the beast, which was clearly deranged. It scraped, stumbled, and slipped on the rocks to assault anyone it could reach.

Ruwena knew this kind of creature. It was a lupuseroja, a violent wolf-boar mix of the Cassius Foundation's design. Ruwena had learned from her former mistress that these hybrids were genetically engineered. The foundation had spliced the genes of a boar into the genome of a wolf to create an aggressive hybrid that would guard the storerooms and weapons depots in the foundation's villages. The lupuserojas were kept chained and hungry to induce the desire to attack anyone who came too close. They were extremely dangerous, and if set loose, they would attack indiscriminately.

Master Xavier ordered all the students to continue their climb as quickly as they could. "Warren will be your guard," he said. Then he, Rachel, and Evan stayed back as a defensive barrier between the creature and the retreating students. They held their fire, hoping the hybrid would stumble into a deadly fall. It would be best not to leave any evidence of their presence—especially their weaponry.

Matron Kavarova challenged the hybrid directly. The lupuseroja found itself facing a large, ferocious mountain wolf. Yet, it seemed not to care. It continued to lunge forward as the wolf fought to drive it back. Ruwena saw this and slipped away from the others. She was almost certain the wolf would be gravely injured if not killed by this creature. Ruwena also knew that Master Xavier was right. There may not be enough time to transform safely. Nevertheless, she took the risk.

The wolf's back leg lost its footing on a slope. She slipped and fell on the rocks sliding toward the lupuseroja. As she scrambled to get up, Master Xavier ran from his post and shouted at the creature to draw its attention to himself. He was too late. The lupuseroja had seen its chance for a kill and leapt toward the wolf. It never reached its quarry. Out of nowhere, a tawny brown cougar, going for a kill of its own, vaulted over the wolf and collided with the creature head on.

As muscular and powerful as the lupuseroja was, it was thrown backward. Both combatants fell downward over the rocks. The surprise attack and the cougar's agility gave the cat an advantage. The cougar's large-padded feet provided better footing on the rocks. Powerful neck and shoulder muscles pulled down its prey. The cougar's powerful jaws gripped the hybrid's throat while claws sank into its flesh. Even though the latter was heavy set and had the thick, muscular neck of a boar, the cougar's long canines reached their target. The lupuseroja fell further downward, dragging the cougar with it until both disappeared.

During the fight, Master Xavier had reached the wolf to help her regain her footing. Then both raced to the edge of a rock formation near where the cougar and the creature had disappeared. There was no sign of them.

*Where did the cougar come from?* Master Xavier asked himself. He knew cougars were native to these mountains, so the cat could have come into the cave seeking a place to rest when it heard the commotion. Since cougars use stealth to hunt their prey, it may have used the ruckus to mask its approach in the hopes of catching prey by surprise or to raid someone else's kill. If so, the cougar may have recognized the hybrid as another apex predator and a rival.

"It should not have been a student," Master Xavier said

sharply as both he and Matron Kavarova abruptly ascended the rocks as quickly as they could. As a wolf, Matron Kavarova advanced more rapidly and was already engaged in sniffing every person, students and staff alike, to account for everyone. Only one person was missing: the *H. sapiens* student, Ruwena. Both faculty members along with Evan and Rachel began searching for her. Before long, Evan spotted Ruwena laying between two rock formations. When he reached her, she could not stand. She was shaking, cold, exhausted, and looked beat up. She, too, had slipped and fallen upon the rocks. Fortunately, Evan was a powerfully built young man and strong—a benefit of his wolf genes. He lifted Ruwena without difficulty and was able to carry her the rest of the way up to the egress from the cave. There, the group rested until everyone, except Matron Kavarova, had resumed their human form.

After they left the cave, Savannah asked Master Xavier what kind of creature had attacked them. "It was a genetically engineered hybrid," he replied. He thought for a moment and then admonished the students. "Do not fault the creature for what someone else made it. It should be pitied, not hated."

*What was it doing here, and how did it get here?* Master Xavier mused. If the creature had simply escaped to run free, it could have traveled here completely on its own. If the Cassius Foundation has moved into the area, this would not be the case. This was cause for considerable concern. *Where Cassius has moved in, Biogenics will soon follow,* he surmised.

Master Xavier's original question still nagged him. *Where did the cougar come from?* None of the *H. transformans* students had any feline genes. Ruwena was the only missing person after the fight with the creature. Although most of her injuries were consistent with a fall, several of her symptoms suggested someone who had forced a transformation too quickly. The cougar which had also fallen on the rocks, was not seen again. *I wonder,* he thought.

The group continued its journey—this time with a heightened alertness and a greater sense of awareness. Both Master Xavier and Matron Kavarova were eager to confer with their colleagues in the northeastern outpost. Perhaps their scouts knew of movements by Cassius and Biogenics.

## The Grotto

The northeast outpost was a small sunken grotto hidden among several large boulders at the base of the mountain. It was inside the forest that formed a boundary with the mountain. The area was dense with hardwood trees, especially oaks, which provided a canopy overhead. Several interconnecting caves had been excavated where crevasses had formed between the rocks. The caves served as meeting places, storage areas, shelters, and living quarters for their scouts. The connections between them were narrow passageways, some of which were natural formations between large boulders. Others were tunnels that had to be carved out deep underground.

There was a single wooden structure embedded between the two largest oaks. It was the outpost's main house. It blended so well with the trees that it could not be detected from outside the grotto. Underground tunnels connected the main house to nearby caves. These had to be excavated around the roots of the two oaks in order to keep from damaging the trees' root systems. The trek through those tunnels was interesting. No wonder the students had to take courses in gymnastics.

Water flowed down a crevice in the mountain's face,, creating a waterfall. The waterfall fed a deep pool from which a brisk mountain stream flowed through the grotto. Later, the stream joined many others that flowed into a river which hosted an abundance of freshwater fish.

The surrounding forest supported a wide variety of wildlife—birds, including raptors, beavers, raccoons, and other small mammals. Woodland deer could be seen early in the mornings and at dusk. The beavers had built their lodge and dam on a small feeder stream, creating a pond nearby. The pond supported a variety of amphibians—frogs, salamanders, and several reptiles: turtles, snakes, and lizards. Happily, there were no alligators.

Farther down from the pond, the stream also supported a family of river otters that had a burrow near it. There, they fed on fish and other tasty stream inhabitants. The pair were quite content to stay where they were and rarely ventured far beyond the grotto except to find food. They were friendly to the scouts who often gave the otters fish. The pair had two pups and were raising them in the grotto's safety.

After their travels, the students felt like they had entered a paradise. It was beautiful, peaceful, and friendly, and there was hot food. The students could roam freely throughout the grotto, but not beyond its boundaries.

"Hybrid creatures have been seen in this region," explained Master Crocius, chief of the outpost, "and they are often deranged. Since they almost always attack on sight, many of our scouts remain in human form, armed with bows and arrows. The scouts are skillful and can bring down most of these creatures with a single lethal shot. Then the creature and the arrow that killed it are burned." Master Crocius paused for a moment and then offered a warning. "Despite what you see here, it is a dangerous place."

*This explains the hybrid creature we encountered in the cave,* thought Master Xavier. Then he asked Master Crocius, "How common are cougars in the area?"

"Not uncommon," replied Master Crocius, "although we rarely see them. They will come down this far to hunt for prey, but usually avoid contact with humans—another reason our scouts do not transform into mammals this close to the mountain."

The students took advantage of their found freedom and began exploring the grotto. Ruwena promptly headed for the stream to look for the river otters. Not long afterwards, a third river otter joined the resident pair and their pups. Ruwena knew she could not be away for long. She could not be missing again.

Later that evening, the students were reminded that this was a field expedition. Erwina maintained close surveillance on its borders with Biogenics and Cassius. This outpost kept watch over the northern and northeastern regions between Erwina and Biogenics. The scouts at the outpost were very skilled in surveillance and would often slip over the border to expand their range of view. All of them could transform into a mammal native to the area that they were watching. Students would be given opportunities to pair with a scout on a routine patrol around the grotto. This was the only time they were allowed outside its boundaries and not farther than 100 yards away from it.

Students also received real-world reports of scouting and

surveillance from well outside the grotto's boundaries. In their surveillance reports, scouts reported on activities in bordering Biogenics' villages, especially any indications that Biogenic's was preparing to mobilize its forces. The scouts would report also on changes in the patterns or behaviors of native wildlife, if any. Sightings of any apex predators (e.g., bears, cougars) remote from the grotto would be noted during a routine report. Any evidence or sighting of a hybrid or a great gray dragon was reported immediately.

Much to Ruwena's dismay, one scout reported seeing a third otter downstream cavorting with the other two adults. This was greeted as pleasant news. If the third otter had been a hybrid, the two adults would have chased it off. Still, Ruwena would need to be more careful.

A Duel in Mid-Air

The area of the stream occupied by the otters coursed through dense brush and trees, which helped conceal the location of their den. The brush also provided cover where they could hide from the few aerial predators—primarily hawks and eagles—that also hunted near the stream and the river into which it flowed. The adults were not at risk, for they were too large and heavy. Their pups would make a fine snack. This meant the parents were always on high alert for predators on the ground or in the air. So, it was a welcome relief for the parents to have a third adult to help watch over the pups. It proved to be a blessing.

One afternoon, when Ruwena was visiting the otter family as an otter herself, she spotted Alan, one of the outpost's scouts. This time, she saw him before he spotted her. She promptly ducked under the water and headed for dense underbrush overlying the stream. There she raised her head above water just enough to watch the scout and breathe. The scout was not looking in her direction. He was looking upward, toward the sky. Suddenly, the female otter barked several warning calls to her pups and anyone else who would listen. She, too, was looking up at the sky. Ruwena did the same and saw a strange creature in flight overhead. She had never seen this hybrid, nor had her former mistress ever described such a creature to her.
It was a lyvulfon—a genetically engineered mix of vulture and lynx.

It was the Cassius Foundation's attempt to recreate the gryphon. Suddenly, the creature dived toward the stream and snatched one of the pups. The pup's mother frantically grabbed the pup in her mouth and tried to pull it back down, but she couldn't. In the water, she had no traction, and the father was too far away to help. Alan saw immediately what was happening. He drew an arrow and took aim. He could not release it—the mother was between him and the lyvulfon, as the two struggled with each other. He would have to wait until the hybrid disengaged from the mother, hoping it would not be too late for the pup.

The lyvulfon finally broke free, with the pup in its talon, and was about to fly away when Alan saw another otter launch itself out of the water toward the creature. Alan watched in amazement as the otter transformed in mid-air into a Cooper's hawk and attacked the lyvulfon.

The hawk gripped the hybrid with her talons and used her beak to rip at its head and eyes. The lyvulfon could not defend itself and still hold on to the pup. It dropped the pup and turned on the hawk. Then the aerial battle really began. The creature dwarfed the hawk in both body and wingspan; however, it lacked the hawk's agility. The latter was far more aerodynamic. Even though the lyvulfon could tuck its back legs under its body, its shape created significant drag during flight and limited its maneuverability. With the two locked in battle, the creature's size and weight was to its advantage.

The hawk was in trouble when Alan finally had a clear shot. He brought down the creature, and when it fell, it separated from the hawk. At first the hawk appeared to be in a free fall itself. Then it recovered enough flight capacity to break its own fall. It fell into the dense underbrush which cushioned it. The lyvulfon crashed into the stream. Alan raced to haul the creature out of the stream before it could contaminate the water.

In the meantime, the mother had carried her pup to the bank and was trying to revive it. The pup was still alive but severely injured. Alan would have to take it to the grotto immediately, for any chance to save it. He picked up the pup and hurried to where the injured hawk had fallen. He didn't find the bird or any sign of it—not even a feather; and he was certain of where it had fallen. Given the pup's injuries, he couldn't take time to look for the hawk. So, he turned away and ran to the grotto as fast as he could with the pup's mother following him.

Ruwena had transformed back into an otter just as she fell into the dense underbrush. While Alan dealt with the dead creature and collected the otter pup, she slipped back into the stream and hid among the vegetation and tree roots along the bank. She was heartbroken. The pup was completely limp and appeared dead.

In an act of desperation to save the pup, Ruwena had exposed her abilities to one of Erwina's scouts. Although the scout did not know who he saw transform in mid-air, he would not report what he had seen. Now she had to get back to the village as quickly as possible to avoid being missed. Yet, she could not do this at first. She was exhausted and needed to remain an otter for a while longer. She slowly threaded her way back through the underbrush, carrying her robe with her, until she could resume human form.

When Ruwena arrived at the main house, there was great excitement at the cave where the pup was being treated. Everyone was crowded around it. She slipped into the students' quarters unseen, cleaned herself up, and changed clothes. Then she joined the others. To her relief, the pup would survive. Her risk had paid off and, with all the commotion, she had not been missed. She was battered in the fight and the fall; however, her smock hid any signs. Compared to a hawk, the lyvulfon was clumsy in flight. Although she had been buffeted by the creature's large wings, she had not been struck by its formidable beak or talons.

Later that day, the creature's body was retrieved and examined. After a specimen of its tissue taken, it was burned with the arrow that killed it. That evening, there was a briefing to which the students were not invited. There were two matters to discuss. Foremost were the two hybrids that had appeared so close together—both in time and location. The faculty and staff were deeply concerned that the Cassius Foundation was becoming more aggressive in releasing deadly hybrids. Whether the foundation's target was Biogenics or Erwina or both was uncertain.

The second matter was Alan's sighting of an otter—most likely the new arrival—that could transform directly into a bird. This level of capability had not been seen in many generations. Neither the hawk nor the otter were seen after the incident, so its fate was unknown. *Neither was the cougar*, Master Xavier noted. He also noted that the third otter appeared shortly after their arrival. *Coincidence?* He asked himself. *I wonder.* All the faculty, scouts, and students—even Ruwena—were well known. *It is not impossible that a lone and remarkably powerful H. transformans could hide in the area*, he thought, *just unlikely.* He did not know that his theoretical *H. transformans* was hiding in plain sight.

It had become clear that the conflict between Biogenics and Cassius was intensifying. An increasing number of hybrid creatures—products of Cassius's genetic engineering experiments—were coming into Erwina's territory. Given the recent incidents with the lupuseroja (at the cave) and the lyvulfon (at the river), the field trip was cut short. The region was far less safe than originally thought when the trip was planned. It was time to bolster surveillance and defenses in the immediate region, and this was not a task for students. Preparations were made for the group to leave the next day and return to the compound. There was much to report to the leadership.

To the students' surprise, their lessons did not end at the outpost. Each student would take turns guiding the group back to the compound. On multiple occasions, course corrections were in order. A student would fail to recognize which way, only to pick the wrong direction. This was expected. Students could make these mistakes until he or she realized the error. Correcting these missteps honed students' attentiveness to landmarks that one day would help them find their way home.

# FROM THE GRAVE

by Sharon Krasny. *Write by the Rails*

I am dead.[1] For 5,300 years, snow and ice hid my body on the side of the mountain I crossed many times. Dying seemed so final. One minute fresh, alpine air breathes. The next minute that same air rattles stale of all oxygen, leaving me gasping and empty.

As I died, no light of the new spring warmed me, only the cold darkness of failure. My murderer's arrowhead pierced an

---

[1] David Kiefefaber.(November 4, 2016).Researchers Discover 5,300-Year-Old Mummy Ötzi the Iceman Was Quite Fashionable. Science. https://www.insidehook.com/article/science/researchers-discover-5300-year-old-ice-mummy-otzi-the-iceman-was-quite-fashionable (image fair use)

artery deep within my left shoulder, paralyzing my arm and filling my ribs with blood. My body staggered, dropping to one knee upon impact. My vision glazed from the attack.

He had hunted me expertly, felling me with only one shot from behind. The slow sound of distant snow crunching under his boots neared. Struggling to stand, the puncture wound set the mark deep. I fell to kneeling, almost praying. He soon would have my life. The past four moons marked his patient tracking. How could I have been so careless?

The hunter had arrived despite all my efforts. He had hidden in wait roughly thirty paces back behind a brace of trees and a large rock. The perfect position to catch his prey. The perfect place to aim his bow and send his arrow to his mark. I wanted to stand, but the will to breathe was stronger. The bitter taste of blood wet my tongue. I tried to form words of a curse, but none came.

The air was too thin and too biting at this height on the alp. Consciousness wouldn't linger much longer. My quickening heart pumped more and more blood through the hole, pooling and gurgling inside like a mountain spring. My chest felt tight heat from the straining of my heart. Sweat soaked through my fur coverings, leaving a deep cold as the blood in my skin retreated to be nearer my weakening heart.

His hand squeezed my shoulder, twisting the arrow's shaft. Pain, pulsing pain, rushed to my brain as the flint broke off, causing me to lose sight for a moment. In the darkness I sought courage and found realization that courage shouldn't matter now. Hope's cry was being drowned out by blood's surging waves in my ears.

He pulled the broken shaft from its mark before grabbing the pouch from the cord around my neck. Snow crunched to cushion my head, but the rock my lips landed on bruised any last words that might have escaped. Drool formed, freezing me to the rock. My eyes struggled to lock onto reason through the haze that was forming; and then I knew.

Life had come to this, and a betrayal never felt so deep. Removing his axe from his belt, he shifted his weight to deal my head a crushing blow. My sight grew dimmer, the haze clouding out the light. Wanting to see the vision of Mara. Trying to picture the flowers that would come soon—the festivals of the people. These images of comfort faded and abandoned me. Fear forced my aloneness in close. I had failed.

Realizing the secret would die with me, I felt tension ease, and I let go. Courage to send my spirit to the afterworld found me. She carried my spirit out, escaping through a sigh before he brought the jadeite axe down heavy upon the back of my skull.

My name was Gaspare, a descendant from an age of tribes. My tribe, Ankwar, was based on the three fathers who had come together—one from the south and two from the east. We groomed the land to reveal secrets of survival, tamed the animals to create herds.

We were not like the Grundiler, who were comparable to beasts living underground. We were curious about the cycles of growth, the potential of life from a seed, the power of a tribesman to grow in status with dominion over these seeds, and the strength of those who had an ability to not only grow life but take it.

Our Ankwar tribe chose peace. Those from within our tribe, like spores that itched with anger, however, broke free, traveled an eastbound wind to the horsemen, and returned to exact revenge we weren't ready to defend against.

I was a son and brother. Some thought me a worthless coward. Someone, I hope, had found me brave.

The mountain became my tomb. Silence alone mourned me. The wind, which had once guided me, brought a gentle snow down for cover. The spirit of Chealana protected my remains. She was present in the snow that lay gently on my shoulders. She howled in the wind that blew more snow, pressing me into the ground. No one found me dead until the numerous blankets of snow and ice receded thousands of years later.

As the icy blanket slid off my lifeless form, my story found hope again to live. My destiny in death was not the absurdity I had relinquished my life to once being. I walked the land long before the birth of pharaohs. The secrets I keep are not from the tomb, but from the times of the first kings, when man felt it his right to rule over other men and to determine the destiny of a people.

Fate's futility melted with the glacier's thaw. I still have a role to play in the saga of men. May this new era bring light into the darkness I once knew and understanding of the power that lies hidden within the hills of the ancient tribes.

I am the Iceman.

## Arrow's Mark

Nothing is more personal, more sacred than a hunter's first kill. One life is taken to provide nourishment and safety for the loved ones of the other. Death enters into love's equation, resulting in a sum of humble respect for the innocence sacrificed. Two autumns ago, when I was eleven springs old, the men of our family went to hunt food for the upcoming frost. The deer were mating, and the harvest from the land was drying. I went to ambush a deer along a game trail my father showed me back in the summer. The red and yellow leaves, bedded down on the trail, crunched as I walked through. My new bow dropped to my side, string loose and resting while I made my way to an opening near two giant oaks.

Cheala was kind and sent her winds to stay on my face with the sun behind. Dusk would be here soon. The woods smelled freshly of rotting leaves after the recent rain, a damp, good, earthy smell. Stepping into the bend in the trail by the first oak, I looked up and saw him. A beautiful, strong buck about thirty paces ahead. He stood perpendicular to me, and his strong foreleg stretched forward, showing me my coveted shot.

Quickly I pulled the loop on my string up to the notches on my bow, tightening the pull. Stepping forward a little to get a more perfect shot, my foot kicked some old acorns into dry leaves. The buck, not catching my scent, became curious. Turning towards me, he took first one and then two steps, stopping to sniff the air. His presentation of his chest was not the aim Father had taught me. The shot would be narrow. A risk even for my older brothers, who were much surer shots. Cheala softly blew across my cheeks, cooling me, and with the sun on my back I just knew. This would be my shot.

In a movement trained from six springs of practice, my legs took stance and my bow arm readied. Bringing the bow straight up on target, I heard father's voice telling me to focus and breathe. My left arm drew back the arrow in a line parallel to my bow arm. The clear air filled my chest as I expanded my breaths to feel the surrounding sounds. The arrow, notched and resting on my fisted grip, didn't bounce as when I was younger. The bow and arrow framed the deer as I watched him steadily. The deer twitched its ear and continued munching on the grass blades it had found. Ears alert, but not scent alerted, he looked at me. The sun's angle made his coat shine smooth. I felt the connection. We were to be one.

Holding the bow parallel to the ground, Father's words came, reminding me to tilt, so I canted my bow slightly to the left, opening my view. The arrow rested, waiting. Ignoring everything else, the arrow and I became one as I placed all my intent on sending the arrow straight to the buck. My eyes never once left the white patch of fur. Inhaling a deep breath and anchoring the pull to the same spot on my left check, I took one last moment not to doubt, but to believe. Everything felt right and good.

Through instinct born of training, I exhaled with the arrow's release and watched the arc and bend of the shaft swim through the air like a fish going upstream. A soft thwack announced the finding of a mark on the lower neck. Just a little higher than I had hoped to place it. The deer dropped on the ground. The arrow had done the task of severing a vein. Awaking from my focus, I realized my fallen deer needed me. Too many tales of the runaway deer quickened my heartbeat, causing me to ignore more obvious plans.

Forcing a calmness I wanted us both to feel, I slowly approached, bent low and whispered, "Kula... kula... easy, boy, easy." The back legs of the deer scrambled against the high grasses to stand. "Kula... kula.... shhh... easy now." The majestic animal lay at my feet, an offering for my skill. Kneeling one knee on the antlers to steady us both, I saw the nervous wideness of the eyes searching instinct for a plan. His nostrils flared and stretched, seeking an answer in the wind. I saw myself and my hopes in him and felt the draw to reach him, touch him, comforting him in his gift to me.

With my hand, I covered his eyes. An old song began in my chest. Starting as a hum, the words came slowly into focus.

"In the shade of ancient oaks, I await your coming ..." The newly low notes of my voice brought promise of rest. "I will pull nectar from the blossoms to feed us. You will weave coats

119

from the stars above..."

While I sang, the blade of my dagger brought final relief. "And we will know together what it means to live free."

The final note of the song signaled the last heartbeats. A sigh, released from the nostrils, marked the passing of a creature most noble. The tension went out of his neck, and he lay still and heavy in my lap. I didn't move. I couldn't move. Reverently, my hand dropped from his eyes, lingering upon his proud neck. A softness was accented with the fall of a leaf. The return of birds and squirrels gradually replaced the quietness.

Life moved all around. I had whistled to Esteban and Father, who were hunting nearby. Before they came, I whispered a thank-you and stood still watching my deer. The gift he gave meant more than food for a few days for the family. He gave a boy of eleven springs permission to feel as a man.

Gabor and Esteban were first to find me. With a low whistle, Gabor stood and took in the size and strength of my buck. Esteban, who had mostly trained me since I was five, came and stood beside me, placing a hand upon my shoulder. We three brothers stood watching and remembering.

ᘔ

As a child of five springs, I received my first bow. Father had made a bow for me, but then didn't have the patience to train me. As a small boy, a smack to the back of the head greeted my whines. I learned to listen and tried to understand. Without Father's guidance, I would shoot aimlessly into the air, using the bow as more of a toy. Esteban had taken pity.

"Gaspare, you must stop and think before you fire your shot," my brother had said. "If not, you might not get a second chance."

"But I am stopping," I replied. Smack. Esteban had been right. I needed to focus.

My mind was on so many things back then. If I ever wanted to please Father and earn my right to help the men hunt once the harvest had been exhausted, I would need to try harder. We had been working on this technique since the new moon, and my aim was not such that I could risk my life or take a life.

"I am sorry. I will try harder."

"Do not drop your head in shame," Esteban said. "That was the way of a boy, and I am training you to be a man. Stand up and look straight. I need you to focus."

My small frame had responded, and I tried to push my shoulders back.

"Esteban, may I say something to him?" asked Gabor. Esteban eyed him for a second, blew out a gust of air, and stepped back, ushering him towards me with his hand. "Two heads are better than one. I am at a rock with him," Esteban noted. He snatched a tall seed pod growing nearby and began chewing on the end to get the juices from the stalk.

Jumping down from the ledge where he had been watching, Gabor strode over to us. My thoughts hedged on the futility of my skill, so I shuffled my feet and waited. As Gabor approached, he reached for the bow and placed a strong hand on my shoulder.

"Hold your finger up in the air," Gabor said. "Just like this." He pointed straight into the air. I mimicked his movement. "Now, close your left eye, but don't stop watching your finger."

I did as he had instructed.

"Did your finger move, Gaspare?"

"I haven't moved my arm, no."

"I mean, did you see the finger from a different side when you closed your left eye?"

I tried again, looking at my raised finger, and I closed my eye.

"No, it doesn't move."

"Now try with your right eye," he said.

Holding my finger up, I closed my right eye, and the finger shifted.

"Hey, it moved, but I didn't move it," I exclaimed.

"Try your left eye again," Gabor said.

Again with my right eye closed, the finger remained still. The left eye closed, the finger moved to the side. Fascinated, I flipped back and forth between moving my finger with the left eye closed and not moving my finger.

"Alright, enough looking. Never mind, just keep both eyes open when looking at your target." I dropped my bow,

121

chuckling, quite pleased with myself.

"Here, let me see you hold the bow more like this."
Gabor placed the bow down by my side, so it was still in my grasp,
but it wasn't ready to fire. "The best shot comes from the perfect
bow, not from the perfect target. You need to focus on the natural
frame your bow makes before you focus on your target."

"But if I am focused on the bow—" A look from both
Gabor and Esteban had silenced my protest. I quickly swallowed,
letting him continue.

"Before you even fasten an arrow into your bow, you
must see what is around you. What do you see, Gaspare?" Gabor
had asked.

"I see some trees."

"Is that all? Look at the movement and the patterns,
understand the wind. Now look again."

I looked again and stopped seeing the big trees and
instead found a single yellow-tinged leaf hanging on a sucker
coming from the base of the tree. I saw one sparrow out of a flock
of six.

"Deep breaths, Gaspare. Deep and slow breaths. Breathe
deep; now close your eyes and listen."

Gabor stepped back to give space.

I could hear movements of the wind. The leaves were not
just rustling; they were shifting with the breeze.

"Without opening your eyes, what do you see?" he asked.

"I see the wind. She is coming from my left and curving a
bit."

"Why do you think she behaves this way?"

"I suppose the wind bends because of the rocks over
there."

"Good, Gaspare. Now open your eyes and tell me what
you know now."

"I know that there is a squirrel in the tree over there, a
bird scratching for food to my right, and the wind is moving
across me this way."

My left arm had arched in a motion to show the wind,
and the bow became more of a tool for pointing, helping me to
emphasize my understanding.

Gabor stopped and said, "Remember how closing your

left eye moved your target?"

"Yes."

"See how you are using your bow to point at different places?"

"Well, yes."

"What are you getting at?" Esteban asked. He stepped forward, curious to see what Gabor meant.

"Did you see how the whole time he was sensing he used his left arm and not his right?" Gabor asked.

"Yes, but that is because he had his bow in his left hand."

"No, Esteban. We pull the arrow with our stronger arm, not hold the bow that way. If you were speaking with the bow on your stronger arm, naturally you would have pointed with the bow as an extension of yourself. He doesn't feel the bow as a part of him yet because he is using it in the wrong way."

Esteban looked at me, and I looked at my hands.

"Switch hands, Gaspare. I want to try something with you."

Gabor took me away from the shooting mark. He asked me to show him the direction of different landmarks, like Grandfather's hut, the well for the family, the tree the squirrel had been in just a moment before, and each time I did I used my left hand to show him. The bow stayed steady at my right side this time.

"I see what you are saying, Gabor," Esteban said. "Hmm, give me that bow."

I handed the bow to Esteban and he, holding it in his left hand, unleashed three arrows to the spot I desired. Each time, he considered the placement of the arrow and the movement of his hands. Then he shifted the bow to his right and tried, but could not fire one arrow to the same place.

"Use your left hand to draw the arrow back and try again. Place the arrow on the right side and tilt just a little to the left. Remember to focus on your breathing and surroundings."

I felt the bow lengthen my right side. I stood tall with shoulders back and felt my chest open wide to breathe deeply three times. I could feel the wind. The bow balanced the stretch of my arm. I could send the arrow where I needed it to go.

"Keep the bow straight out in front of you. Don't over-raise the bow, moving it up from your side."

As Gabor reminded me, I dropped the bow to my side and fixed my foot spread while slowly bringing the bow straight up on my right side, stopping directly level to the ground. My small boy-sized body felt big and strong.

"Use the bow as a frame to help you focus on your target, Gaspare."

I dropped the bow to my side, repeating the lift with my right bow arm, stopping precisely level with the ground and framing out the inner dip of a knot in a tree.

"Good, Gaspare, now add the arrow to the bow as you pull it up."

The arrow didn't cooperate much, bouncing along my pointer finger. The small muscles in my left arm twitched from the strain.

"Pinch tighter with your left fingers on the notch of the arrow. Hold it on the string."

Raising the bow one more time with the feathered arrow, I pulled the string back, testing the arch. The arrow quivered and bounced once or twice before I steadied the shaft, pinching tighter with my thumb and middle finger. A slow inhale expanded my chest and cleared my head. I ignored the muscles twitching, and I breathed deeply again, pulled back to my cheek, took aim and released.

The arrow flew straight and hit the mark just two knuckles' lengths away from where I had aimed. Esteban handed me another arrow and told me to aim for the first arrow. Repeating the shot sequence, I did, and the arrow shot straight towards the first and landed next to the mark. He handed me a third arrow and again I shot. The arrow plunged deep into the mark directly under the first two. I had made a cluster shot, and I knew that Esteban was pleased. He walked over, ruffled my hair, and took the bow.

"Look at you, Gaspare. There's nothing wrong with your arm when you use the stronger arm." Both Esteban and Gabor turned to head back for afternoon chores. I followed, but Esteban held up his hand to stop me.

"Not you, Gaspare. You have some practicing to do. Three little shots will never save your life or put food on the

124

table."

"How many do you want me to do?"

"Stay until you have shot forty with more clusters than stray arrows. Can you do that?"

For the first time since our training had started, Esteban smiled when he looked at me. I remember that smile even now all these springs later. He had been pleased, and I had wanted to make him proud and make Father proud. I still did.

"Yes, of course, Esteban. I can do that with my eyes closed."

"And I want you to stop by the viburnum on the way back home. You need to select ten more straight branches for more arrows."

They laughed, shaking their heads, saying something about having eyes closed, and departed while I ran to retrieve my three arrows. I had seven arrows. Esteban's order would take a while. But I liked the feel of the bow in my right arm. It felt like a weaker part of me had been strengthened by the job of holding the bow steady. The soft wood of the yew branch was pliable yet sturdy. I could feel the tension when I pulled on the string, but I could also feel the compression of the wood in the bow. There was life in the wood, much like a heart, and I held that heart in my hand. That day so many days ago, my legs had stood firm and spread like Esteban showed me. My back went straight with shoulders back and low. I began to breathe like Gabor said, and I notched the arrow. The draw came, and arrow one found its mark.

જી

Today, with only two more full moons till my Mennanti, I looked to those feelings and memories. Even now, two winters after my first kill, I sought perfection. I strung the bow with the precision of many repetitions; I pulled back, anchored, and released my arrow to find the first target. Thirty-nine more to go.

Chealana trotted along with me to get the arrows. "Girl, you had better learn how to retrieve these arrows quickly for me, or we will be here all night." She looked at me and then got distracted by a rustling in the leaves and went to investigate. When I got back into position, I gave a quick whistle. Chealana came and lay by my side with a quiet groan.

"I hear you, girl. It will be a long time before we leave, but I want you here with me so I don't accidentally shoot you. You wouldn't want that, would you? Of course not. Whatever squirrel or bird you were investigating will just have to wait. Besides, who would keep my feet warm at night if you go off and get yourself shot?"

Chealana pivoted her ears to listen, but kept her chin on her forepaws. She then rose and came closer, smelling the air. "What do you see, girl?"

She stood still, but her head and face focused on learning what was on the wind. Her ears pivoted forward and backward, and her nose twitched to catch the scents the wind sent. Voices from the past came back to memory.

"She is not using her eyes as much as she is using her senses."

*That's right, Gaspare. You need Chealana to teach you. She understands the wind. Better than you, I told myself. Deep breaths, Gaspare. Deep and slow breaths. You are not Chealana, but her master.* If I was to take the actual role of a man in our village, I needed to work hard and know inside that when the time came, I would be ready. I needed to claim my role as master.

A butterfly late for the season flitted by. Without releasing, I traced the flight with the bow and arrow taut. Never letting my eyes miss the unpredictability, I watched the delicate wings. When the butterfly flew in front of a small burst of green color midway down a rotting stump, I found my mark and I released. Thwack. Pieces of bark burst from the trunk as the sharpened flint found the center of the moss. Now thirty-eight more marks to find.

## SUSIE DICKSON'S PRAYER
by Bonnie Harris, *Valley Writers*

Today is my third day of being seven years old.

The first day was a good day. Granny gave me a beautiful doll. Rita Faye's eyes were blue like the water Jesus walked on and her hair was red just like mine. But the second day was full of red... hot... thunder... pain. It all started when I sat Rita Faye in my little-girl chair outside in the warm sun.

"Rita Faye, you stay here while I help Granny pick tomato bugs." *Moms just can't always be around. Some only show up every now and then. Some Moms go away and don't ever come back.*

I drowned about a thousand wormy bugs in my coffee can of soapy water. I held some tight and squished the yellow out, dipped my fingers in the can, then wiped them on my shorts. After dinner Grandpa was headed to the barn with a wagonload of hay. I climbed on and twisted myself down into the middle of that sweet smell. All afternoon I jumped from the barn loft and landed in the big pile of hay. My legs were scratched and red, but the thrill was worth the aggravation of it all.

Aunt Mabel drove up in her new Ford Fairlane. "Lord, child, just look at your legs! Go get cleaned up. We're all going to a revival meeting."

I was so excited that I jumped up and down. Then I remembered Rita Faye. My heart crumbled into a thousand pieces when I saw her. The hot sun had melted her arms and legs, her beady insides were all bumpy under the sticky goo. But Rita Faye was smiling, her Jesus-water eyes fixed on me. *Children still love their mothers no matter what.*

Grace Tabernacle was full of people, their eyes shut tight, waving arms above their heads... loud singing... drums pounding... dancing in the aisles. *We stay in our seats at Pleasant Valley Church. We don't get up and run around.*

Brother Turman jumped up and down so much

his hair fell down in his eyes and shiny sweat ran down his face. He stomped his feet and screamed about the flames of hell and how hot it is. My chafed legs burned like when Granny had poured green alcohol on them. My whole body got hot like Rita Faye's when she melted.

An apple-faced woman ran up front hollering that she was going deaf. Lightning flashed and thunder boomed in the hot darkness outside. *Is this the end of the world?* Brother Turman closed his eyes, looked up, and said words I had never heard before. His big hands grabbed that woman's head. He almost shook it off her shoulders. With a quick jerk, he let go and she fell backwards. Two men caught her, laid her on the floor, and just left her there. *Pleasant Valley Church doesn't have all that commotion. We sing Amazing Grace and songs about crystal water, streets paved with gold, and pearly gates. Pastor Delaney says God heals broken hearts.*

At the end of my second day of being seven, I prayed.

*Now I lay me......*
*If I should die...*
*I don't want to be thrown in the forever-burning fire of hell.*
*I want to sit by that big rock listening to your stories.*
*It probably wouldn't be a good idea for you to let me be a mother.*
*I am much better at picking tomato bugs.*
*If it's not too much to ask, I really would like to keep my hearing.*

*Susie Dickson. Amen.*

# POETRY

L'ILLUSTRAZIONE
ITALIANA

Anno XXI. - N. 1. - 7 Gennaio 1894.

Centesimi Cinquanta il Numero.

Per tutti gli articoli e i disegni è riservata la proprietà letteraria ed artistica, secondo le leggi e i trattati internazionali

# FIND ME A STONE
by G. W. Wayne, *Blue Ridge Writers*

Find me a stone, not a rock, but a stone:
beach stone, river stone, ocean stone, desert stone.
A solitary stone in a wilderness of grass.
To fit my palm. My soul to calm.
Should you be far, and shadows pulse.

Find me a stone, not a rock, but a stone:
smooth and oval, uncornered, unedged.
Experienced by sand, water, wind, heat and now
lessened in size to the sleek of its soul.
Weathered to wisdom, secure and shatterproof.

Find me a stone, not a rock, but a stone:
plain gray or mottled brown.
Striped, its inner layers teasing curious
or sparkling polished quartz about its belly.
Please find me a stone.

So, when I threaten to crack, to shoot out splinters and maim
under the crush of collapsing time
or cheap words seeking battle,
I can run my fingers across this stone.
Find cool comfort in the forging it has borne.

Find me a stone, not a rock, but a stone,
that you have tested for patience,
for solace, for strength, endurance and dignity,
in crises of character where you have triumphed,
and I will stay whole.

Please, find me a stone.

## CLOUD PHYSICS
by David Anthony Sam, *Riverside Chapter*


Alto cirrus clouds break
light in fractional arcs,
part rainbow
of divided spectrum,
part half-moons
of pure ice-white.

Just the right waves
to catch in the eye's mind
and become an image
still unfragmenting
its reality.

# SHARDS 24
## by David Anthony Sam. Riverside Chapter

The tall grass rolls into itself,
generous wind inseminating
the future.
                    I am a good place to hide.
Digging into the red clay
brings blisters of rebound
and glues of mud.

My hair wears wild wind
with grace of springtime.
Pollen dusts me
but I still remain the sterile
mad eye.

Carves of flesh statue me
into the oldest tree.
Druid memory.

A salt lick is pillar enough
to leave memory for hope.
As I look back, the dark sky
forks lightning, and I
boil into the mystery of stone.
Garnet perhaps–not diamond.

The mirror of my face
looks into the granite,
turning solitude to slow dust.
Clarities of color
plumb my shallow depths
for a wayward galaxy,
unspiraling itself into
the knowing silence.

Tall leaves of grass,
too tall to fit in a short line.
I hide            a good place to be.

# BECOME THE ANCESTOR

by David Anthony Sam, *Riverside Chapter*

The full moon bays
in the voice of a wolf.

Black waves break pale gray
against the last shore.

The pennies of the eyes
see only remnants.

Who has the halt
in a high tree
where ghosts of ancestors
have climbed
and feather the night
like sleeping vultures?

I crouch in the brush
fearful of pale shadows
that bear silence
as a dry tongue.

Night sees in deep awareness
as thickening air
wearing itself
as dew on my flesh.

The moon bays
and I feel it
in my throat and teeth.

# COMPOSITION FOR LOGS AND FIREPLACE
by David Anthony Sam, *Riverside Chapter*

The bad news of the year
ignites at the touch of a match.
A kindling of soft pine
spits and sparks in first fire.
An incense of cherry and birch
writhes wet smoke up the flue
with enough escaping into
the darkened room where I sit.

My ears still echo from the chop,
the shriek of grains straining
to stay together, then giving.
The wedge had split wood,
grown from our exhalations,
storing decades of carbon
in the knots and grains
of white oak and silver maple.
The maul had driven the wedge
deep through their history.

My arms still ache from each
swing and rebound, from
the weight of carrying logs
through two feet of snow
into the mudroom to wait
the evening's needed fire.

Now cold logs sputter juice
into a steam that cracks against
the silence of this winter night.
The sun spanned the day
in its December weakness,
but gets resurrected in this fire.

I open another chapter where
I am not mistaken for anyone
who can ever be quoted.
A loud snap drives a hot coal
out against the mesh screen.
It falls to glow, then die
into the gray remembrance
that must always cover the floor
of anyone's hearth-or life.

## RETAIL POETICS
by David Anthony Sam, *Riverside Chapter*

I can't bundle words
into the coolness of a marketplace
because I try to join things as one
and capitalism needs separate products.

I carry too large an inventory
to be profitable,
and the turnover is insufficient
to clear the shelves.

The delivery from an old dictionary
that sputters with clouds
of gray exhaustion
simply fills the storeroom.

I bundle large themes with small,
two-for-one metaphors,
symbols and the implements
that make them ring.

Customers seldom open the door,
so I spend my day rearranging
the weight of time or decorating
the display window with weak light.

Special of the day:
am extended analogy
at the same price as 1968.
Get it now!

# THE ESSENTIAL OXYMORON
by David Anthony Sam, *Riverside Chapter*

Purr of cat
Brush of lover's lips
Blaze of dying maple leaf
The presence of absence
The absence of presence
The permanence of brevity
The firmness of fragility
The knowing of unknowing
The blood beneath the paper of skin
The green river of it
The pulse of it
The purr of lover's lips
The brush of cat's paw
A sunset before night has decided
on its ending in another sunrise

## BORDER DREAMS
by Devin Reese, *Northern Virginia Chapter*

Carrying hope in a silver cross,
dangling under a dirty blouse.
Burned skin, and blistered feet,
are not sufficient to defeat
the vision of an imagined life.

*Sueños* of tree-lined streets and cars,
of restaurants and movie stars,
*La casa* with shutters and a lawn,
no longer someone else's pawn.

*El empleo* that pays you living wages
to care of your *papá* as he ages, and
ensure that your sweet son can grow
without the hardship of outdoor living.
*Campesino* no more, he'll feel driven
to find his path in this promised land,
*immigrantes* dealt a starting hand.

You glance at *el niño* and feel prid
walked and bused and hitched 3000 miles
*de Honduras* to these huge spoil piles
that mark the final *extensión de* terrain
between you and the U.S.A. of fame.

The coyote *espera* in the *cholla* patch,
and escorts you to another batch
of *viajeros* hunkered down in a truck.
Under the flap, you and *el niño* duck.
Quite rank *adentro*, with all the migrants,
clothed in unwashed shirts and pants.
But the boy's sweet head *tocando* your arm
affirms your faith *en un mundo* free of harm.

Tailgate closes, cramped *espacio* goes dark,
in your *corazón* you feel a growing spark
of fear, yet *alivio*, you're almost there
to a place where you can *finalmente* share
*la vida* you've dreamt of since he was born.

Rumbling along, the truck grows *caliente*.
Wishing for windows, you pant and sigh.
A chorus of moans answers from the dark.
*El niño* on your arm begins to cry.
*¿Qué te pasa?* you are asking,
He says "I feel sick, and
the truck just keeps rocking.
My tongue feels thick."
The heat fills up your limbs,
pain prickles your *cabeza*.
You reach for your *agua*,
but find it all gone.
To *distraerse* from the thirst,
you sing an old song.

| | |
|---|---|
| <u>Vuela Alto</u> | (translation) <u>Fly High</u> |
| *Llegar a la meta cuesta* | Achieving a goal has a price, |
| *te cuesta tanto llegar* | it costs you so much |
| *y cuando estás en ella* | and when you are there |
| *mantenerte cuesta más...* | it's even harder to maintain it. |

Everyone has gone *quieto*; it's
calming them down,
soothing their *espiritus*, maintaining *la fe*,
while onward you roll *hacia* an unknown town.

Your son *esta dormido*, you feel so exhausted.
The song trails off, your head lolls around.
You let yourself *callerse* into sleep with no sound.

*De repente*, the truck slows, comes to a halt,
tailgate flung up, bright *luces* in your eyes,

Border police looking in, you fear an assault,
reach for *el niño* and find only his leg,
squeeze it to *levantarlo*, you may have to flee,
adrenaline rises, you've heard what they'll do,
take *niños* from their *mamás* and lock them up too.

Taking your son would be taking your heart,
You prod him again as they grab people out.
Your son is so tired, you cannot awake him
and plead with the guards to leave him alone.
The one who speaks Spanish comes forward to help,
Takes your son by the *hombro* and gives him a shake.
then shudders and turns to you, *cara* aghast.
"*Su hijo no vive,*" he says. "He has passed."

I cannot say *qué pasó* after that time,
I know your *corazón* closed up tight as a clam.
I'm told you were singing more words of the song.

| *Vuela Alto* | (translation) Fly High |
|---|---|
| *Aquí no regalan nada* | Nothing is given for free here, |
| *todo tiene un alto precio* | everything has a high price |
| *peldaño que vas subiendo,* | a step that takes you upwards |
| *peldaño que hay que pagar.* | is a step you have to pay for. |

# INSIDE AND OUTSIDE, DIVIDED BY FEAR
by Devin Reese, *Northern Virginia Chapter*


Inside

Bright smile, Aunt Atatiana, matching nephew smile.
leaning forward eagerly, his turn, joy stick dancing.
Laughing into Zion's wiggly body, her turn, heart happy.
Screen shapes play along, joining aunt and boy through
the vivid colors and sounds of video game excitement.

Outside

Dark dread pulling forward, hugging the curb.
Officers on duty, jumpy, instincts dandered up,
predatory, targeting the source of the alarm call,
leaving reason aside for the terror of the chase.
Guns already drawn, hand trembling in anticipation.

Inside

A break to get nephew some juice, padding to kitchen,
glancing out a window, feeling the night breeze.
Sweet juice poured, small cup for small hand of boy.
Eagerly slurping, innocent eyes beaming on Tay,
disarming warm eyes gotten from his mama, Amber.

Outside

Front door ajar, but no other signs of trouble.
Clutching weapon, stalking around to the back,
Aaron Dean's pupils dilated like a cat's hunting.
Nothing amiss, except Dean's thumping heart
as he creeps through the side yard, fixated.

Inside

Crunching sounds in the yard, Atatiana turns.
"What's that noise?" she wonders aloud.
Zion jumps up to check out the scene.
"No," says Tay, "Let me do it," her pulse
rising as she turns towards the window.

Atatiana fumbles for the handgun,
best be ready in these uncertain times.
Dark night, could there be thieves?
Zion watches expectantly, trusting, as
she bears the weight of protecting him.

Outside

Shape in window, silhouette of prey, spotted,
growing larger as blind draws upward.
Time to pounce screams Dean's wild id.
Adrenaline pulses to raise arm perpendicular, |
stark salute before trigger pulled hard.

Inside
At the window, sensing people outside,
she hears men's voice yelling. Alarm!
Raising the blind to get a better look,
Tay feels the impact like a train hitting.
Crumples to the ground, agony, shock.

Inside

Small boy screaming. Blood seeping out
of his beloved Auntie Tay, his protector.
Shot down. But in Halo the bad guys die.
Tay is all good, his aunt, she is his defender.
Small boy with no defenses, abandoned.

# RANKS AND FILES
by R. Morgan Armstrong, *Blue Ridge Writers*

In ranks and files, we wait to board.
Anxious to learn our destination, we search and seek,
But all we see are lines of our comrades, waiting,
All of us are the same, equal in worry and frustration.

In ranks and files, we begin to move, but, oh, so slowly.
A creeping movement forward and then a halt,
We want to hurry, but that is not allowed,
We are governed by the law of nature.

In ranks and files, the departure arrives,
Up, up, we soar as we leave our warm homes,
And into the unknown, with faith alone, we fly,
With little to guide us on our journey.

In ranks and files, we our destination see,
At last our goal is near,
The landing brings us within our purpose,
And entry is finally gained.

In ranks and files, we are welcomed by our host,
Welcomed as friends and not the enemy,
But we are by nature not allowed,
A friend to this being be.

In ranks and files, we capture one, then another,
Replicate and mutate inside each part,
Until in waves we overwhelm and kill,
As is our purpose and marching order.

In ranks and files, we are labeled by the host,
And become infamous to that species,
Our name is not what we call ourselves,
But Covid 19 is what they call us.

# GHOSTS
by Pamela K. Kinney, *Richmond Chapter*

Sliding through the ether
Is that a breath of cool breeze?
No, it's just a lonely specter
Haunting corners;
trying to get our attention
A lost soul no longer existing
Sometimes, their words
come over radio waves,
Disembodied voices trying
To reach the living,
Losing the battle, other times, winning.
Ghosts, specters, phantoms,
Orbs, apparitions, revenants,
Haints, shades, shadow people.
So many descriptions, so many names.
It doesn't matter;
for haunting is what the dead do!

# COMMITMENT
Paulette Whitehurst, *Hanover Writers Club*

I will scale the tallest mountain
to capture a snowflake
as unique as your smile,
swim into the deepest ocean,
dive under the cool turquoise waters
in search of pearls
worthy of your attention
I will comb dense forests
for the golden feather
that will touch your imagination
I will take flight through misty clouds
to bring you the brightest
stars in the constellations
I will lead a quest for truth
in the eyes of beggars
on street corners of
large cities and small villages
I will seek perfect words
in the crumbling pages of wisdom
to lie at your feet
You have only to dream
along with me

# HAIKU TO VIRGINIA BEACH
by Cecilia Brown Thomas, *Hanover Writers Club*

When my body leaves,
You may witness my spirit
Dancing on the shore.

# EMERGENCE
by Cecilia Brown Thomas, *Hanover Writers Club*

Red and yellow, brown and beige –
Every color, gender, age;
Tall and skinny, short and wide –
Grateful just to be outside!

All are smiling, no one cares
What he thinks or what she wears.
Ocean spray and joyful squeals;
Unity that fills and heals

Divided souls, afraid and sad,
Alone too long and going mad.
Now we gather at the shore
Appreciating life once more.

Salty breeze and foamy breakers,
No more thoughts of troublemakers.
Gulls that draw us to the sky—Let us spread our wings and fly
Together!

# WE SHALL SURVIVE
by Cecilia Brown Thomas, *Hanover Writers Club*

Relentless scenes of chaos and destruction steal our peace
And the void in our hearts is filled with fear.
Accusatory words from talking heads that never cease
Gouge persistently like maggots in the ear.

No matter where we turn it seems the message is the same,
That the human race is splintered and diseased; so
We look upon each other with uncertainty and blame
And believe the haters cannot be appeased.

Then what are we to do about the global angst and pain
Or the overwhelming riptide of despair
That pulls our spirits under and then under once again
As we frantically seek out a breath of air?

I turn my eyes to Heaven with a plea for signs of hope
And I wonder if a prayer is even heard.
I say we all need something positive to help us cope
And I'm drawn toward the sweet song of a bird.

Spontaneous joy, a simple thing, as clouds of war depart
And my panoramic view begins to shrink;
And the chant of, "Hear now, here now" beats in rhythm with my heart
As a mindfulness reminds me to unthink.

Unthink the threats of angry words, unthink the ugly faces;
See miracles and beauty all around.
Divinity and dignity transcend the age and races
Of all people, and so easily are found.

A chuckle shared with strangers, or a twinkle of the eyes;
A simple, "Please" or "Thank you" with a smile...
The daily interactions of the civil, kind and wise
Nullify the squawking voices of the vile.

147

I know I'm not imagining that in these days of stress,
The majority of people are prevailing
By sharing love and laughter in the simple ways that bless
One another when we think the world is failing.

Chaos, fear and hatred always have and will be part of
Our unending quest for meaning in our lives;
But tiny signs and wonders all around us are the heart of
Reassurance that humanity survives.

## A MISTAKE
by Linda Hoagland, *Appalachian Writers Guild*

When Ellen looked up from her table with
all of her books spread before her, she caught
sight of a fleeting figure that faded
into the increasing crowd of shoppers.
She saw him do absolutely nothing
wrong. He just looked guilty. Guilty? Of what?

She was sitting at a table in the
middle of the mall watching people walk
past her as they shopped for items that
obviously did not include her books.
She glanced into the crowd searching for the
fleeting figure. She spotted him. He was
off to her left and skulking with his head
lowered but his arms were filled with a child.
She saw him reach to cover the child's mouth
to muffle the screams emanating
from the tiny, squirming, onesy-clad body.

Off to the right she saw a lone woman
standing in the middle of the central
circle of the mall hub frantically
searching the passing people for Johnny.
"Johnny" she screamed swinging her head from side
to side searching the arms of passersby.
The squirming, crying child tried to turn his
head toward the screaming, distraught woman.

Ellen had no clue as to whether or
not the man stealing away with the child
had a right to do so.  It was clear that
the unhappy child did not want to go
The only thing she was sure of was that
she was unhappy about the odd scene.

Children have a loud way of expressing
displeasure.  The screams coming from the child
that was in the arms of the skulking man
were tinged with fear.  One quick glance toward the
child, sweeping across his eyes, told Ellen
that this display should not be happening.

Ellen had to make a choice.  Should she sit
and do nothing?  Or, should she try to help
the screaming, panic-stricken, old woman?
Neither one of these choices did she like.
The only thing left for her to do was
try to stop the man who was holding the
screaming child, headed for the nearest exit.
She jumped up from her chair running after
the skulking man holding the squirming child
hoping to have read the scene correctly.
She ran after the man toting the child.

"Stop!" she screamed.  He quickly turned toward her.
"Where are you taking that child?" she shouted.
"Home," he replied.  She heard the old woman
hysterically screaming for Johnny.
"Johnny," she said and there was no sign of
recognition of the name from the child
who was spreading a peculiar odor
that wafted up and assailed her nostrils.
"Excuse me, sir.  I seem to have made a
mistake," she apologized as she walked
to the table where she saw a streak of
fuzzy brown in the form of a small dog
named Johnny run past her field of vision.
She smiled as she sat down to sell her books.

# A PHONE CALL

by Linda Hoagland, *Appalachian Writers Guild*

Celebrating my seventieth year
is my goal for this year.  Today a phone
call forecasted that possibility
was within my reach because the doctor
from Duke University told me the
major surgery that had been proposed
by two different local doctors was
not necessary— yet. The dark cloud that
had been following me around for the
past year had finally shrunk in size and
lighter, whiter clouds were moving in to
occupy the same space.  There are still some
clouds, but they are not quite so menacing.
So that little bit of good news paves the
way for me to move onward and upward
to the signing and selling of my books.
When I am out there meeting and greeting
people, I am not so very alone.  I
am a widow and have been for ten years
with few family members to keep in
touch by a drop in visit or two.  So—
in order for me to be able to
hold a face-to-face conversation with
real, live human beings, I must be out
there selling my books. As long as I am
still able to do so, I will fulfill
my goal of meeting and greeting many
people in my seventieth year.

## A HOLE IN MY HEART
by Linda Hoagland, *Appalachian Writers Guild*

No one warned me of the cavity,
the big hole in my heart that would form
following the death of my husband.
The cavity grew and grew until
I found something to fill it and that
was the love of my two adult sons.
The hole will never disappear but
it is smaller and I am grateful.

## A BETTER LIFE
by Linda Hoagland, *Appalachian Writers Guild*

With suitcase in hand, he was running
to catch the bus that would propel him
into a better life. He wanted
nothing to be placed in his path to
a much needed change. As he started
to board the bus, he was pulled from the
long line where he was placed in handcuffs.
He didn't make it.

# REMEMBER THAT I LOVE YOU

by Linda Hoagland, *Appalachian Writers Guild*

Staring down at the cold, stone floor in the
waiting area of the airport, I
contemplated my future with my son
who was preparing to get on a plane
to fly to New York to visit for two
weeks with his biological father.

I almost lost him permanently at
the hospital at the age of fifteen
after he was struck by a car.  Now, once
again, I'm standing on a precipice
of fear that I would lose him. Even though
his ticket was round trip, I was afraid
that he would be persuaded to stay there.

"Bye, mom," he shouted with glee as he walked
to the steps to climb aboard the airplane.
I had promised that I would not make a
scene by crying at the public airport.
I didn't keep my promise but I'm mom.
Mike came back home two weeks later, thank God.

Again, fifteen years later, I'm standing
inside an airport staring down at the
cold, stone floor waiting for my son as he
prepares to board an airplane.  He is flying
to Omaha to visit his brother.

I wanted to strengthen the bond between
the two of them so that Mike would someday

want to live close to Matt.  I wanted them
to be there for each other at all times.
My reasoning was that I would not be
around forever and family needs
to stick together to help each other.

"Mike, remember that I love you.  Tell Matt
and Becky that I love them, too," I said
as he walked to the area for the
passengers to await to board his flight.

When he returned, I greeted him with love.
"Did you have a good trip?" I asked with hope.
"Yeah, it was great," he answered with a smile.
"What do you think about big Omaha?"
"It's big, a lot bigger than this little town."
"Would you like to live there to be near Matt?"
"I don't think I would, not yet anyway."

I smiled an outward smile but cried inside.
This time I wanted Mike to plan to leave.
We drove Mike back to his house and as he
was getting out of the car I whispered,
"Always remember that I love you, Mike."
"Love you too, mom," he replied with a smile.

# MANTRA FROM THE CITY OF BROTHERLY LOVE by James F. Gaines, *Riverside Chapter*

The teacher says
When you wake to find
Imprints of concrete
Distorting your face
This mutilation
Robs your force just now
When fingers on
A keyboard promise
Another sterile afternoon
Remember the Change
Lives before you and long after
Through you also
Shut your eyes tight
See stars and red atomic bands
Rotate in blackness
A dream only a blink away
Never farther
Than your eyelids
Switch these realities
You will realize
Suffering is only fitful sleep

# UNSEASONAL

by James F. Gaines, *Riverside Chapter*


I can't pretend to know late snowflakes
Or to predict where they will land in April
Unsure as I am of other destinations
Their needling presence needs no other proof
Nor does the light nor I to lay a claim
On heritage in this uncertain time
Clouds perish oblivious and so slow
Students plod by towards a graduation
Crystalline orphans still how many
Realize a choice needs to be made
This much I do already and precocious
Boughs leaf out above my crumpled paper
Whites disjointed under chimes
So shall we find our harvest fields picked over


# GREEN ON BLUE AFGHANISTAN by
James F. Gaines, *Riverside Chapter*

It is all done with filters
Green the color of order and status quo
Green the color of astral vision and upheaval
Blue the color of benevolence and learning
Blue so violent it thickens to sightless black
No wonder target practice becomes target praxis
No wonder smiling teachers need a vengeful shadow
To paymasters quartermasters taskmasters
Colors words uniforms are interchangeable
Only the clotting blood remains the same

## ACTING OUT
by James F. Gaines, *Riverside Chapter*

He was a Hollywood heavy who once
Tried to steal Jimmy Cagney's girl
I remember him chasing
Crazed beatniks who squirted
Selzer in his face as he pursued
His wife's deranged rapist wondering
If he could stomach looking at the child
Later he thought he owed himself
A luxurious star's vacation
So he cast off in a yacht
With a trio of pubescent hookers
To hook marlin during the day
In the depths off Guatemala
Then came the storm accompanied
By a bout of rasping pneumonia
Two weeks before the corpse
Waked only by hysterically mewling teens
Drifted into a cove among mangroves
He reflected between feverish visions
That he really would have done better
To bring along a different kind of mate

# SOPHISTICATES ON BEACON HILL
by James F. Gaines, *Riverside Chapter*


On Newbury Street the Trendies meet
To snark the peons down below –
So light on their feet, devoid of heat,
Like leather tooled to an auburn glow.

Profusely high, they saunter by,
Yet hit their marks with every throw.
Don't even try to figure why
No worries dog them as they go.

In woolen skirts and chambray shirts,
They match the ads their networks show.
A harmless flirt can never hurt,
Provided no gross glitches grow.

If pleasures stall or the stash is small,
They cannot fail to score new blow.
They're in no jeopardy at all –
Protected, innocent as snow.

## Y POR ESO DICES QUE NO ENTIENDES NADA

by James F. Gaines, *Riverside Chapter*

When you had gone without departing
But something inside you left
Unblissfully I was unaware
As when I step off a ladder
Against the hickory tree's solid grasp
From what I assume is the last step
Into nothing falling on my back
A moment of pure shock
Then reassess that things are not so bad
Worse if I fell on a dozing copperhead
And only when I start to walk away
Do I realize some pain will linger?

# BREVITY
by Sofia M. Starnes, *Chesapeake Bay Writers*

1

Brevity in the breaking of a shell —
in a girl's giggle whisked out of silence,
in an ache that wanes, after some brief
well-wishing. Forgo metaphors:
it takes no time to trade dusk for intense

mornings, sunset for the sight of children.
They gambol about, agelessly, chastening
 our unbelief, our attempts at one thing
only: to count the hours; while in a garden,
the past, neither quick nor long, keeps changing.

2

Brevity in a fledgling and its flight —
And it tempts us to look away from this
day, to fallow playrooms and porches, light
and airy, to springtime energies and missing springs.  Who among us recalls the distance
between a nest and a path, a loose latch
and a stranger's door, an overgrown patch
of nettle and full-blown blue irises?
No one.   So we sit here in starlight watch,
barter tales with the evening child in us.

# ADAM

by Sofia M. Starnes, Chesapeake Bay Writers


Against all odds, let us subvert this inclination to lie low. It is that time
of day when He comes out to stroll, to win
us over with white irises, after climb-

ing, steady, to our hut.   Was it a crime
to pluck our share of garden, seed and fruit?

To crave possession of our knowing, put
an end to unsettling conversations? Love,
He said, bears neither fruit nor flower without
words. And now, this hollow in the gut, above

                              my shame.


# EVE

by Sofia M. Starnes, Chesapeake Bay Writers


He's leaving, having stitched new garments for
us out of grass. His eyes, both dark with ire
and weeping unabashedly. Now, more
than good and evil, I have learned despair—

a taste of it—this side of Adam's anger.
We'll work it out, but though I've sworn to tell

our children how it was, my mind's a shell—
shatterproof, yet stripped of pearl and worth.
Some nights, I see God sitting by a well;
His eyes, alit. In Judah, they'll call forth

                              a girl.

# VALENTINE
by Sofia M. Starnes, Chesapeake Bay Writers


Cacophony of ice on brittle grass,
a snow-crunch on the sill, where in summer
a bird sits, peers in, unable (for it has
no way of knowing) to be the hummer
humming of our joy.  We barely know where

birds go when it's cold; and less, where a
museum of words can wax eternal. The
usual answer—*in your hearts*—rests all its trust
on muscle, on fragile spigot and flue.
On throb and toll. On God pinching the dust.

## TWO POEMS
by Elizabeth Spencer Spragins, *Riverside Chapter*

## Spirals

a nautilus shell
comes to rest on winter sand—
imperfect circles
reflect upon the luster
of a journey not complete

~San Francisco, California

## Caverns

a secret sculptor
wanders limestone galleries—
alabaster falls
into folds that hide hard rock
just beneath the lake of dreams

~Luray Caverns, Luray, Virginia[2]

---

[2] Dream Lake, the largest body of water in Luray Caverns, is only 18 to 20 inches deep. This crystal-clear pool reflects the stalactites on the cavern ceiling with the clarity of a mirror. As a result, visitors often believe that the water is quite deep and that stalagmites cover the floor.

## QUARANTINE
by Katherine Gotthardt, *Write by the Rails*

Days of quarantine upon us,
I find myself wearing different shoes.
Nothing matches,
not the fear-filled air
with pear blossom`s in bloom,
nor sun's heat paired
with coolness of early spring,
nor my footwear.
Cooped up but in the yard,
I stand in pjs, camera in hand,
capturing the world unturning.
these flowers leaving me yearning
for something I used to call normal,
the things that got me out of bed:
sunrise, early commute,
light in my eyes,
tearing up and sneezing.
I'm starting to lose faith,
ask where my God went
when all has turned to silence.
I'm starting to resent my family,
nitpick, hate my dog.
I want to rip up the carpet,
demolish the bathroom tile,
repaint the kitchen,
anything for a change
and why oh why
can't they just put their toys away?
Instead, it's back to the yard.
Back to a twig sanity.
Open the lens.
Breathe. Click.

# FIRE DRILL

by Katherine Gotthardt, *Write by the Rails*

Remember when
we were in Catholic school,
and suddenly,
a winter fire drill?
Those were some days, no?

We'd line up,
fight the primitive urge to run,
trip-walk single file
through sullen double doors,
gather out front in awe of the cold
and this unexpected break,
elbow our friend, and wait.

We worried about what we left inside:
puffy coats, our favorite pencils and backpacks,
soggy-breaded bologna and cheese, brown bagged.
We dared not bring our belongings.
Teacher would have yelled at us:
"Who cares about jackets if there's a fire?"
eyes alive, knowing all along
this wasn't the real thing.
We were ill-prepared to survive,
standing outside by the flag, shivering with it,
waiting for the all-clear that seemed to take a lifetime,
no idea how short a lifetime could be
when you always follow directions:
"You'll stand here quiet until they say it's clear.
If you're talking, they won't let you back."

Amazing, those things that silence us.

# PETROGLYPHS, OR,
## A LAMENT FOR LOST CULTURES
by John D. Broadwater, *Chesapeake Bay Writers*


The park ranger points
    to a large, auburn stone.
The sweating visitors,
    talking and giggling,
        pause only briefly to gaze.


A child cries;
    a camera clicks.
The lone photographer
    glances at the image,
        then quickly follows the crowd away.
        I cannot move.
The stone holds me,
    entreating me to hear its ancient songs.


The panorama before me
    spans many centuries
    and countless lives.


Antelopes scamper in stop action,
    chased by still men on frozen horses.
Shapes and symbols unchanged,
    Impervious to wind or sand or sun.


My mind races with questions:
    Who were these people?
    When were they here?
    Where did they go?

The stone is silent.

Reluctantly, I move on,
        turning back for one last look
                at the timeless, incomprehensible
headstone
        on the grave of a lost, obscure race.

# MRS. CREEKMORE'S MAY PEAS

by Pamela Brothers Denyes, Hampton Roads

Stormed hard this morning
After that tragedy yesterday where
Anger boiled and two guns killed
Twelve, a first in my hometown.

Not sure Mrs. Creekmore had the
May peas I wanted, but she did. I know
When I go there that she will sell me
Whatever's going to be on my stove tonight.

Mrs. Creekmore and I didn't speak of it,
The nearby slaughter, only pretty peas, red
Potatoes for my pot, and strong young
Onions, thinned from her garden.

Home from the farmer's market,
I shelled peas in silence and in pain.
Shelling peas gives you time,
Time enough to think about yesterday.

Sweet May peas fell from my fingers
As I released them from sturdy pods,
Gently freeing them, so as not to bruise
Nor break nor bleed nor kill.

What unspoken ugly pain wracked this
Killer of twelve co-workers?
Why did no one notice his anger,
So crazy it erupted in unholy murder?

Surely this sick man's murderous spree was
Not about work, but about fear and anger.
Can't we be mindful of each other's pain
And choose to ask the hard questions?

I went to Mrs. Creekmore's again today.
She had mama and all her sisters there, and
Somebody's husband, all together, keeping
Each other close, like peas safe in a pod.

*The Farmers' Market*

# EVENING ON THE AVENUE
by Pamela Brothers Denyes, *Hampton Roads*

From inside a rented Haussmann apartment
on swanky Avenue de la Bourdonnais,
the Eiffel Tower is visible, but just the top,
as it is one block plus a park away. Each hot day
I walk the city, awkwardly gawking at landmarks.

From the corner Italian restaurant, richly herbed
tomato-based sauces and pizzas scent the air,
climbing to our third floor flat, which has all
windows open on this very warm June evening.
French wine flows as the first order of the evening.

Stepping over the French-door threshold
onto the small wrought iron-railed balcony,
I watch two proud waiters below, who smile up at me.
They are selling tonight's specials in English,
then serving them in French to tourists like me.

Across the street, a lone saxophone rehearses.
Later, songs not in French or in English float up
the avenue from the restaurant closer to the Seine.
With my half-full glass and a Mona Lisa smile,
I am fully content absorbing life on this Paris avenue.

# TRIMMING FOR STRENGTH
by Pamela Brothers Denyes, *Hampton Roads*

Outside my picture window, old trees sway,
April leaves fluttering dark-pale-dark green
In the spring-scented gale.

One tree was topped last week in a similar
Blow; pathway blocked for several days.
It was a weak tree with top-heavy growth.

I get that way, too, all new sprouts with
Little attention to the core of me,
Too much in my head with no balance.

Then something in me topples and I must
Pay attention to what stabilizes me,
What strengthens and grows me.

I must rest more or sometimes work harder,
Define the health of body or mind, or lightly
Move on from what was once important.

Life is to be shaped carefully, regularly
Trimmed by the owner, in a gentle dance
With any gods or guidelines one chooses.

Fertilize the roots of your tree of desire, trim
Weak branches of body and psyche, and
Sway in the breeze, knowing you are strong.

# A PRAYER FOR LESS LOVE
by James W. Reynolds, Valley Writers

I've heard what you say in the name of love
and your favorite word is no.

I've seen what you do in the name of love
because the purple bruises still show.

You say you're a man of love
but that sounds dangerous to me,

so bring me no more love
and show me simple courtesy.

# NONFICTION

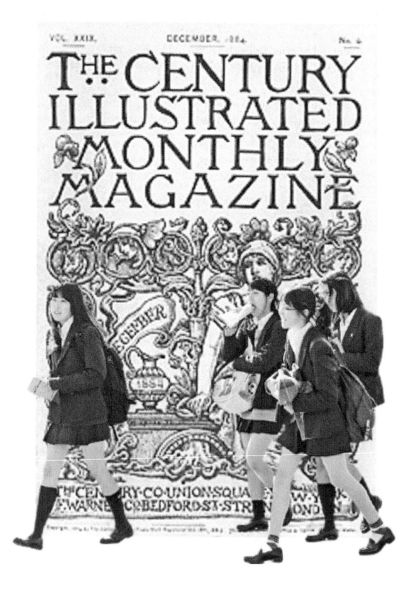

## Connected by Strings

by Danielle Dayney, *Riverside Chapter*

My sister Brittany and I pulled into a parking lot with an innocuous building just off a busy street near the mall after eight in the evening. I had driven past that shop hundreds of times when I lived in Ohio. It had different names over the years, but the building outside looked mostly the same. Gray cinder blocks, blacktop parking lot, graffiti sign with a clever name mentioning needles and roses.

I tapped my foot nervously on the floor of my sister's SUV.

"Ready?" Brittany asked.

That year was full of firsts for me. My first time quitting a job to become a writer, my first time seeing a therapist who helped me see I was enough just as I was, my first time driving myself and my two daughters eight hours to visit family, and my first-time getting tattoos with my sister.

I glanced over to Brittany and unclenched my jaw to answer, "yep." I had three tattoos already, but I got no less nervous. Still a needle, still permanent.

After climbing out of the car, I unbuckled Reagan. She had begged me to let her come. My youngest, Ashlyn, stayed back with Brittany's husband, Zac, already asleep on the air mattress in my niece's room.

Inside, the waiting area was nothing more than a couple black leather love seats and a small table with a stack of Rolling Stone magazines. The walls and tattoo chairs were black as well, and the floor was black and white tile. In fact, the only color in the whole place was that of the obligatory framed tattoo drawings on the walls. The shop was clean, something that I assume is extremely important when dealing with needles and skin. A smell of disinfectant mixed with stale cigarette smoke filled the space. Cigarettes. I hadn't smoked one in years, but it suddenly sounded like an okay idea. Heavy rock blared from speakers near the entrance, still the buzz of the tattoo machines was louder. I couldn't hear myself think. Maybe that was a good thing, otherwise I might have continued to talk myself out of getting the tattoo.

Hours before, I told Brittany I wanted to get feathers. Something for us, and something also to remember Mom. But feathers are generic and overdone, so we went with Brittany's idea.

A female tattoo artist approached us and said, "Welcome." I didn't catch her name. "Do you have an appointment?"

"We do. The sister tattoos I called about earlier." Brittany took the lead, and Reagan hid behind my legs, clutching the new-to-her stuffed polar bear she'd acquired from my stepdad earlier. We had stopped by his house to sort through some of Mom's things, and Reagan found it in the bedroom bay window next to some old throw pillows. I left his house with a pile of old photos and a few antique bowls, and Reagan left with the bear.

"Why don't you come on back and show me what you want done?" the female tattoo artist said as she tucked a strand of dark hair behind her ear. She was in her early twenties, dressed in black to match the walls. We followed her back to a separate room with a couple of art tables. She pushed aside some old Chinese food to pull out a sketch pad. I opened my phone and showed her the two images of stick figure girls. One was talking through a tin can and the other was listening. We live hours apart and mostly communicate through phone conversations. If Mom were still alive, she'd be happy with how close we stayed. When Mom first passed, Brittany had a dream where Mom was teaching her to fold a fitted sheet. In the dream, Mom made Brittany promise to stay close to me, as close as Mom always was to her siblings.

We are forever connected by both losing her and our common desire to stay close.

"Cool," she said. "Let me draw them up real quick. You can wait in the lobby."

"Thanks," I said, ushering Reagan out of the room and towards one of the couches.

"How long will it take, Mommy?"

"Not long. You just snuggle with your new stuffy and wait right here while Mommy gets her tattoo, okay?" she nodded.

"Who wants to go first?" the tattoo girl asked when she returned.

"I will," I said. "Otherwise, I may back out." I settled into the black leather chair and it groaned when I turned and pointed my left ankle up toward her. She shaved my skin with a cheap Bic razor and added the ink copy of my stick figure.

"Do you like how it's positioned?" She asked, re-tucking the hair behind her ear. I gazed down at my ankle

"Looks good to me." I shrugged.

I glanced behind me to see that Reagan had already fallen asleep on the couch with the large polar bear nestled under her head. The kids had stayed busy that trip. It exhausted Reagan.

"Ready?" asked the tattoo artist.

"Sure." I nodded.

The tattoo gun buzzed to life as she pressed the pedal with her foot. I looked away, toward my sister, and cringed.

"Does it hurt?" asked Brittany with a sarcastic smile on her face.

"No," I shook my head. "Just don't enjoy watching." Brittany laughed. She was used to needles. She followed Mom's footsteps toward a career in the medical field, working as the manager of a small general practitioner's office. I, on the other hand, get a sour feeling in the pit of my stomach at the sight of blood.

Ten minutes later, after she cleaned the fresh ink, tattoo girl asked, "what do you think?" I looked down at the stick-figure girl wearing a striped dress and a high ponytail. I smiled.

"It's perfect," I said to her.

"Cool." She smiled back. "You're up," she said to Brittany. My sister took off her cross-body bag and sat it on the chair next to Reagan, who looked so peaceful snuggled up to the bear almost half her size. I glanced around the parlor. It was empty except for another tattoo artist, a thin, bald man with two full sleeves of tattoos and several face piercings who was pushing a vacuum across the floor toward us.

"I have to clean the floors," he said as he unraveled the cord. He winced and nodded his head toward Reagan.

"She's fine. I doubt you'll even wake her." I waved him off, swatting the air in front of me.

He shrugged. "If you say so," he said and plugged in the cord next to the door, vacuuming the black rugs near the entrance. By the time he finished with the vacuuming, Reagan was still asleep, mouth gaping with a bit of drool slipping out, and

Brittany was also finished getting her tattoo. I examined her ankle and the stick-figure girl with a polka dot dress and a high bun, listening to a can. There forever. I smiled.

After the tattoo was clean, we lined up our ankles; connected the strings. I hugged Brittany, and tattoo girl snapped a picture.

*The tattoo artist*

# Duty
by G. W. Wayne, *Blue Ridge Writers*

Gustave Groeger, late in 1894, had dared to name his last child after himself, defiant of the curse that had plagued his father, Gottlieb, and his uncle, Charles: namesakes predeceasing their parents. Diphtheria had harvested his older brother, Gottlieb junior, whom Gustave could barely recall, having been a toddler in the tenements of Hell's Kitchen at the time of his passing. His cousin, Charles junior, had died en route from Silesia to New York City's golden door long before Emma Lazarus had penned her poem. Charles had entered the frigid deep of the North Atlantic in a weighted flour sack several days out of Bremerhaven. Cholera, the family history insisted.

Why had I been spared, Gustave sometimes pondered when talk about the Groegers' tragedies in the flight from the poverty of a weavers' village and during subsequent hard times in Manhattan emerged after rich desserts at birthdays, anniversaries, and weddings at table in Paterson, New Jersey?

We've escaped fate's net, Gustave believed during those occasions as Wilson kept America safe and his own fortune grew: a manager's position at the Pelgram and Myer Ribbon Mill and a solid home in the Second Ward. Four grown offspring: Anna, Emily, William and, finally, Gus junior.

Then, the Zimmerman Telegram and unrestricted submarine warfare. In April 1917, war declared. Registration of young men. Inductions. Anti-German sentiment encouraged. Gustave felt it behind his back at work. He saw it on billboards glaring down on Market Street: Smash the Hun.

Papa Gus left the very Germanic Workers' Gymnastics Club. Left the First German Presbyterian Church for the First Baptist Church. Forbade speaking German at home. Hung Old Glory on the front porch for holidays and on Sundays. Always talked up his adopted land. "We have a duty to be loyal to our America," he would say repeatedly when asked about his new habits.

Was that why Gus junior had enlisted? Was it my fault, Gus senior worried as the family gathered at the Railroad Avenue Station to see his son off on a chartered train.

Just before boarding, father and son had talked and

179

embraced on the platform. The enlistee had whispered into his father's ear, "I have a duty too." It had caused the older man to close his eyes and inhale deeply.

Please, God, don't let him die in this war, Gustave prayed as the train carrying his youngest pulled out of Erie Station to head to newly established Camp Dix, near Trenton. It was September fourth, 1918. So late in the war to join, the patriarch thought. The Allies had pushed the Germans back in August victories. Second Battle of the Somme. Second Battle of Bapaume. The Battle of Amiens, where Americans took casualties. By the time Gus junior would be ready to ship to France, this whole mess hopefully would be over.

To his right, Gus' wife, Carolina, held onto his sleeve. He heard her sobbing softly. On his left, his other children: Anna, Emily and William, waved to their brother's passing train. Gus senior caught the flutter of the small American flags as they waved out of the corner of his sight. "Gus, Gus, Gus," they yelled suddenly.

There he was, Gus junior, slight and small, leaning out of a Pullman car window. Carolina released her grip on her husband and moved in front of him, madly flailing her arms at her youngest. "I love you. Take care of yourself," she shouted into the din of the steel wheels rumbling on the tracks, into the cries of the many mothers, fathers, brothers and sisters massed on the platform. Papa Gus raised his own hand in farewell, and then lowered it slowly as the last car slipped into a descending plume of stifling coal smoke that drifted toward them from the distant, huffing locomotive.

Gus prayed. Lord, bring him back to us soon. He wiped away a tear.

On Sunday afternoon, the eighth, Papa Gus sat in his easy chair facing the window of the quiet, tidy living room. In the dining room Carolina clattered the dinner dishes off the broad oak table to carry to the kitchen to wash. She spoke softly with Emily, who had joined them that day while husband, Sergeant Alvin Thetge, was on duty with the Paterson police. Emily's light laughter led him to envy his daughter's position. Police were exempt from conscription, and still maintained high regard in the community.

Anna and husband, Theodore, had stayed at home this

Sunday, having dinner with Anna's mother-in-law, Julia, who doted on the couple's son, also a namesake. Married with a child, and gainfully employed, Teddy was unlikely to be conscripted, reasoned Papa Gus. William and wife, Cora, also celebrated at their house with three-year-old Willian junior. With a son, and as foreman of a silk mill, he was also probably immune from service.

No letter had arrived from Gus junior yet. Not that the elder Gustave expected one. He regretted not having installed a telephone in his home. Neighbors Joseph and Anna Slack had such a fancy device, and managed a call from Joseph's brother, Arnold, at Camp Devens in Massachusetts, almost weekly. A great expense, Papa Gus thought, but worth it in these times. Arnold was about ready to ship out, having completed all but a week or so of the half-year basic training. The coming event was obvious in Joseph's eyes as he and his neighbor had exchanged small talk over their backyard fence while tending garden yesterday. Joseph's voice strained; he stared beyond Papa Gus as they compared notes about planting fall spinach and lettuce.

Six months, thought Gus senior, would keep his son stateside until early March next year, if he would even be needed that long.

Papa Gus picked up the Paterson Sunday Chronicle. The usual war headlines hogged the first page. 25,360 Men Will Register In The County Next Thursday. Silk Workers Raise A Flag. Local Soldier Receives Wound. French Smash Ahead In Five Mile Advance. Yanks Smash Enemy. The family patriarch pondered. An easy gesture of patriotism to raise a flag in a park. Was the wound a bullet, or the depredation of a gas attack? Five miles forward, then soon to be given back in this trench warfare. The Yanks had only retaken a breach in their lines, not quite the heroic "smash" of the banner.

On page fifteen the Chronicle had printed The Nation's Honor Roll. 5,240 Killed in Action. 1,532 Died of Wounds. 1,686 Died of Disease. 784 Died of Accidents. 14,277 Wounded in Action. 3,224 Missing in Action or Prisoners. Papa Gus wondered if the statistics included those who had suffered stateside.

Several soldiers at Camp Devens had recently perished due to an aggressive pneumonia, the elder Gus recalled from his fence talk with his young neighbor, whose brother was preparing

181

to be a medical corpsman. The young trainee had witnessed an autopsy on one of the victims. Lungs blue and swollen with foamy surfaces.

Gus junior was only about five feet three inches tall. Weighed just over one hundred pounds. Subject to fits of asthma.

Papa Gus hardly slept that night. Or the next. No letter came that second day, or on the tenth, the day after. The nervous father reasoned the activity and confusion of settling in at camp had delayed his son's writing home. On the eleventh, he took leave from Pelgram and Myer at noon to rummage at his mail box for a letter. Nothing. He tried to keep his worries from his wife, though he could sense from her tossing in bed, and the lack of her usual smile, that she was troubled too.

They held hands frequently.

Finally, on Thursday, September twelfth, one day after their soldier son's twenty-fourth birthday, a long letter about life in the barracks and friends already made delighted the couple in their Garrison Street home.

Gus junior instructed them how to address a letter to him. They mailed one the next day with double postage to cover the weight of their relief in five pages of happy gossip and news from Paterson. Correspondence followed every several days.

"All is well," each of the ensuing messages from camp began. Those simple words relaxed Gus senior and Carolina after they had nervously torn open the envelopes. Word of the pneumonia Papa Gus had heard about from his neighbor was creeping into the newspapers in early October. Camp Dix was not exempt.

On Saturday, October fifth, no letter arrived from Gus junior, Nor on the seventh, or eighth, or ninth. On Thursday, the tenth, the neighbors Slack let Papa Gus use their telephone in a vain attempt to reach their son. The plague of pneumonia, now admitted to be the Spanish Flu, was raising lurid headlines in the newspapers.

Finally, on Friday, the eighteenth, a telegram came late in the day to Carolina at home, who ran to her husband at work.

*The Secretary of War desires me to express his deep regret that your son, private Gustave Groeger, junior, died of broncho pneumonia on October sixteenth. Letter follows. Hugh L. Scott, Commanding Camp Dix, New Jersey.*

ℰℴ

In the several days that followed, before Gus junior's body was returned to him, Gustave Groeger bought a large family plot at Laurel Grove Cemetery in nearby Totowa, New Jersey. Eventually, a large, solemn headstone with only the family surname would loom massive in its center. On the day of Gus junior's interment, only a simple wooden cross stood in its muddy middle.

When later asked why he had purchased the gravesite, Papa Gus would reflect that Groegers had been scattered in different cemeteries during the years immediately after their immigration. Some lay in Queens, mostly the Lutheran Cemetery. His mother rested in the old section at Laurel Grove. One had been buried in Yonkers. "We need to assemble our souls going forth in one place," he would say. 'We need to form an honor guard for Gus."

Sometimes, the old man would sob softly, then add, "We have a duty to be loyal... to one another."

**World War I Casualties: Descriptive Cards and Photographs**

**Gustave A. Groeger**
**Residence:** Paterson, Passaic County, NJ
**Place of Birth:** Paterson, NJ
**Cause of Death:** Disease
1 photo; 1 descriptive card; correspondence
**Card ID# 972**

# THE UPSHOT OF COURTSHIP

by Devin Reese, *Northern Virginia Chapter*

She had become accustomed to rebuffing his advances. It's not that she didn't find him attractive. But he had been a later bloomer, and she had gotten to know him before he had bloomed. Just two years ago, he was tiny, scrawny, and shy, and she would not have given him the time of day.

Admittedly, Peter was so remarkably transformed that she must have noticed. Now that he had grown up, he was macho – strong limbs, intense eyes, fierce-looking face, dark skin. Daily, he tried to woo her, showing up suddenly, following her around, and singing in his resonant voice.

Perhaps her reticence was not an aversion, but just laziness. With such a persistent suitor, she didn't need to expend much energy in response. It seemed like Rosemary just went about her business, resting, eating parfaits of fresh fruits, bathing, and otherwise leading her simple life.

Eventually, he won her over. While we did not witness the moment of truth, she began to act odd, like women do when they are anticipating a baby. She was agitated, always in motion, and rearranging things in her environment, as if in expectation of a change not yet visible to others.

One warm day, sensing her restlessness, I let her go outside. It was an uncharacteristic November day in Virginia, sunny and in the 70s, alleviating my worry that she would catch a chill. From the kitchen window, I watched her greedily stretch her legs out, revealing their soft skin, to soak in the sun's warmth.

However, when Rosemary began to dig, I got concerned. Taking her time, but working steadily, she dug a hole about eight inches around and six inches deep. She must have sensed the slight crisp in the air after all; she was digging a burrow. As I headed out to rescue her, I was stopped in my tracks.

She had backed up to the hole, positioning her rear end over it. Surprised, I saw her body begin pulsating, a gentle rocking forward and back. A seed of an explanation was forming in my mind, recalling something I'd seen elsewhere, but before I could assimilate it, a shiny, white egg dropped into the hole.

My eyes widened, my face brightening as a delighted voyeur. Peter had succeeded in his mission to mate with Rosemarie, remarkable because he was half her size and mounting must have been difficult. A feeling of awe and pride rose up in me, since I had nursed Peter from near-starvation to his current good health.

Out came another egg and another until there were ten eggs in the hole. My son had come home by then, astounded and gaping. The two of us, shameless, hung on Rosemarie's every movement, reminding ourselves to breathe while we watched her labored breathing as her head thrusted in and out, making space for more air.

The rain was coming, and temperatures were dropping. I knew that the eggs would not survive in those conditions, since they naturally should have been laid in a tropical jungle rather than a Virginia back yard. So, Guy and I waited anxiously for Rosemarie to finish and move away from the nest.

Finally, she lumbered off, seemingly satisfied with her accomplishment. She had meticulously covered the nest with shifting right and left movements of her legs, tossing small piles of dirt on it. By shimmying her body back and forth like a putty knife, she had leveled it with the surrounding soil.

Guy and I crouched closer to the nest. How were we going to move the eggs without harming them? I had read that, if they are rotated, the eggs will not hatch properly. Working quickly but carefully, I plucked each egg out of the nest and handed them to my son, who gingerly set them in a box of soil.

Eight eggs made it intact, while two were broken. We shepherded those eight inside, clutching this box of unexpected, rare treasure. Incubation was the next challenge. They would need to be kept warm, of course, but how? Rosemarie and Peter's indoor habitat, which was heated, was the only logical place.

There the eggs sat for a week perched in their box of soil, looking like a science fair project to see whether ping pong balls will sprout. Rosemarie and Peter peered at them through the clear wall of the box. Whether they were aware of their offspring was tough to determine.

Regardless, the eggs were separated from their parents once a proper incubator arrived in the mail. In went the eggs, one by one, delicately, our fingers trembling with the prospect of small lives brewing within. Then, the long wait began.

On through Thanksgiving, Christmas, the New Year, Guy's birthday, and still the eggs sat looking like ping pong balls. The big laying event had been exciting, but our expectations ebbed with the passage of days and weeks and months. Two months...three months...was it possible they were not alive?

On day 100, I noticed the cracking. One of the eggs had a cracked shell, and blood-like liquid was seeping out. My remaining expectations were crushed. I was dreading having to remove a dead hatchling, but would cross that bridge when the time came, i.e., when things started to smell.

On day 107, I peeked into the incubator window and saw the crumpled eggshell with a trail of brown liquid, as if it had literally exploded. How disgusting. My sigh was interrupted by a small movement in the corner of the incubator.

A hatchling! A wiggly hatchling, a perfect, tiny copy of its red-footed tortoise parents!

# IN PRAISE OF SHAME
by Carole Duff, *Blue Ridge Writers*

We talked a lot about the ducks during freshman orientation at this all-girls college, before the sophomores, juniors, and seniors arrived that fall. Every evening, we six dorm mates from the second floor sat together in the dining hall that overlooked a large pond, home to several pure-white ducks and a motley-colored goose. I don't remember our exact words but imagine they went something like this. Names changed to protect the innocent, although as it turned out, none of us were.

Linda: "Aren't the ducks cute? I love how they puff out their little breasts."

Pat: "Chest, it's chest, I can't say that other word." Asking for a "chicken chest" in line at the cafeteria got laughs, too. Linda and Pat roomed together.

Debbie: "Ducks make me nervous."

Sue: "Yeah, they're disgusting and crap everywhere." Debbie and Sue roomed together.

Me: "Ducks are okay but watch out for the goose. Geese are larger than ducks and have longer necks, bodies, and legs, notched bills, low-positioned nostrils, and that distinctive honk and hiss, and they can bite. When I was a toddler, living on a farm, my older sister taught me to bark at the geese to chase them away. That worked for us—you might try it, too."

Sandy said nothing and never did unless she felt called to. She and I roomed together. The six of us—four white girls, one Middle Easterner, and one black girl—lived all four years with our respective roommates.

Soon after the rest of the students arrived on campus, we met Mary Jayne, M.J., a junior who lived on the third floor in our dorm. She sat with us during dinner and, like a big duck, took us under her wing. We happily followed her lead.

M.J.: "Feather pecking is normal, though it can damage plumage and injure a bird's skin." M.J. was a biology major.

Sandy, my quiet roommate: "I don't think they want to hurt one another."

Roommates Linda: "I just love the creamy white plumage

187

on their wings and breasts," and Pat: "Don't say that word. Chest, it's chest."

Roommates Debbie: "Their yellow beaks and orange legs and feet make me nervous," and Sue: "Yeah, and they crap everywhere."

Me: "Those birds must be hearty, because I've seen nobody tending them, other than the cafeteria staff hosing pee and poop off the sidewalks and terraces or tossing out stale bread. I always root for the ones at the bottom of the pecking order. And when I feed ducks, I try to give everyone their share of the bread."

Maybe there were too many birds for the food supply, because feather pecking happened often, even outside of mating season. And when the pecking drew blood, usually a larger bird picking on a smaller one, it quickly developed into a vicious frenzy with others joining in.

Later, I would read that abrupt changes in the composition of a flock can stress ducks and lead to aggression. Adding ducks of different ages, breeds, colors, sizes, or traits can further upset the order and increase pecking, unless they've been raised together. But back then, I didn't know any of this. I thought ducks were ducks, and people were people.

Until I got pecked on. One day, early in the first semester, I was taking a shower in the mid-hall bathroom that served the entire second floor.

There were several sinks and toilets but only three shower stalls, often in full use during mornings and evenings. To avoid the wait, I took my shower before or after lunch, depending on my class schedule.

The bathroom was quiet after lunch that day. No whoosh of the bathroom door opening or thump as it closed, no water flowing from sink faucets, and no one calling "flushing" before flushing the toilet so people in the showers knew to step away from the spray and avoid getting scalded as cold water diverted to the toilet.

When I pulled aside the shower curtain and stepped from the stall into the dressing area, my towel, clothes, and keys were missing. Someone had taken everything. I considered pulling the shower curtain down and using it for cover, but that would have put the shower out of commission. And even if I ripped the curtain down, then what? I still didn't have clothes or keys. Maybe if I waited for someone to come into the bathroom—unlikely since the thief was probably outside, preventing anyone from entering. I visualized parading down the hall in all my glory, accompanied by snickers and sneers of on-lookers. Humiliation isn't any fun unless it's witnessed. I knew that much.

My gut roiled as I thought about how I would miss my afternoon class, how my parents sacrificed for me to get an education, how someone had stolen the most valuable thing I had: time. I closed the shower curtain, pushed my long, wet hair back, thrust out my chest, crossed my arms over my naked breasts, and planted my feet.

Chin held high, I shouted, "Bring back my things. Bring back my towel. Bring back my clothes. Bring back my keys." On and on I yelled, louder and louder, the same words, nonstop. Then I barred my teeth, flexed my arm muscles, and bellowed.

"Bring. Them. Back. Now... Now... Now... Bring. Them. Back. Now."

Tears streamed down my face, and my body shook not from the chill of being wet but from rage. I was glad no one could see me, because if they saw any sign of weakness I would likely suffer another pecking incident, maybe even ostracism. Since shaming is about gaining status and power at someone else's expense, I figured two could play that game.

It seemed a long time but was probably less than ten minutes until my clothes, towel, and room key magically reappeared in the stall's dressing area.

"Thank you." I yelled, not in anger but vindication. I had won. After drying myself off, I wrapped my wet hair in the towel and put on my clothes.

The hall was empty when I left the bathroom. I don't remember anyone saying anything about the incident, but nobody living on the hall looked me in the eye for the rest of the day.

Their shame, not mine, I said to myself. But from then on, I kept an eye on my things and never fully closed the curtain when I showered. So, maybe my win was Pyrrhic, because the cost of victory felt more like defeat.

Today, between one-in-four and one-in-three students, ages 12-18, report being bullied at school. I would posit that all of us experience bullying of some sort in our lives. Like ducks, humans can use their power to control or harm others. Human bullying can be verbal: saying mean things, teasing, name-calling, taunting, threatening; or physical: hitting, spitting, tripping, taking someone's things; or social: leaving someone out, telling others not to be friends with her, spreading rumors, embarrassing her in public.

Bullying often happens more than once or has the potential of happening more than once. But again, as a college freshman, I didn't know any of this. Or that the next incident would be a textbook case, pure but not so simple.

Because I forgot to watch out for the goose.

Back then, I was a slow eater, a positive quality in my family. We took our time when we gathered for dinner and didn't get up from the table until the last person finished. Maybe I was especially slow, eating dinner with my friends that evening, because I had a paper due the next morning, a paper I hadn't written. I'd asked my roommate Sandy to sub for me, cleaning tables in the dining hall for an hour after dinner. As a scholarship student, I worked campus jobs, but that night traded money for a little extra time. In retrospect, I'd realize my friends took advantage of my predictable behavior. They ate in record time and returned with M.J. to the dorm. I followed minutes later.

"One, two, three, four..." I counted the steps to the second floor, dragging my feet. Only fourteen hours until the paper was due. I ran my hand along the smooth, acrylic-painted cinderblocks. The scent of disinfectant common to all institutions filled my nostrils. As I squared the turn at the U-shaped landing, I thought about how much I missed my mother's cooking, my father's voice, and the comfort of my bed.

When I reached the second floor, M.J. raced out of Pat and Linda's room, directly across from the stairs. "Quick, something's happened to Sandy." At that moment, my exacting sense of time faded into the background, like a tiny figure at the vanishing point on a painting's distant horizon line. Then my brain short-circuited, as it has in similar circumstances since I was a child—and still does. But that deep hurt is another story.

"What?" I asked, my heart pounding as I walked into Pat and Linda's room. Sue and Debbie were there, too, but not Sandy. My gaze bounced from person to person. Pat and Linda sat on their desk chairs facing me from the far end of the room. Sue and Debbie perched side-by-side on one bed to my right. Sue clutched a pillow to her chest. M.J. stood in the center of the room. Why were they staring at me?

"Sandy fell down the stairs," M.J. said.

I froze. "When?" That word brought time back to the foreground, and intuition kicked in. Something wasn't right.

"She fell down the stairs," M.J. said. "We took her to the hospital." How could they have taken Sandy to the hospital and come back so quickly? I took little time to finish dinner and walk back to the dorm, had I? They wouldn't do this to me, would they?

That's when my intuition shut down. "Where? Is she all right?" "Don't you want to go see her?" M.J. asked.

I saw my friends scoot to the edge of their seats. A sick feeling roiled my gut as my brain flipped from one neuronal pathway to another, like a computer gone haywire among an endless loop of conditional, if-then statements. If Sandy, then stairs. If stairs, then the hospital. If the hospital, then sub. If sub, then Sandy. I stood in the middle of the room while others waited for me to say something but couldn't make sense of anything or find a path to a coherent answer.

"Don't you want to go see Sandy?" M.J. pressed. "Don't you want to go to the hospital?"

Hospital. My brain skipped to the hospital's if-then statement. "I need to get someone to cover my shift tonight," I said. "Sandy was going to sub for me."

A roar of laughter swept through the room as my friends smelled blood. I felt the sickness in my gut twist my face into a painful smile, a rictus.

M.J. pointed at me as she looked at each of our friends. "See, I told you she didn't care about anyone but herself."

"No, no, I want to go to the hospital to see Sandy but first need to..." More roars of laughter.

"See..." "No, no, I..."
"See?"

I felt the sharp bite of the goose. This time, I shut my mouth and waited.

After the laughter died down, M.J. called, "You can come out now." Sandy emerged from the closet behind me. Another wave of laughter filled the room.

"I'm sorry," she said to me over the roar, "I didn't want to do this."

I didn't feel called to say anything. At that moment, it crossed my mind that M.J. had an older sister, too, one who'd graduated from this college. Maybe M.J. was doing to me what had been done to her. I remembered what she'd said when we first met: "Feather pecking is normal." For ducks and geese but not for us, I thought, because humans can control their behavior. This was no longer about winning or losing, but a lesson we needed to learn.

Instead of barking, as my older sister had taught me, I stared at each of my friends in succession. Laughter and finger pointing stopped. Linda studied her shoes. Pat picked her cuticles. Debbie hid her face with the pillow she'd been hugging. Only Sue met my stare. We both recognized crap when we saw it.

We held that silence for a minute, though it was probably more like seconds.

I glanced at Sandy and said, "It's okay, I understand." Then I gave M.J. my full attention. "That. Was a dirty trick." I turned on my heel and left the room.
Sandy followed me out the door. "I'm sorry, I didn't want to do it." "It's okay, Sandy. I really understand."

That night she subbed for me in the dining hall, and I pulled an all-nighter. It took me a day or so to recover from the loss of sleep. But I never recovered from the shaming.

That. Was a good thing.

Now I'm not an advocate for bullying or shaming—quite the opposite. But good came of it. For one, the shaming and bullying among us ended. I got better at taking my lumps rather than asking others to sub for me when I over scheduled—which I still do. And I never pulled another all-nighter, because the cost of winning—a day or so of foggy sleep deprivation—felt like another Pyrrhic victory.

I'd also like to think I was a little less of a self-centered, know-it-all after the incident. From then on, I invested time in my friendships while pursuing a degree in history. Historians know that for 99 percent of human evolutionary history, humans lived by foraging and therefore had to learn to work together to survive.

Did we freshmen and M.J. survive the shaming? Yes, and we remained friends, too, often eating dinner together in the dining hall, though I don't remember us talking about the ducks after that. Some of us also stayed in touch post college as we pursued our professions.

M.J. became a veterinarian. "I feel sorry for animals, because they can't tell you where they hurt," she told us. Maybe because I knew the same was true of people, I became a teacher.

Year after year, I taught at least one class of high school freshmen and took them under my wing.

"We have to learn to live and work together," I told my students and colleagues. And I always made sure everyone got their share of the bread.

## HARD CIDER
by J. Thomas Brown, *Virginia Writers Cub*

No sooner had The Beatles appeared on the Ed Sullivan Show in February 1964, when my family was off to England. Our move from Pennsylvania was complicated by a shipyard crane dropping the shipping container holding our furniture. My mother turned it into an opportunity to replace the bent and broken things with English antiques acquired at auctions. The English set the bar for an antique to be four hundred years old or more. She was able to get bargains on two-hundred-year-old grandfather clocks, tables and chairs, dinnerware, and crystal that were sought after in The States where it was difficult to find things over a hundred.

We house hunted in London, but the homes were gloomy and smelled like cabbage. Finding schooling was difficult. Canes of various thickness stood racked outside the headmasters' offices. It was not reassuring to hear that canes were hardly ever used anymore. The English schools would not allow me to enter the British education system. By the tenth grade, American public schools were two years behind the English. The British students were preparing for O and A level exams and on a path to university or trade education. My younger sister, Lydia, and brother, Jeff, were not yet beyond hope and were accepted.

My parents fell in love with an eighteenth-century manor in Sundridge, near Sevenoaks, Kent. It was called Greystone Court and was divided into three separate homes. Greystones was approached from a single driveway leading to three separate courtyards in the back. The front was kept in its original state, facing the beautiful Kent countryside. Our third of the manor had a huge expanse of lawn, a gazebo, and a sunken rose garden. A solarium opened onto a wide veranda overlooking hedged gravel paths. In America it was my job to cut the grass and rake the leaves, but I could not get the English lawnmower to start. There was a flame thrower to control the weeds, which I managed to ignite. It incinerated half the main path but fizzled out and I never could get it going again. We let the weeds grow until forced to hire a gardener.

The living room was used to entertain Mom and Dad's

friends and business associates. It had a sunken floor with an ornate fireplace and French doors opening out to the veranda. The bedrooms were on the second floor and we were one short. I was assigned the library on the third floor for my bedroom. The walls were lined with English history, mysteries, and contemporary literature, including the unexpurgated version of *Lady Chatterley's Lover* banned in the United States.

ॐ

New Beacon Boys' School in Sevenoaks took my brother in. He did well and got good at soccer. "What do they say about losing the Revolutionary War?" I asked one day.

He cracked a grin. "They had to let us go because they were too busy ruling the world."

Lydia enrolled in Combe Bank Convent, where nuns daily smacked the students' knuckles with rulers and dealt verbal blows. Before her first year ended, she and three other girls hopped on a double-decker bus outside the school entrance and made it halfway to London before the nuns caught up with them and hauled them back. They nearly got away. All were placed on disciplinary probation. I am proud of her for being the ringleader of the rebellion. Dad was, too. She was a leader.

Far into the school year it was decided the best solution for me was a boarding school in Bury St. Edmunds, Suffolk, called Herringswell Manor International School. Boys were required to wear a blazer, tie, smart trousers, and leather shoes; girls a blazer, white blouse, skirt below the knees, and calf socks. No sneakers or dungarees.

The Sunday before I was due to leave, I convinced my parents I was old enough to buy my clothes myself. They gave me the money to shop in London at Selfridges. But this was the era of Swinging London, so I made my way to Carnaby Street instead and bought a double-breasted Edwardian pinstripe blazer and matching bell bottoms, a flowered shirt and paisley tie. And a pair of leather Mod boots with high heels. Technically, it was a suit— and the boots were leather.

When I got back home in the evening, Mom was upset. It

was my first *you-did-what?* "Whatever possessed you to do such a thing? Your father will be furious. It's a good thing he isn't here right now." I imagined Dad's eyes bulging out of their sockets, but he had already left for the airport.

Mom was willing to play it by ear. I wore my Carnaby Street suit as we headed out to Herringswell Manor by train on Monday morning. Built in the early 1900s, the estate had been acquired by two partners with ambitions to establish it as an international school catering to Canadians and Americans: an Irishman named McDermott and a retired American colonel named Villiers. Mr. McDermott greeted us at the entrance and gave us a tour. For all the mock-Tudor grandeur of the outside, the interior of the main house was austere and pervaded by a damp chill. Once white walls were tinted with age and the dark-stained woodwork plain. The snooker table in the pool room looked promising, but the turn of the century easy chairs sagged to the floor. Cue stick racks lined walls covered in scuffed wrought leather. The girls' dorm was on the second floor, off limits to the boys. Mr. McDermott showed the classrooms and the lounge, then drove us over to the boys residence hall.

The house was split in two. One side was the domicile of the dorm parents, the Andrasanins. Mr. Andrasanin was also the biology teacher. In the lounge, the smell of curry comingled with the odor of burning coal from the fireplace.

Mom gave me a brave smile. "I'll send you a hot plate and some cans of stew."

"Sorry, hotplates aren't allowed. Biscuits and chocolate are fine, though," said Mr. McDermott.

The boy students' rooms lined the hallway spanning the second floor. There were two beds to a room with a coal fireplace between. In the bathroom was a clawfoot tub with a water heater mounted above on the wall. The bathroom was heated by an electric space heater. I could see my breath in the air. Mr. McDermott led me to my room and explained the rules: smoking was allowed but use the ashtrays, no alcohol, curfew at 10 p.m. Supper was at 5:30. It was here my mother took her leave. They left me to unpack.

I laid my suitcase on the bed closest to the fireplace. As I hung up my clothes my roommate walked in, a short wiry fellow with a beard and curly hair. He introduced himself as Jon Rauss and told me I was on his bed, but to take my time. Jon pulled a pack of Gauloise from his shirt pocket and offered me one. "They're strong," he said, watching with interest as I inhaled.

I nodded, trying to control my choking. "Where are you from?"

"Switzerland. I have dual citizenship with the U.S., actually."

"Why did you pick this school?"

Jon shrugged. "My parents picked it. I got expelled from Lausanne for drinking." He took a deep drag and propelled the lungful across the room in perfect rings. "What does your dad do?"

"He works for World Trade Corporation. He's in marketing."

"My dad is John D. Rockefeller's lawyer. Winnie Rockefeller is my best friend. I'm flying to New York next weekend to see him so you'll have the room to yourself." I couldn't top that.

⅋

We assembled in the main lounge of the manor house in the morning to wait for breakfast. I walked in with Jon and he introduced me. Seven boys and seven girls made up the student body. I was number fifteen. I found a warm spot by the fire and lit a Player's, trying to fit in. The others were dressed according to code in clothes from shops on Saville Row and shirts hand stitched in Hong Kong. At least I was the tallest in my high-heeled boots.

A few weeks later I had settled-in to the school routine properly dressed in a two-button blazer, charcoal pants, and black Oxford shoes. English and biology became my favorite subjects, because of the lack of textbooks. Creative writing exercises helped me develop my imagination to write fiction and didn't require a textbook. Drawing specimens from the Linnaeus classification system was interesting, despite not being able to understand what

Mr. Andrasanin was saying.

Colonel Villiers played the role of physical education teacher and conducted class in a raggedy sweat suit from his military days. He led us on runs about the grounds, then lined us up to shoot hoops on the concrete driveway of one outbuilding. I wasn't good at basketball and made the mistake of getting in his way, bouncing off him as though he were a brick wall. Get up, moon child, he ordered. I got up and took a shot, missing by a mile.

The weeks turned into months. To pass the time after supper, we played pop tunes and lip synched to The Spencer Davis Group, Neil Diamond, The Hollies and The Yardbirds. The winter wore on and the short breads and chocolates from home no longer took the edge off the tasteless boarding school diet. The rumblings in our stomachs were accompanied by grumbling. One evening we decided we had enough.

"There's a pub half a mile down the road," said Jon. "They have fish and chips."

Larry always talked about the cookouts back home in Oregon. "A steak would be nice."

"I've lost eight pounds," I chimed in.

"You up for it," Larry asked.

"Don't look at me."

"Since nobody's volunteering, how about drawing straws?" Larry pulled a box of wooden matches from his pants pocket and broke the end of one. He handed the bunch to Jon. "You do it. Shuffle them."

Jon lined up the heads and held them out in his fist. Mine was the short match. "Okay, I'll go."

"Get some beer, too," said Jon.

Everyone put in a couple of pounds and I stuffed the notes in my pocket. I turned off the outside lights and closed the front door slowly behind me to avoid creaking it, but it let out a long, throbbing, groan. I looked over to the door leading into the Andrasanins' apartment. All clear. Fifteen minutes later, I walked up to the bar of the Whitehart Tuddenham.

"We can't serve you," said the bartender.

I could barely pass for sixteen, let alone eighteen. "Do you serve fish and chips?"

"We're fresh out."

I didn't give up. "I'm from the school down the road. The food's terrible." I pointed at the meat pies on the bar. "Can you sell me those?"

"What the bloody fuck." He motioned with his head. "Walk around outside and meet me at the back door."

It was several minutes until the door opened. "Best I can do, mate." He handed me a box of meat pies and a bag with three bottles of hard cider. I fished out the wad of money from my pocket and handed it to him. "Ta," he said and closed the door. I rapped impatiently.

The door opened a crack. "What now?"

"What about my change?"

"Is that the thanks I get? Piss off. Consider yourself fortunate."

When I got back to the dorm, the front door was locked. The lounge was empty. I went to the Andrasanin's side of the building and threw pebbles at Larry's windowpanes above their kitchen window. He opened the sash and leaned out.

"The door's locked," I whispered.

"Climb the trellis."

I looked up at the ivy covering the latticework. "I need two hands to climb."

Several heads appeared near the window and huddled together. A minute later Larry lowered two sheets knotted together. "Tie them in these."

I made the end of one sheet into a sling and loaded the contraband. The bottles clanged cheerfully against the side of the building on their hand-over-hand journey upward. I climbed the trellis and scrambled over the sill behind them. We polished off the pies and cider and were deeply satisfied.

The next morning Mr. McDermott called me into his office and pointed to the seat in front of his desk. "You were seen climbing up the side of the building after hours last night. Mr. Andrasanin found cider bottles in the trash. Am I missing something?"

After my full confession, I was suspended for two weeks.

The train back to Sevenoaks was empty in the middle of the day and clattered noisily over the rails. The familiarity of the passing landscape served as a reminder I was getting closer to home and my father's anger. My anxiety grew.

I lugged the suitcase from the bus stop in Sundridge up the hill to Greystones in a drizzle and was let in dripping by Mrs. Hedges, our housekeeper. Mother was out shopping, so I went upstairs and unpacked my clothes and the notebooks I needed to keep up with schoolwork. Two weeks banishment is a lot of time, but on the shelf over the desk was the means of escape: *Ape and Essence, Catcher in the Rye,* and *Lady Chatterley's Lover*; the uncensored version.

Mothers of murdering sons sentenced to hang have countless times pleaded the innocence of their child, yet I was uncertain of the outcome. All the bad stuff in my entire life added together could not hold a candle to getting suspended. I told Mom the entire saga over roast beef sandwiches and tea when she got home.

It turned out Dad was in the Hague for another two weeks, so there was a reprieve. She listened patiently as I told my side of the story. "Mr. McDermott called me this morning to let me know you were suspended. Now that you told me about the food situation, I'm giving him a piece of my mind. All the money we pay them~ if they fed, you better, none of this would have happened."

Mr. McDermott confessed it was Colonel Villiers who wanted to expel me permanently, but he had argued for a three-day suspension. Two weeks was the compromise, but he could not change that. He agreed to talk to the cook. My humiliation was over.

Mother was busy shopping for antiques during most of the time of my exile, and I was on my own. An old Lambretta motor scooter that wouldn't start was tucked under a tarp in a corner of the courtyard. Mrs. Hedges's son, Charles, took me on a bicycle tour of Sundridge and showed me a garage that stocked scooter parts. With a new spark plug and carburetor float, it sprang to life and I could take scooter rides on the back roads.

Most of the time I had the place to myself and did a lot of

reading. My library bedroom had French-style windows that open outward to the steep hip roofs of the manor. To the left, it was all twelve-pitch terracotta. To the right, you could see the front lawn three stories below and tiny catt
le grazing in the distance.

The end of the first week I finished *Catcher in the Rye* and was halfway into *Lady Chatterley's Lover.* It was 27 degrees Celsius (eighty-one degrees Fahrenheit,) unusually warm, and I opened the window. I like to read in bed and flopped down, returning to my place, the part where the lover is stripped to the waist and washing himself while Lady Chatterley is watching. I continued reading for all the wrong reasons. There was a tapping on the windowpane.

"Hello. Do you mind if I pop in?"

Startled, I look across the room. In the window, with the sunlight pouring in, is a brown-haired girl my age crouching on her haunches on the sill. She wears a dark pair of tights and blouse.

Before I can answer, she hops to the floor. "I'm your neighbor. I live next door in the middle."

I'm reminded of her strong resemblance to Emma Peel from the Avengers. Not sure if she is real, I slide from the bed and stand there facing her, wondering what to say.

"Did you walk here over the roof?" We don't shake hands. "Along the gutter, actually. You're a Yank, aren't you?" *Like, don't you ever walk three stories up along the gutter, too?* Her eyes rest on the can of Three Nuns pipe tobacco on the desk and she smiles. "Are you on holiday?"

I dig for something to impress her and panic. At first, absolute dead air nothingness, then decide to play the victim. "I was suspended from school for drinking—hard cider."

"For that? How awful."

Names are exchanged. Hers is Amanda. It turns out she was let out of her school early to attend a funeral that afternoon. "I must get back before they notice I'm gone. It was really nice meeting you, Tom." She hops back on the sill and steps catlike onto the roof, smiling. "Cheerio."

Early the next morning I played Beatle songs downstairs

in the living room on our grand piano. With the top up, real loud. Halfway through "I Want to Tell You" the phone rings. "Yes, hello, I'm your neighbor. I hope you don't mind me asking, but do you like The Beatles?"

He hadn't given his name. It seemed he must complain about playing too loud so early in the morning. "I apologize. It's much too early."

"Oh, not at all. Good choice, I enjoyed it. Do you mind if I ask, but how old are you?"

"Seventeen."

"I am so happy The Beatles caught on with you Americans. So glad we had this chance to chat. I won't disturb you any longer. Goodbye."

The phone clicked. *How polite.* I never saw his daughter again.

Greystone

# WHAT DOES COURAGE LOOK LIKE?
by Rev. Dr. Larry Buxton, *Northern Virginia Chapter*

*[King] David went and brought up the ark of God from the house of Obed-edom to the city of David with rejoicing; and when those who bore the ark of the Lord had gone six paces, he sacrificed an ox and a fatling. David danced before the Lord with all his might; David was girded with a linen ephod.*

*So David and all the house of the Lord brought up the ark of the Lord with shouting, and with the sound of the trumpet. As the ark of the Lord came into the city of David, Michal daughter of Saul looked out of the window, and saw King David leaping and dancing before the Lord; and she despised him in her heart.*

2 Samuel 6:12b-16

What does courage require of us? Every day we face choices at home and at work that boil down to this: "Do we keep doing the same thing? Or do we try something different? Is this the time for the tried and true—or the time for variety, the spice of life?" As we wonder how best to influence our children, strengthen a marriage, or improve an organization, we rarely think of a "Dancing King" (apologies to ABBA) as a source of wisdom.

But he is.

King David's half-naked public dancing is one of the great scandals of the Bible. A soldier-become-monarch in his inaugural parade strips off his clothes and, surrounded by dignitaries and warriors all dressed in their finest, undulates along the parade route into the capital city.

David's half-naked public dancing is also one of the great mysteries of the Bible. What leads a warrior-king ascending to the throne of a newly formed country to throw dignity to the wind and boogie his way into power? What leads a beloved public figure to disgust his wife on one of the most important days of their lives? Is there a greater purpose to his embarrassing himself? What could it be?

In this provocative event, David points us to deep

questions about leadership. What does courage require of us? When should we buck convention and upset tradition? And when should we restrain our impulses and practice self-control? Does good leadership shake things up or does it smooth things out? There is our dilemma in a nutshell: Rock the boat or calm the waters?

These are tough questions for all of us—current Presidents, former Presidents, business leaders, Moms and Dads. David's daring exhibitionism opens a host of questions on how we decide what to do and how to do it and who will be affected by our actions. Answering them is the work of a lifetime.

Setting the Scene

We enter the story some years after the death of Israel's 11th century monarch, King Saul. David had been the king of the southern territory known as Judah, but upon Saul's death the tribal leaders of the northern territory (Israel) installed Saul's son Ishbaal as king. Ishbaal's forces had frequent skirmishes with David's soldiers, and Ishbaal proved to be an ineffective leader. When he was assassinated by soldiers seeking David's favor, the military leaders of the 10 tribes of Israel came to David to make peace and pledge their loyalty. In receiving them, David united the two former realms into one new country. He became the first monarch of a united kingdom.

David has determined to make newly captured Jerusalem the political and religious capital of this new nation. He recognized that the Ark of the Covenant, the historical vessel in which God was believed to dwell, is the perfect symbol to bring into Jerusalem. It announces continuity with their sacred past and hope for a God-blessed future.

The big event begins as David leads a large group of warriors to the nearby village of Kiriath-jearim (also called Baal-Judah), where the Ark of the Covenant has been stored for 20 years. After a short layover in the house of Obed-Edom, David readies the inaugural parade to bring the Ark into Jerusalem. As the procession gets underway, the new king shockingly strips off most of his clothing! He then accompanies the Ark into the city with whirling, twirling, reckless abandon. He dances before God in ways that some describe as being "with all his might" and "to the glory of God." Others see it as vulgar.

David's near-naked, ecstatic dancing has numerous explanations. He may lay aside the royal robe to exhibit the skimpy covering of a priest stepping out of his royal identity to claim also the entitlements of a religious leader. He may imitate the sacred dances of prophets, adopting a prophetic identity. Either of these options would proclaim that David intends to be not only a political leader but a spiritual one as well. Or is he stripping himself of all kingly attire to be just an ordinary citizen, to say, "I'm just like you, my people, we are all the same before God"? Or is he co-opting ecstatic practices more commonly associated with idol worship—and if so, for what purpose?

Other guesses abound, but his action is clearly daring and risky, one that requires bravery and nerve. We can identify David's daring boldness and nerve as "courage."

Courage is the *sine qua non* of leaders. No one leads by always playing it safe. Leadership is a risky business, and leaders can be found in many places along a "risk continuum." While David's dancing puts him among so-called "risk-inclined" leaders at one end of this continuum, courage is often required of "risk-averse" leaders at the other.

Risk-Inclined Leaders

Some leaders are drawn by risk. They're invigorated by daring actions that cut against the grain. They think leadership by definition is moving out ahead of the group, showing independence, and challenging others to adopt the leader's reality as their own. The leader as outlier, visionary, and futurist is intentionally de-stabilizing. David's daring dancing fits here.

Risk-inclined leaders are needed when an institution has become wedded to an unproductive status quo. Leaders can "shake things up," force novel approaches and reward innovative thinking in ways that other members of the organization cannot. It requires courage to break away from the forces of groupthink to innovate, to step forward (often alone) and invite others toward a different and unforeseen future. It was risk-inclined leadership that led Senator Robert F. Kennedy to quote George Bernard

Shaw so often in his 1968 presidential campaign: "Some see things as they are and say, why; I dream things that never were and say, why not?"

For all their value, risk-inclined leaders would do well to examine their motives for what compels them to disrupt the status quo. Some leaders thrive on chaos and keeping others off-balance. Former President Trump prided himself on being "unpredictable" and clearly governed with an appetite for turmoil. Some leaders cling to a variation of "Woe to you when all speak well of you" (Luke 6:26), finding virtue in the very act of fomenting discontent.

Sean Martin, professor at The University of Virginia Darden School of Business, writes, "[Some leaders tend to] demonstrate self-confidence and comfort with risk-taking—and sadly, these traits may lead to the initial perception that they are impressive. But studies show that they are also more likely to disparage others, take more than reasonable credit, hog opportunities for themselves, engage in impulsive behavior and respond defensively to feedback." [3]

Risk-taking by definition creates uncertainty, and it may be hard to know just where the leader stands on any day. Jeffrey Miller, in *The Anxious Organization*, states, "A boss's displeasure is an objective survival threat to anyone who depends on a paycheck." [4] Risk-inclined leadership has its dangers.

Risk-Averse Leaders

Leaders on the opposite end of the leadership continuum will be more risk-averse. They may believe that cohesion and stability are far more important to an organization's mission than disruption. Leaders who are steady free their organization from anxiety and uncertainty so they can do their best work confidently. Often the

---

[3] University of Virginia Darden School of Business. (2019). Teamwork: UVA Basketball Coach Tony Bennett's 5 Pillars of newswise. https://www.newswise.com/articles/teamwork-uva-basketball-coach-tony-bennett-s-5-pillars-of-success

[4] Miller, Jeffrey A., *The Anxious Organization: Why Smart Companies Do Dumb Things.* Facts on Demand Press, 2008, p. 179.

culture itself contains so much "whitewater" that organizations value a steady steering hand.

Steadiness is contagious. When an organization has a clear mission and vision, the leader who adheres to those principles promotes predictability, trust and focus. Predictability in an organization increases its effectiveness; members can stay attentive to the mission without being distracted by anxious uncertainty. Effective leadership today often stresses mindfulness, collaboration, teamwork, trust, relationship-building, and similar skills.

Risk-averse leaders will find it important to examine any inclination to *not* act boldly when circumstances change. If challenging the status quo is called for, they could examine themselves to clarify what's at risk by *not* stepping out in faith. Are they backing off of some higher principle to remain comfortable? Are they exaggerating the consequences of risk? Are they being led by fear? Leaders who are used to collaborating, trusting others, seeking clarity, and speaking openly will find these to be tremendous assets when making these sorts of decisions.

The point is, courage can be shown by both behaviors. The risk-inclined leader shows courage in holding steady, restraining impulses, trusting the process, and maintaining security. The risk-averse leader shows courage in stepping out, breaking the pattern, challenging expectations, and disrupting the status quo.

It is difficult to pin either label firmly on King David. A warrior can't be all one or the other but has to embrace both options. As a teenager ready to battle Goliath, David may seem to be risk-inclined, except that he never regards his challenge as particularly risky at all; he never sees victory as anything other than a certainty. As a psalmist his poetry both celebrates contentment and stability *and* welcomes change and newness as gifts from God.

Rarely is effective leadership doing one thing or the other consistently. Rather, effective leadership is having the courage to act either way as different circumstances require.

The Risk of Rejection

Life itself is a risky business. In the best of times, we know that our future can turn on a dime, that life can end as easily as inhaling a virus smaller than a dust particle. When we're feeling fragile or vulnerable, the slightest bit of constructive criticism feels devastating. And if we're living in grief or depression, struggling emotionally, and suffering deeply, simply facing another day is exhausting. Ordinary life often requires, in Paul Tillich's phrase, "The Courage To Be."[5]

Leadership is an especially risky business. Risking the disapproval of people important to your heart and your work is an occupational hazard. The Greek philosopher Tacitus said, "The desire for safety stands against every great and noble enterprise." Without the support of co-workers, staff, stakeholders, friends and family, leadership is lonely. If someone's disapproval leads to their withdrawing from you, it may provoke that primal fear we all share, the fear of abandonment.

David learns that the hidden cost of leadership is sometimes rejection. Despite one's best intentions, anyone's actions can evoke someone else's condemnation. Let's look at the reaction of David's wife Michal toward his "courageous" dancing.

Michal sees David "leaping and dancing before the Lord," and she is disgusted. With brutal honesty, one translation says bluntly, "she despised him in her heart." Michal regards her husband with contempt. She loses respect for him and scorns him. Why? Her reaction and the reasons behind it are ripe for speculation.

Earlier in the David story, we're told that Michal falls in love with David. Never is it said that David loves Michal. So we may glimpse a marriage long troubled by unreciprocated love. 2 Samuel 3 names six wives of David; depending on the timeline of these marriages (also disputed), Michal may well have felt sidelined or ignored. Michal is Saul's daughter, a king who was respected for his humility and modesty. David's dance is anything but humble. Nor is it particularly regal behavior. She might be disgusted by her husband's refusing to act with the same regal

---

[5] Paul Tillich (2014). The Courage to Be. Yale University Press.

dignity that the moment required and her beloved father would
have shown.

When the dancing is over, Michal confronts David at
home. She blasts him as a "shameless" and "vulgar" man. David
fires back, "It was before the Lord, *who chose me in place of your
father* and all his household... that I have danced." It is a pointed
insult. David essentially says both, "It's none of your business"
and "God chose me over your 'beloved' father, anyway." Michal is
trapped forever in the Saul vs. David antagonism, and to David
she will always be Saul's daughter. That we are immediately told
she remained childless all of her life (v. 23) may be a judgment on
her for her contempt, or a judgment on David for never again
approaching her physically as a wife.

The intentions behind David's dance are also fodder for
speculation. Was David showing off? Was dancing so recklessly
David's egotism on vivid display? Was he arrogantly
demonstrating that the King was above the normal rules of
decorum? Or was he selflessly acting before the Ark of Almighty
God like an ordinary commoner ("vulgar fellow" can also mean
"an everyday sort")?

Another possibility: David was demeaning himself in
order to elevate God. "If I go lower," he might have thought,
"God goes higher." This is how John Wesley, the founder of
Methodism, understood David's message.

John Wesley Emulates King David

Until the spring of 1739, John Wesley was a proper Anglican
priest. Born in Epworth, England in 1703 and educated at Oxford
University, he was a firm believer in the spiritual power of the
Anglican liturgy and gathered worship. But that spring, riots
around Bristol rose to a fever pitch, with coal miners taking to the
streets to protest high food prices, low wages, poverty, and
discrimination. Revivalists such as George Whitefield saw in the
crowds of miners, rich opportunities to preach the gospel of
salvation. Whitefield encouraged Wesley to reject the safe
confines of parish ministry and join him in outdoor preaching.

Wesley wrote in his *Journal*, "I could scarce reconcile
myself at first to this strange way of preaching in the fields, of

which [Whitefield] set me an example on Sunday, having been all my life (till lately) so tenacious of every point relating to decency and order, that I should have thought the saving of souls almost a sin if it had not been done in a church." [6]

But through prayer, signs of Providence and the encouragement of others, Wesley put the mission of Jesus Christ above the conventions of his tradition. Quoting this very passage, Wesley wrote, "At four in the afternoon I submitted to 'yet be more vile' [2 Samuel 6:22, KJV], and proclaimed in the highways the glad tidings of salvation."[7]

David's twirling in public inspired by Wesley. He shifted his approach to his ministry. David's courageous dancing, which he saw as David's lowering himself, risking criticism and contempt, to elevate the Lord God Almighty. Giving honor to Yahweh superseded any concerns for dignity and propriety. Wesley followed David's lead and preached outdoors, in roads and fields, risking contempt to share the message of Jesus Christ. A risk-averse leader, "tenacious of every point relating to decency and order,"[8] Wesley became an iconoclastic leader for economic justice.

This is a pivotal moment in Methodism, and in American and European history. Methodism became known for "field preaching," for going where the people were instead of waiting for people to show up in church. Methodism's growth in America was rooted in its preachers' willingness to forsake the settled life to travel into the frontier and preach the gospel to American pioneers.

Being a Methodist circuit rider, continuing Wesley's work, took courage.

The Courage of Jesus

Where would Jesus fall on this continuum of risk-aversion to risk-inclination? Jesus himself was often called "Son of David." He is

---

[6] "Journal of John Wesley". (nd)
https://www.ccel.org/ccel/wesley/journal.vi.iii.i.html
[7] *Ibid.*
[8] *Ibid.*

both the religious and spiritual heir of King David and, according to Matthew 1, his physical heir. The mission he accepted and the suffering he endured in faithfulness to that mission required considerable courage. Those who followed him required bravery and nerve as well, and Jesus gave it. "Take courage!" he said. "I am here. Don't be afraid." (Mark 6:50).

Without pinning either label on him, we can see Jesus exercise both aspects of courage in his ministry. True, the nature of his work was intentionally provocative. His divine mission was to overturn the old reality and inaugurate the kingdom of God. His confrontational entry into Jerusalem on Palm Sunday and his overturning the moneychangers' tables in the Temple are classic examples of courage that challenged, provoked, and antagonized. These are ways he showed leadership to his followers.

Jesus also exercised restraint when restraint was more strategically effective. Jesus's mother urges him at the wedding in Cana to step in and solve the running-out-of-wine problem. He replies, "Woman, what concern is that to you and to me? My hour is not yet come." In the Garden he restrains a disciple from swinging his sword. He refrains from answering Caiaphas, resists the entreaties of Pilate, endures ridicule and punishment, and allows himself to be crucified. All of this took courage. Just as it sometimes takes courage to act, often it takes courage not to act.

Doing a New Thing

Doing anything new takes courage. The new thing often asks us to minimize our ego needs to serve the greater mission of the organization. David inaugurated his new kingdom by making the Ark of the Covenant—the presence of God—as the focal point of the new nation. Jesus and John Wesley both put their mission—honoring God—above their personal preferences.

Patrick Lencioni, a Christian business advisor, says, "For a Christian leader, this subjugation of self to mission is paramount, because the only reason to challenge a process is to serve Christ."[9] David, of course, lived 1000 years before Christ, but his challenge to "process" (i.e., the way things are done around here) was equally God-centered.

You may or may not include yourself as someone following a process "to serve Christ." But the "subjugation of self to mission" remains paramount. Is there a missional challenge before you now, asking for your attention? What large call might whisper in your ears?

We have a nation to heal, and most of us have feelings of anger, sadness, disgust, woundedness, confusion, and countless others. We need to keep our principles and still take an additional step toward making our country strong and whole. Or we may blend families, combining adults and children into a new configuration. The central mission is to create one new family out of two, and it will require courage to subjugate personal preferences to this greater task.

The same holds true when we combine work teams, integrate departments, merge companies, blend congregations, or just get married. What is paramount is the "subjugation of self to mission?" Leadership is the name we give to the simple action of focusing our influence toward a large and worthy goal.

We've learned that effective leadership does not come without cost. One cost is asking ourselves challenging questions. What is the highest good I am aiming to achieve? Is this goal high enough? What old ways do I need to challenge and even discard to meet this new moment? What within me balks at moving forward? Should I stick my neck out or keep my mouth shut?

Where you are called to act with courage will be unique to you. You may do easily what is called for implicitly. The right thing may come naturally to you. Give thanks!

---

[9] Patrick Lencioni, 2004. "Challenge the Process." In Christian Reflections on the Leadership Challenges. John Kouzes & Larry Posner (eds). John Wiley & Sons, Inc. NY: 71-84.

For myself and the rest of us, I draw encouragement from the plaque my brother had for years on his kitchen wall:[10]

Why were the saints, saints? Because they were cheerful when it was difficult to be cheerful, and patient when it was difficult to be patient. Because they pushed on when they wanted to stand still, kept silent when they wanted to talk, and were agreeable when they wanted to be disagreeable. That was all. It was quite simple and always will be.

*John Wesley, Founder of Methodism*

---

[10] Know Your Quotes. www.knowyourquotes.com/Why-Were-The-Saints-Saints-Because-They-Were-Cheerful-When-It-Was-Difficult-To-Be-Cheerful-Patient-When-It-Was-Difficult-To-Be-Patient-And-Because-They-Pushed-On-When-They-Wanted-To-Stand-Still-A-Source-Unknown.html

## LIFE BEFORE RICHVALE
by Linda Hoagland, *Appalachian Writers Guild*

"My name is Ellen and I am a resident of your small town filled with its small-minded people who really don't give a hoot about whether I live or die," were the words Ellen wanted to shout over the microphone at every public gathering.

Ellen had been living in Richvale for fifteen years without a past that she wished to discuss with her friends and acquaintances. No one cared enough or was interested enough to ask.

Her close friends knew she had spent many years in Cleveland, Ohio. Her acquaintances knew she had moved to Richvale, Virginia, from somewhere up north. Actually, she had been living in a small town in southern Ohio just prior to moving to Richvale.

No one knew her true background and how she ever got back to Virginia, her roots, or why she needed to return to Virginia and a life she had never really known. She worried about what they would think if they were aware of her past decisions. She also worried about them not caring.

She knew not to say too much to the Bible-belters that she lived around and worked with daily. They would prejudge her and hang a sign on her telling the world that she was different. Doors would be closed to her and friendly embraces would be held back, allowing only the most fleeting of handshakes to express the how unwelcome they were, that she would be subjected to for the rest of her unwelcome days in Richvale.

Being branded as different isn't always bad.

In Richvale, different is bad.

She knew she was different. She had to fight, scratch, scrape, and struggle to survive. She was proud of the fact that she was continuing to fight for what she wanted, but she wasn't willing to tell anybody about it, not there in that small town where they have the small minds to match.

She was afraid to tell anybody until now.

So get ready, Richvale. Here it is.

She wants to write a letter to the powers that be in a small town that was and is no more a large part of her life.

&

Dear Richvale Founding Father
Wannabees:
    Much to the chagrin of many
people with whom I have spoken, I was
born in Virginia, in Charlottesville,
to be specific. I am a true Virginia
native. Ironic, isn't it?
    I know I don't sound like a
local native, but I had no control
over that part of my life. I was two
years old when my parents moved me
from Charlottesville, Virginia, to a
rural area in southern Ohio called
Twin Valley where I lived until I was
twelve.
    Then, we moved to Cleveland
where my accent of an Ohioan expanded
to being one northerner with the
correct pronunciation for words,
rather than the slurred accented
sounds of the south.
    I spoke in a tone that branded
me an outsider, and I could not lose
the tone enough to make myself blend
in with the people with whom I dealt
daily.
    "Where are you from?"
    "Why?"
    "You weren't born in Virginia."
    "Why do you say that?"
    "You don't talk like a
Virginian."
    "Do Virginians sound like you?"
    "Yes."
    "I'm glad I don't sound like a
Virginian."

"Where were you born?"
"Charlottesville... Virginia."
"Oh."

Not being accepted in Richvale was one of the hardest ordeals I have ever had to deal with in my eventful life.

I was a lonely, fat teenager who was determined to survive no matter where I lived without regard to my surroundings. I didn't want to be associated with the three "R's" in Cleveland. The "R's" were Reading, (W)Riting, and Route 23 because of the heavy flow of West Virginia coal miners traveling north to find jobs. I was from Virginia, not West Virginia. There was a difference.

My parents did the best they could in a period that was aimed toward progress no matter the cost.

My father used to be a coal miner but worked on the railroad when he found the opportunity to do so. Layoffs of miners were forcing many miners to change and discover a new way of making a living. The progress of machinery constructed to replace men in the mines forced them into a new life.

The railroad job was great and gave dad an opportunity to make a living wage without crawling into the bowels of the earth to extract coal through the man-made mouths called mines. Again, progress discovered my father when coal powered steam engines were replaced by diesel powered locomotives. Layoffs in the name of progress for the railroad industry forced my father to search for a new way of life.

He had heard of work in Indiana where he traveled to from southern Ohio and applied for a job as a machinist which was the type of work he had always done except that it had been done on a variety of machinery. He was getting ready to move us to Indiana to be with him when, once again, progress took over and redirected his life. This time, the progress was different. The American workers and their unions had forced wages too high for the companies to pay, therefore progress cost dad his job when the company closed shop and moved to Mexico where they could pay for cheap labor and continue to produce a quality product.

He heard of work being available in Cleveland, Ohio, and off he went to search for a life in that huge city. That's where he found a job and where he stayed until he retired. That's where I was moved to when I was twelve years old and about to embark on my adventure into the world of high school in a major urban area.

I graduated from high school not having attended my senior prom, never having gone on a date, and not having any idea about what I was going to do for the rest of my life.

I found a job which was difficult because of my size (which was an eighteen), my age of seventeen, and my total lack of experience which couldn't be remedied until someone hired me, believe it or not.

Dieting was my new goal because I was tired of being lonely. I really

wanted to be asked to go on a date.
You had to know I was naïve.

The first man I dated was Joe, a
gentleman who will always remain in my
heart as my first love.

Ed, the man I married, was the
second man I dated.

Before I married Ed, I dated a
third man named Tim. I had met him in
a bar, and I thought he was nice. I
was testing the waters because I
wasn't sure if I really loved Ed.
After being plied with drinks and
sweet-talked all evening, Tim drove me
to a motel where I was forced to pay
for my drinks. I didn't know where I
was going when I got into Tim's car. I
didn't know what he had in mind or I
wouldn't have trusted him. I didn't
know until long after the repayment of
my debt of drinks that what he had
done to me was called date rape. Back
then, I was too embarrassed to say
anything about it. I was afraid of
what people would think of me. I was
blaming myself for what Tim did
because I was sure others would blame
me.

I was pregnant when I married at
twenty-one. It was the price I had to
pay for my first indiscretion. Ed was
my first plunge into sex. Not Tim, who
was disappointed to discover that he
was too late.

The father of my baby married
me, and we spent five very unhappy
years together with the product being
my two sons whom I love with all of my
heart.

My husband was drinking heavily
during his lunch hours and after work

before he came home. I'm guessing the
alcohol triggered his abusive behavior
toward our eldest son, but when the
abuse started, I knew it was time to
get out and start over again.

I had a problem. I was pregnant
for the third time and I couldn't
afford another child, nor could my
soon to be ex-husband afford another
obligation. I was afraid if I told Ed
about the pregnancy, he would delay
the divorce.

"What are you going to do?"

"What am I going to do?"

"You let yourself get pregnant?"

"I believe you had something to
do with this. It wasn't an immaculate
conception."

"What do you want me to do about
it?"

"I don't want you to tell the
judge or your lawyer or anybody about
this. I want an abortion."

"I'll help you pay for it."

There wasn't much discussion. He
didn't want the additional problem to
grow inside of me and become another
liability.

It was hard to do, but it needed
to be done.

When I was divorced, I ended up
with my four-year-old and two-year-old
sons. I had a job that didn't pay
enough to feed me without even
discussing the nutritional
requirements of my two sons.

I was working in an office when
I filed for a divorce. My boss took it
upon himself to tell me I shouldn't go
through with it because he didn't want
any of his girls suffering through an

ugly divorce.

"Mr. Dear, you don't have to live with that crazy man, and I don't either. It's none of your business what I do with the personal life," I said as I tried not to cry.

"This will interfere with your job," he continued.

"No, it won't. I quit," I said as I walked out the door never to return to Cleveland State University again where I was also a night student trying to earn a degree and a better life for me and my sons.

Maybe it wasn't the best choice I could have made for the direction my life was to take. I've never regretted the choice.

I was a single mother of two sons without a job and no friends because my previous friends were the fickle friends of a defunct marriage. When the marriage ended, so did the friendships.

I met a single mother of three children who needed a place to live, so I offered my home with the thought that we could share the rent, utilities, and food costs.

I wasn't ready to return to an office where another Mr. Dear might be working.

Bertha, my housemate, led me to bars and restaurants where I could get a job and meet men who would fill the space that my former husband vacated.

I met and became associated with some of Cleveland's Finest. I also learned not to trust most of Cleveland's Finest because they were out to get anything they could any way they could get it.

I found a job at a restaurant and I was quite content with the work until I could no longer survive on what little money I was bringing home. I applied for food stamps or any kind of government assistance I could find.

My former husband would not pay his child support, which was the paltry sum of fifteen dollars per child per week, totaling one hundred twenty dollars a month.

To get help, I had to quit my job so I could get my sons on a medical card, receive food stamps to feed us, and get a few dollars to put towards the rent and utilities.

Still, that wasn't enough.

I met and fell in love with Jack, who told me he was separated from his wife. I believed him.

Bertha quit her job, and I asked her to leave because she wasn't helping me. I had to feed her and her children because she did not get another job or get help from the government.

I started tending bar in the afternoon where I was being paid under the table so I wouldn't have to report it on my income taxes or to the welfare people who would look upon the extra income as an attempt to defraud the government.

I wasn't trying to defraud anybody. I was only trying to survive and raise my two sons the best way I could.

With encouragement from Jack, when my sons got old enough to go to school, I went in search of an office

job again. I wanted to make a decent
living for my boys and me.

Baby-sitting became a problem
because those people I found were
unreliable.

One week when I was without a
babysitter, I asked my former mother-
in-law to watch my boys until I could
find a new sitter.

While she was watching and
caring for my sons the first day, my
ex-husband picked up the boys to take
them to a picnic area where his
parents owned a couple of lots for the
future building of a summer home. A
wading pool and play area had already
been constructed in the complex, so
picnicking was fun and easy to do.

When she told me that Ed had my
sons, I became scared. If he came all
the way from Pennsylvania on a Monday,
a workday, to take the boys out to
play, I knew he wouldn't bring them
back to me.

Well, he didn't bring them back
because he had stolen them and taken
them out of state.

After two weeks and several
threats, his parents returned my sons
to me and I immediately made plans to
leave Cleveland so he would no longer
have easy access to his sons.

Uprooting and facing change
seemed to be the norm.

I packed my boys up and took
them to visit their grandparents, my
mom and dad, in southern Ohio while I
tried to figure out what I would do
next.

I left the boys with my parents
for their planned two-week visit, and

I drove back to Cleveland to plan my next step.

My decision was made for me when I returned to my burglarized home. My clothes, my food, and everything that belonged to my sons that I hadn't packed up for the visit were gone. My babysitter, who lived in the house in front of mine, moved to Pomeroy. When she packed up her belongings, she also took mine two hundred miles from Cleveland.

My relationship with Jack was a wild ride on a roller coaster. I discovered he had never moved out of the house and physically separated from his wife and that I was in love with a married father of six children.

While I was riding on the adrenaline high of the roller coaster, I became pregnant with Jack being the father. Again, I faced the problem of a baby.

"What are you going to do about it?"

Déjà vu all over again.

"What do you want me to do?"

I knew I wanted this baby more than anything I could ever want. I wanted this unborn child growing inside of me because it was part of Jack. It was his seed, which was a product of his love for me and my love for him. It was my dream, my wish, my desire, and my wrong.

"Get rid of it. I left my wife because she was pregnant with our seventh child. She stopped taking her pills. I wouldn't go back into her bed until she got an abortion. I want no more kids, not yours or hers. Do you understand?"

To continue my relationship with Jack, I had to get an abortion. I didn't want the abortion. I wanted this baby. I loved Jack, so the baby had to go. I guess it was God's way of getting even.

I quit my job and left Cleveland within a few weeks. I was moving in with my parents so I could find a job and a life in southern Ohio, a place I didn't want to return to, not yet, not with my tail between my legs.

I couldn't find a job in that small corner of Ohio, so after two months of dragging myself from business to business and office to office, I went back to Cleveland to work.

I had to go back to Cleveland because I had to prove to myself that the city did not chase me away. I had to dictate my own terms for living and leaving.

So, I found another job and renewed my relationship with Jack. I proved to myself that I wasn't afraid of anything Cleveland shoved at me. Then I walked away, moving my life back to southern Ohio away from Jack. This time it was of my own choosing.

Believe it or not, I loved Cleveland. It was more my home than any other place I lived. Someday I want to go back there to live, but not now.

Southern Ohio would not be my permanent choice for a home. I wanted to leave there whenever I could and go someplace, any place where I could start over with my boys.

My sons were garnering friends in Twin Valley that I didn't want them to be around, but there was no one else in the area. I could see the trouble starting, the attitudes changing, and the lack of respect being tossed in my direction.

Eight years had lapsed between my marriage to Ed and my second marriage to Mike. Mike was a wonderful man who came equipped with two daughters the same age as my two sons. During our courtship period, our children got along wonderfully and promised to continue to get along after we were married.

Well, that didn't happen.

Katie, Mike's eldest daughter, resented my assuming the role of her mother and did everything in her power to make her feelings known to me. Cindy was happy with the joining of families. My youngest son was like Cindy and accepted Mike openly. My eldest son resented Katie and her actions towards me, and he refused to get along with anyone.

The marriage was short-lived, lasting only six months before I threw in the towel.

I met my third husband in the law office where I worked as a legal secretary. He was filing for a divorce from his wife and I was attracted to him from the first moment I saw him.

Sonny came with excess baggage as four children. When we married, I was caring for his three sons and my two sons. His daughter, who was pregnant and planning to marry the father of her baby, remained with her mother.

As with all blended families, it was difficult for his sons to adjust to me and mine. They wanted the freedom to run without accounting to me about where they were going and what they were planning to do. I wouldn't allow my sons that kind of freedom, so naturally, I wouldn't allow Sonny's three sons to roam freely.

After a few months, they each at separate times returned to their mother. Our family comprised Sonny, my two sons, and myself.

After my dad died, I asked my mother, who I knew would have to live with me, if she wanted to go back to her birthplace in Richard County, Virginia.

She thought it was a great idea, and we moved to Virginia. My mother was returning to her home place and I, along with my two sons, was returning to my native state. My husband whom I met and married in southern Ohio came along for the excitement.

I was searching for a loving small town. That was the atmosphere I wanted for my sons.

We arrived in Richard County to stay with my Uncle Jim until we could buy a mobile home, and have it set up near my uncle's house on property that belonged to my mother and would eventually descend to me.

My uncle did not want us on his land, and we were forced to set up our mobile home on a lot in Richvale. It was the only lot we could find on short notice. We moved out of Uncle

Jim's house during a snowstorm.

Uncle Jim had not welcomed us with open arms.

Richvale was a small town full of people who should have been living in a large city, maybe Cleveland or New York, where it can be dangerous or costly to be friendly. A small town doesn't have the right to adopt the airs of the city dwellers. A small town needs to take care of its own, and that includes the newcomers who have moved into town and have become one of them merely by moving into the neighborhood.

Richvale was unfriendly to me and my family.

We could never be a part of anything without forcing ourselves into the inner circle.

We were outcasts, outsiders, and northerners who didn't belong. We didn't have family scattered over the county. We had only ourselves.

Well, Richvale, we have now moved on after fifteen years of being unwelcome to another town where we are welcome.

I hope someday the people in Richvale discover they are a small town and learn to act like the friendly, inviting, sharing, and loving small town they should be because it is not a good place to visit nor to live if you're not one of their own.

Regretfully yours,
An Unwelcomed Former Resident

She wanted to write that letter to the inhabitants of Richvale and let them know how she felt about not being welcome. She wanted to scream at them and tell them she didn't need them for any reason, but she will not do that. She wanted them to know that she hurt inside because they weren't interested in her or her life enough to find out why she was in Richvale. Her life was hard, but she's not ashamed of it. She decided, probably not the same ones others would have made, but they weren't walking in her shoes and living her life.

Survival in Richvale was as lonely an obstacle course as it was in Cleveland. There were many more physical dangers lurking around the corner waiting for your arrival in Cleveland. Richvale offered the same lonely quiet dangers of solitude and neglect as did Cleveland that ate away at your mental wellbeing and pride.

She always pictured a small town as a cocoon that opened to welcome people into its warm, inviting fold to be covered from all harm. Richvale was a cocoon that remained closed.

She still lives relatively close to Richvale, and she continues to see former acquaintances with whom she shared space in that small corner of the universe.

She will never mail the letter, nor will she ever forget or forgive Richvale.

*She wants to write a letter to the powers that be in a small town that was and is no more a large part of her life.*

# OUT IN THE COLD - A COMMONS ESSAY
by K.F. Shovlin, *Virginia Writers Club*

The thing about being a community leader is that you are never, really, a community leader. At least if your heart is in it. And so it was, 9 pm on a cold and icy night, that I walked in circles on a small stretch of ice covered sidewalk on the island that divides the lanes at the entry of one of our seven streets.

It snowed last night. When I woke up at 5:38 am, I saw the fluffy blanket of white that the meteorologists were predicting over everything outside. I was already scheduled Telework for the day, but my agency was closed additionally. In the before times, this would've meant a snow day, but those don't really exist anymore. So I worked, and I listened. It's a Thursday and Thursday is a trash day. No one on my block has set out their trash, but mine sits behind the door, ready to go at the first sound of the truck. That sound never comes. Instead, I hear the plows. First it was the plows on State Road 600 that carries heavy traffic east to west through our part of the south county. I'd put that at about 9:30. Then it was the county road that flows throughout the community. That's about 10:15. Finally, I hear a plow on my street. It's 11:30 am. Hey, it's done. I will not nitpick. But I was wrong.

First came the text message. Our Treasurer watched the truck move down his street at full speed, slamming directly into the speed bumps. Two years ago, this action destroyed a bump on one of our streets. I had noticed damage on the one he cited while walking the community the previous Friday. It's 11:37 am. This is OK, so maybe some asphalt damage. At least the roads are done.

After my full eight hours of telework, I spend thirty minutes shoveling the front walk of my house and of my neighbors on either side. I usually do the entire block, but there's a quarter inch of ice under this snow, and my asthma is flaring. I finally relax, put on a movie, and attempt to eat leftovers for dinner. At 7:20 pm I get "the call."

"Hey, just wondering when to expect the snowplow on [my street]," I hear from a concerned community member who I rely on.

I tell him I wasn't aware their street wasn't done. He laughs that he assumed I'd tell him that I was already on it after receiving several messages. I did not receive any messages, though. No one called our management company, posted on our website, sent a message to the manager, or even posted on NextDoor. Then the kicker. He tells me that when the company was out for the snowstorm two weeks prior, the driver pulled over to talk to him while he was out with his son and realized there were two streets he wasn't aware of. Well, this time they got one of those two.

So now I'm lacing up my boots, throwing on my coat, my HOA hat (yes, I literally have an HOA hat), and my mask, I head out to see it firsthand. I text the Board to let them know. I can safely assume the first four streets I pass will be clear, it's the back three I fear. Success as the two adjacent are plowed, but that leaves one in question. I walk along it and it is all ice. I watch as three vehicles slide while navigating it, one almost going headfirst into a mailbox.

It's the third Thursday of the month. Before our current manager took over, this would be the week of our Board meeting. I'd be sitting in a Board meeting. I'm sure this would've come up if we had. To accommodate our manager's schedule, we moved up a week. I failed to consider this as I called her and left a message. Some text messages follow, and she sends the number of our snow removal contractor. I call them, and without a hint of desperation and anger (the old honey over vinegar aphorism) I ask that they remedy, "post haste!"

Ninety minutes later and there I am: standing at the entrance to the street, pacing on what once was snow but now is ice, awaiting a truck that should've come eight hours prior. My hands get stiff, so I put them in my pockets. My ears get cold, so I put up the hood of my hooded sweatshirt. My nose gets cold, so I put on my mask. Then my right big toe got cold, and that was enough for me.

I'm not sure when the plow finally arrived. I assume it was right after I left, but I'm sure I'll hear about it later. I long passed the hypothetical 'how long is too long to wait for' consideration. For 102 minutes I waited in the cold, nodding at every vehicle as they took the turn, counting the buses (five), the delivery cars (four), the pickup trucks could have a plow on the front (four, but technically three as the one drove back), the dump trucks (one), the police cars (one), and dozens of other vehicles.

Character is when you do the right thing. When no one is looking. Leadership is when you do the right thing when everyone is doing the same. I probably could've held out for another half an hour, but would it really matter? Now, as I prepare to turn in for the night, I hope the street was plowed. I'll look tomorrow. For now, the job is done.

# THE CAKE
by Judy Light Ayyildiz, *Valley Writers*

The white shingled house finds itself cleaned-up and ready for company with Aunt Faye and Uncle Pete, who ride the city bus for an hour to come from Huntington to visit.

The two of them never forget to bring us presents for being such good kids. Uncle paints houses five days a week to make a living while Aunt stays home and whips up stuff like macaroni salad with home-made pickles in it or pecan pies that are just to die for.

Their house sits on the tip of a huge hump called Eight Street Hill. Uncle Pete painted his whole front porch as blue as the summer sky. Sitting there, we can hear cars coming from down around the bend of the red brick street before we can even see them. JD and I make a guessing game out of whether a motor groan is a car or truck, and Little Pete gets to guess what color it might be. Sometimes we even get it right. The porch has a white wooden swing with silver chains that's plenty big enough for four people.

Three bird cages hang in their house—a yellow, an orange, and a green to match the feathers of Aunt Faye's "song babies." She talks to her pets in a special high-pitch silly language. The little birds tweet back. They understand. Uncle calls them "Fancy Tail," "Bright Bonnet," and "Twinkie Toes." He makes up little ditties for them. "Oh, what are we going to feed to you that won't make so much birdy-poo?" We laugh and laugh.

Each bird has its own name, its own cage, and its own part of the house to live in. Aunt says, "That way there's always singing wherever you go in our place." We can't figure out how she can always tell which bird is making a fuss. When we kids visit to stay all night, she lets us help cover them, so they shut up and go to sleep. As soon as that cloth that fits the cage to a T goes on, each bird conks out like a light bulb. No dog would do that. Though, some wild birds sing at night.

Aunt and Uncle also have two little yippy dogs with perky ears, big wet eyes, long tails, and sloppy tongues to lick faces whenever they jump onto laps. Aunt Faye and Uncle Pete have five rooms to their house, and a bathroom with a flushing toilet. Even the dogs get baths in the tub. Maybe the next time we get to go home with them, we can help give the dogs a soapy dip in the big white tub. One time, Daddy wrestled Old Ruff into our washtub that was full of soap and vinegar because the dog had an "unpleasant encounter" with a polecat. "Some people call them skunks," Daddy said, "but the smell is the same no matter what you call them." And Momma answered, "You don't ever want to call them."

This week is the Fourth of July; and the whole bright world looks it. The three of us race out onto the gravel road when the bus stops. Aunt Faye and Uncle Pete are standing there on Route 60 when the bus moves on. Each one holds big package. They've crossed the road when we get up to the highway.

Our guests don't put down their bundles; so we kinda dance around them. Aunt Faye hugs big rectangular box wrapped in pink Happy Birthday paper that we know is for me. They missed my birthday back in winter and sent me a note by U.S. mail saying they would make it up come spring. Uncle Pete grips the handle of a grocery bag that he opens with a wink to let us get a peek of a cake in a special plastic holder. "Faye slathered this cake with boiled egg-white frosting," he says.

"And," Aunt chips in, "I colored it red and white to celebrate the Fourth!"

When the five of us sashay past the sawmill and straight on the gravel road to our house, we smell Momma's chicken and dumplings along with her green beans cooked two hours with bacon. "oo-wee," Uncle says in a girly voice, "Brother Jewel's Gladdy has whipped us up another fine mess of eatins!" We all giggle. Little Pete runs chug-chug steam engine circles round us all the way to our front yard.

With needles, JD and I helped string those green beans. Six chains of them strung on a thread have hung in the kitchen since last September so that they could be dried and then cooked with a taste as good as fresh. This pot finishes off last years' beans.

Momma will stick her pan of yeast rolls in the oven twenty minutes before we gather round the table. That way, the rolls will stay warm throughout dinner. Momma let me help her from the rolls. As if they were pieces of clay in an art project, I rolled three balls of dough and then stuck them together. When the dough slowly raised up to three times the size of the balls, the dough became one big puffy three-leaf clover. To eat, stick a plunk of butter into the middle on the top and let it ooze down into the center. And then pull each part off one at a time.

As we come to the creek-rocks walkway to the front door, the screen flies open and Daddy is out with a big wide smile of welcome. Uncle and Daddy do pats on the shoulders and look each other in the eyes. Faye hugs Daddy at his elbows. She's kind of short. He taps his fingers on top of her head. JD and I stand back. We each hold a bag with the presents.

Inside, we trail from the living room, through Momma and Daddy's bedroom, and into the kitchen. JD takes the cake out of the bag and hands it to Momma. I slip over to my cot in the corner of the kitchen and lay my birthday present in its pink wrapping there. I am very anxious about opening the present, but I know it's not proper to insert what I want into the welcome of guests. The tasty big meal smells almost ready. After, we'll get to have the yummy cake. The present will get opened in time.

Everybody talks all at once in the kitchen with everybody hugging everybody. And then Momma starts giving directions to laying out the food on the table. Daddy darts out the door to the back porch and just as quick is back inside waving a big bottle of brown whiskey in his hand.

"The Fourth of July celebration begins with a toast to 'Give me liberty or death, Patrick Henry—and to the patron of liberty, Jim Beam." Daddy holds his hand with the bottle above his head like a prize. Aunt and Uncle are all smiles and moving toward him as if he's just invented the world. I'm in the middle of putting the bowl of slaw on the table.

"JD, get us down three tall glasses and a pitcher of ice water." Daddy speaks in his most happy voice. Momma just slowly shakes her head. Aunt Faye catches Momma's look and adds, "Well, it seems appropriate to have a fast one to toast while the table's being set."

"And a refill to top it off will highlight this fancy meal that Glad's fixed-up." Daddy adds.

Aunt Faye edges right fast over to smooth a hand on Momma's arm. Momma nods, yes—although they'll never get

Momma to drink.

By the time the last dumpling is downed, our happy group jangles loose enough to let the usual tall tales bring up lines from songs we sing together. JD and Momma start gathering up the bowls and plates. Daddy tops-off glasses again while Little Pete sidles over to the sideboard and quietly takes the cake out of the bag.

Sitting on a dark blue plate, it's sure a beauty, with curls of red tipping off the waves of white frosting. I'm dying for a mouthful when Faye, Pete, and Daddy stand with arms linking shoulders, urging me to join them. They weave side to side. "You're our soprano on this one," Aunt says, motioning with a finger, "And Little Pete, you need to learn this one, too." Little Pete declines. What can I do but join them? Else we'd be all evening getting to the cake.

With the heated kitchen smelling heavy with chicken and dumplins swimming in whiskey and cigarettes, we croon together in the harmony of wilting flowers as we slide words to "Yankee Doodle Dandy."

"We are Yankee Doodle Dandies, Yankee doodle-doo-or die. We all children of our Uncle Sam, born on the Fourth of July...."

Uncle whines the high harmony in his stringy tenor, Faye, the alto, and Daddy and me, the melody. Last fall, I learned "Golden Wedding Day" and "Near the Cross." Even Momma would do an alto if we got into "Near the Cross." My silly brothers care more about playing X and O with school paper than singing old songs and hymns. But they will play in the penny poker games while Momma and I do the dishes.

"Let's have into it again, and this time sing, '... dandies who will really try!'" It is agreed, and so we do two times onward.

And then, we sing, "Amazing Grace, how sweet we sound the songs we sing like this—" when Momma steps in to say in no uncertain terms, "I think that's enough singing for one afternoon. 'Amazing Grace' is my mother's favorite." The drinkers pause for a tad of a top-off, and Little Pete springs over to the cupboard to bring forth, finally, the cake. It must be eaten; and then, someone will ask to see what is in the birthday box.

Momma clinks down a stack of dessert dishes onto the table beside the cake. Aunt Faye trips around the side of the table.

She is full of herself with something to say, her face lit up like a Halloween pumpkin with a church candle in it. "I just came up with the most original game we could play on a day like this!"

Nobody says anything, but we skate our eyes back and forth to figure what she means.

"It's called 'Hide the cake!'"

Grinning, Momma cocks her head at Faye. "Well, I can say for sure there aren't many places in this house where a person could hide a cookie, let alone a cake as big and fancy as this." None of the rest of us move a muscle. Faye raises her arms, claps her hands together over her head. Her long, shiny balls of red earrings swing to and fro.

"Not in the house on a hot day like this!"

"We are in a mess of puzzlement as we stare at her. Uncle grins wide. "Now, my girl has something fun in store...."

"Oh yes," Aunt chirps, "and you're all going to love it—in the woods! The ones just over between the C n O and the patch of trees near The Canyon—and I get to be the hider!" With that, the little woman takes two steps and swoops the cake from out in front of Momma, plops it back into its plastic holder, and lifts it up by the handle.

"The finder gets the first and biggest piece!" she yells over her shoulder as she throws open the back door. "Give me about ten minutes," she adds, before she bounds off the side of the porch with Old Ruff leaping ahead of her and barking back.

Momma doesn't let us wait the whole ten minutes, sure that this whole idea could be a bit dangerous considering Faye's companion, Jim Beam.

The six of us fan out into in the woods, not so much looking for the cake as for Aunt Faye. Those woods there go from flat to uneven and then become a small hillside above The Canyon.

Finally, it's Daddy that hears her moan and he and Uncle Pete rescue Faye at the foot of where the woods start to climb the hill. She might have been knocked out a bit as she rolled back down the hill. Pete and Daddy get her to her feet, and she lets out a yell. Momma turns to dash home for something to wipe Faye off with. JD finds her black high heel shoe up on the side of the hill where it looks like she slid. A person has to know how to clomp through these woods. Sliding on the wrong shoes is not funny.

After she's back in the house and lying on the living room couch, the adults agree that she hasn't broken anything. Momma makes an ice pack out of a hot water bottle and gives her two aspirins. The three drinkers switch to hot tea laced with just a drop of Jim Beam for their nerves, and to take away concern for Aunt Faye's slightly sprained ankle. "Well, her ankle along with her 'sprained pride'," Daddy kidded.

"Don't joke. Could have been a lot worse," Momma says, as she plops down in the rocking chair and lets out a "whoo-eee" of breath.

After some resting and talk that turns into jokes and laughs, Momma looks around to us kids. "I think my children have waited long and good enough to taste of that hiding cake."

Everybody agrees. Us kids run to bring into the living room the prized cake, dishes, and forks and knife. The red fireworks on the frosting tips have sort of flattened out to penny shapes, but it is still perky as can be. "Use your imagination," Aunt says, laughing.

Momma does the honors of dishing out the cake in big portions. "Eat up, we need our strength for climbing!" she says, handing the plates to Little Pete, who serves them around. It is as good as it looks; and so, some of us have two pieces. It's allowed because of celebrating. There's only a big wedge left by the time everybody gets filled-up.

Aunt Faye, revived and sassy again, asks, "Would someone tell me why the Happy Birthday girl hasn't asked to open her present?"

"I've been waiting all afternoon to do just that—if I'm allowed," I answer in the humblest voice I'm able to concoct.

"JD, will you bring it here?" Momma says.

When Aunt Faye hands it to me, she says that she will give me a nickel if I guess what it is. I study the shape of the box and give it a shake.

"Plastic dishes!"

Aunt Faye pouts. I get a chill from my hair to my knees. Maybe she won't give them to me for knowing the surprise like that, because it was true. "Now you've gone and spoiled the fun," she says. My tears well up. Why can't I ever pretend?

And so I beg. "It's not my fault I guessed what I wanted."

I did wish for some real ones to put up on the rock shelves of my hide-out. I had seen some in a five and dime store. The box there shaped itself just the size of Aunt Faye's present—which also rattled like plastic—not like it takes brains to know what is in that box.

I do my most pitiful face and manage to let some tears slide down my cheeks. "Getting them is like a dream come true," I whimper. "I've wanted them since before Easter when I found the box in Wimple's Five and Dime. You don't have to give me the nickel."

Still holding onto the box with my fingers under the ribbon on the side, I could grab and run with it if I had to, but I counted on her letting me have them. To say the least, I luck-out, with all the adults saying I should keep the dishes, and with Uncle Pete giving me a dime instead of a nickel. I look over at JD and Little Pete. They both know that I have played it just right.

End of the Fourth

Aunt and Uncle always throw a hissy-fit, insisting at the end of the day that Little Pete and I get to ride the bus home and spend the night with them. JD isn't interested in the birds or nippy dogs. Little Pete and I look at going almost anywhere as an adventure. Also, we don't get to spend much time with Momma and Daddy's families that we hear talked about like they are characters in some story books.

They all live in Huntington, Teays Valley, Saint Albans, or in other far-off hills up and down the rivers and hollers of West Virginia. Like us, they might not own cars. Our home is too small to have visitors overnight. Maybe not everyone wants to be near a slaughterhouse or railroad tracks, at least as near to them as we are. To me, it's a shame that most of our kin cannot see what a nifty spot we live in. Our Aunt Faye and Uncle Pete stand to represent most of our big families. Daddy's mom and dad are dead and gone, but they had ten children before a couple of them died. On Momma's side, Granny and Granpaw had twelve—but the oldest, Fonso, got killed in the mines and the youngest, Helen. died in a car wreck.

I haven't yet had a chance to open the plastic dishes. They are blue and white and have teacups and saucers and little forks. I almost want to stay home in order to take them to my hideout in the tall weeds between the railroad tracks. I slide the box way back under my bed after I pack my nightie in a paper bag.

As Little Pete and I shrug on shoes to leave with our guests, I, in a by-the-way voice, ask, "Aunt Faye, what about the cake cover?"

"Got it already stuffed in my shopping bag, Sweet Pea."

Little Pete, me, Aunt, and Uncle ride on the wide back seat of the bus all the way to Huntington. Aunt Faye stretches across Little Pete and Uncle. She snaps open a little white and red metal box. One at a time, she shakes out to our three hands a peppermint breath mint. "You remember," Aunt laughs, "how we get off at the stop up the hill from our house?"

"I'd know where to get off all by myself," Little Pete brags. He squashes his mint between his jaw teeth.

Aunt leans over again. "After we get off the bus and start down the sidewalk, listen. Those two smarty pants doggies of ours will start whining and whelping."

"They'll do it louder when we walk up the steps to the front porch," Uncle adds.

They are proud that those fancy house dogs can hear and smell so good. I think how hound and bird dogs just naturally the same thing without anybody thinking it's special.

"I'm dying to see them," I answer with a cheer. "It's so super great they can smell us coming—even being locked inside the house."

"You two have treats and games and birds and dogs all waiting for you," Uncle tells us, giving me a little elbow punch on my arm.

Aunt Faye hugs Little Pete with her arm around his shoulder. "We'll cavort all evening."

He smiles with his eyes twinkling. As they start telling it all again, I just grin, thinking of when I will get old enough to be a waitress or secretary, how I'll get my pay and go first thing and buy me a plastic cover with its own handle.

At the house, Uncle brings out a box of Fourth of July sparklers. We've seen them set to spewing rays of yellow fire, but these are the first that we've ever got to light ourselves. We dash all around the back yard for the most of an hour with the two yippy dogs along with Uncle making sparkling zigzags and circles. Aunt begins to hobble a bit and then, finally, takes a sit-down on the steps where she continues to wave sparks and cheer us on.

After, Little Pete and I get big coffee cups of chocolate milk and crackers, while Aunt and Uncle favor themselves with just a small toddy to help them sleep good and tight after such an adventuresome day.

Tomorrow, we can play with the dogs and watch the cars come over the hill. Aunt Faye will fry-up pancakes with syrup. Tonight, we only get to see the birds as they are put to sleep. Everybody's plumb tired—but the day is one to remember.

Little Pete and me already guess, cause we've come to know that the next morning after a sleep-over at Aunt and Uncles house, sure as that sun comes up, they get up in a cranky mood—even though, we hadn't done anything wrong. One of them will end up putting us on a bus to home before noon.

After the End

The two of us hop off the bus at our Rt. 60 stop and cross to walk out our gravel road a couple of hours later, feeling like we just must have done something wrong. We had cereal and toast for breakfast instead of pancakes. Aunt Faye was still hobbling. Aunt and Uncle didn't act none too happy to have us jumping around and trying to play with the dogs and sing. They said they got up with a bad cold and needed to go back to bed. Most of all, unfortunately, this time, we were going to have to leave early. Uncle Pete took us to the bus stand. "It's not anything you guys did," he said, and gave us a hug before we get on the bus.

Little Pete and I come to understand what Momma means when she uses the word, hangover.

JD clues us in.

"Puke," he says, scrunching up his lips like a butt's hidden hollow.

"Oooh, yuck!" Little Pete yells.

JD doesn't open his mouth and pulls the scrunch into a big smile all the way up into his freckled jaws. "Well, then, does 'vomit' suit your ears better?" he asks.

"I don't get it one bit," I answer, knowing he's just making a big deal out of the secret.

"What do you have to do when you throw up?" JD asks, eyeing first me and then Little Pete.

"Get a bucket or go out in the yard," Little Pete answers.

"Bend away from yourself, or else get it on your shirt," I add.

"Oh—hang over?" JD almost can't contain himself. He opens his lips to a big-toothed, silent hoot.

"Old people who drink too much whiskey to celebrate always have to hang over after it's done with."

But the night's adventure into the city, the firecrackers, and Aunt and Uncle's house was just fine with Little Pete and me. We set our minds on taking advantage of any bright upshot come our way. We take the good with the bad. I still have most of the day to set up my new dishes in the hideout.

Being as how, now, I understand, it becomes clear as mud why JD, who is more in line with the ways of the world, doesn't want to bother with going off to the city with them, just to get sent home early. As for me, I'll most likely do it again. Aunt Faye and Uncle Pete are fun to be around for any amount of time they allow.

# AUTHOR NOTES

**Judy Light Ayyildiz** is a graduate of Hollins Writing Program and the author of 11 books in five genres. She is the recipient of many awards and accolades, including the 2018 "Golden Nib Award" Her memoir *Nothing But Time* is a required reading in the Chaplaincy Department of UVA. In 2011 she released *Forty Thorns* based on the life of a woman who was a fighter in Ataturk. Please see http://www.judylightayyiildiz.com.

**Robert Morgan Armstrong's** recently published novel *A Serving of Revenge* through Dementi Milestone Publishing, Inc. with a literary review in Kirkus Reviews is available through Dementi, Amazon, Ebay, and Barnes and Noble. Written from two points of view, a boy growing up in the 1950s witnesses and mayhem, runs through boss politics in his small mountain village in central Virginia, and intertwines with a mountain resort hotel's colorful cast. Morgan is a retired Virginia General District Court judge and draws from his rich experience dealing with the kinds of characters who populate his book. *A Serving* is the first of a three-part series.

**John D. Broadwater** is a maritime historian and archaeologist who writes mostly nonfiction articles, book chapters, and books about shipwreck projects he's directed or participated in. He is currently writing a book on the excavation of sunken British ships in the York River, and his next project will be to write middle grade adventure fiction based on his experiences at sea over a fifty-year period. John's Amazon Author Page: https://tinyurl.com/y4vrj6xd

**Larry Buxton** is a retired United Methodist pastor, part-time seminary teacher, and active clergy coach. His article was adapted from his second book, *30 Days with King David: On Leadership* (Front Edge Publishing, 2020). You can reach him at www.larrybuxton.com (and subscribe to his weekly videos "Leading with Spirit"), www.facebook.com/larrybuxtoncoaching, and www.linkedin.com/in/larrybuxton/. In addition to writing, he enjoys traveling, genealogy, reading about rock music history, and rooting for the Washington Nationals.

**J. Thomas Brown** lives in Henrico, Virginia, and has co-produced local TV writing shows and coordinated poetry readings at the Richmond Public Library. His short stories appear in *Scarlet Leaf Review* and Everywhere Stories: Short Fiction from a Small Planet. He has contributed poems to *Lingering in the Margins: A River City Poets Anthology* and *North of Oxford*. His other works include Saint *Elmo's Light: Collected Short Stories of J Thomas Brown* (Fenghuang Publishing, 2021), *Driving with Poppi: A Patremoir* (Fenghuang Publishing, 2021), *Mooncalf* poetry collection (Fenghuang Publishing, 2020), *The Hole in the Bone* (Fenghuang Publishing, 2019), and *Land of Three Houses* (Austin Macauley Publishing, 2018).

A futuristic novel is in progress based on the Hayflick Limit and immortal HeLa cells. The story is told by someone 450 years old. To connect with the author, visit www.jthomasbrown.com.

**Stacy Clair** writes she once had a teacher tell her class, "If you're religious or suicidal this class is not for you." She writes, "I feel the same can be said about my writing. I use poetry and short stories as my outlets; creating pieces around self-harm, suicide and violence as a cathartic way to release negativity. I find comfort in these dark words being put to paper." Please take caution when visiting her site and heed the header warnings for every writing: https:// rahlahasscars.wixsite.com/stacy. Her family-friendly published human interest pieces through Our Life Blogs here: https:// www.ourlifelogs.com/search-results/q-stacy-clair/qc-blogs

**John Cowgill** is a railroad photographer and author who writes on his site, 'John Cowgill: Stories of the Railroad' (https://johncowgillstoriesoftherailroad.com/). He also writes for The Trackside Photographer and writes day trip articles Prince William Living. His short stories and poems and appear in the Virginia Writer's Club Synopsis and the Spilled Ink Synopsis. His Facebook page is 'John Cowgill: DC Railroad Examiner', and his photography page is 'John Cowgill: Photographic Journeys'. for (https://johncowgillstoriesoftherailroad.com/).

**Pamela Brothers Denyes** is an emerging poet. "Evening on the Avenue" and "Trimming for Strength" are part of a larger body of work titled *Renewal: Cultivating My Better Self*, which won an honorable mention in a 2020 National Poetry Writing Month contest. "Mrs. Creekmore's May Peas" won first place in poetry in the

2019 Hampton Roads Writers' poetry contest. Other works are published in several editions of the *Virginia Bards Central Review* and the international poetry journal *Childhood, Vol. 1*, published by Robin Barratt/The Poet Magazine. These published works are available on Amazon. pamelabrothersdenyes@gmail.com.

**Marco Faust** has been teaching science and engineering principles to aspiring Licensed Operators of nuclear power plants around the country for 35 years. Although not yet retired from that, he aspires to establish a second career authoring science fiction set in the not-too-distant future. The Prologue to his first novel, Neurophile, is presented here. He can be contacted at marcofaust@chronodex.com

**James Gaines** resides in Fredericksburg. He has published work in regional and national journals since the 1970's. In addition to poetry he writes science fiction with his son John as J. M. R. Gaines, including the Forlani Saga novels *Life Sentence* and *Spy Station*, as well as short stories.

**Katherine Gotthardt** is President of Write by the Rails, the Prince William Chapter of the VWC. An award-winning author, she has nine books to her name and dozens of publications in print and online journals. Read more about her work at www.KatherineGotthardt.com.

**Warren Groeger** writes as G. W. Wayne. He often works in historical fiction or nonfiction. He has two novels available on Amazon: *Katie, Cara, and KT*; and *KT Rising*.

**Jane Harrington** teaches word craft at Washington & Lee University and is a fellow at the Virginia Center for the Creative Arts (VCCA). She has published four books for children (Scholastic, Lerner), and her literary prose has appeared in a wide range of journals and anthologies. Winner of the 2019 Brighthorse Prize, her novel *In Circling Flight* (excerpt here) will be published this year. For more info and links to some of Jane's work, visit www.janeharrington.com.

**Linda Hoagland** has worked most of her adult life in various jobs, from bartending to clerical duties in large metropolitan areas and the small town that I love. She earned three Associate Degrees from

Southwest Virginia Community College. She is the mother of two adult sons. She writes fiction, nonfiction books, essays, short stories, and poems. Visit her website:lindasbooksandangels.com.

**Denise Moreault Israel** is a recently retired clinical psychologist who has rediscovered a passion for writing. Born in Quebec and raised in New York City, she has lived in Michigan, Georgia, South Carolina, Maryland, and Virginia. Her writing is influenced by these microcultures and the stories she has heard. She has written a novella about the lives of her great-grandmother and grandmother. Now she is focusing on short stories.

**Pamela K. Kinney** gave up long ago trying not to listen to the voices in her head and has written award-winning, bestselling horror, fantasy. science fiction, poetry, along with nonfiction ghost books ever since. Her horror short story, "Bottled Spirits," was runner-up for the 2013 WSFA Small Press Award. Her horror poem, "Dementia," that was published in HWA Poetry Showcase Vol VII in 2020, made "Best Poem," in Critters Readers Poll 2020. She has horror, fantasy, and science fiction stories published in various anthologies and magazines, an urban fantasy novel, a science fiction novella, and a collection of horror short stories published too. She has nonfiction ghost books, five published by Schiffer Publishing, the sixth by Anubis Press, and will have a nonfiction book, *Werewolves, Dogmen, and Other Shapeshifters Stalking America* coming soon from Anubis Press.

Along with writing, Pamela has acted on stage and film and investigates the paranormal for episodes of *Paranormal World Seekers* for AVA Productions. You can learn more about her at http://www.PamelaKKinney.com.

**Sharon Krasny's** "From the Grave" is the opening chapter and "Arrow's Mark" is chapter 11 drawn from her debut novel Iceman Awakens. Based on the real life Ötzi, the Iceman found murdered and forgotten in the Tyrolean Alps 5000 years ago. Iceman Awakens, a historical fiction, is based on five years of research and consultation with expert primitive archers and an archeologist, who has worked on the mummy's research. You can reach Sharon at www.sharonkrasny.com or by her linktree https://linktr.ee/skrasny9. In Iceman Awakens, Young Gaspare tells his story as the Iceman, as he faces the rites of passage of an ancient tribe, the longing for love and deepening friendship, and the scars of cowardice. Gaspare's four challenges will test his wit, strength, and the love of a mother for her son. If he is to find his place in the changing tribe, he must understand his greatest fear.

**Devin Reese** is a Ph.D. turtle ecologist who grew up in the D.C. area and now writes science articles, video scripts, curriculum, prose, and poetry. Devin tends to view humans through the lens of animal behavior and is inspired by how science illuminates our own lives. She currently writes nonfiction for a variety of outlets, including PBS-Eons, SciShow, and Engineers and Scientists Acting Locally. She lives in Alexandria, VA, where she and her hydrologist husband have raised their three kids. See her work here: https://writers.work/devinareese

**Janell E. Robisch** is an editor, graphic designer, and published author. She began her career in college, helping an author put his book together for publication, and worked for publishers such as Oxford University Press before striking out on her own. Janell has been a freelancing publishing professional since 1998 and has specialized in helping indie authors since 2015. She writes fiction under the pen name J. Elizabeth Vincent. You can find Janell at https://speculationsediting.com and https://jelizabethvincent.com
.

**David Anthony Sam** has six collections in print: Dark Land, White Light (2014, 1974 Dark Land Publishing); Memories in Clay, Dreams of Wolves (2014 Dark Land Publishing); Early in the Day (2015 Dark Land Publishing); Final Inventory (Prolific Press 2018); Finite to Fail: Poems after Dickinson, 2016 Grand Prize winner of the GFT Press Chapbook Contest; & Dark Fathers (Kelsay Books, 2019). Webpage and blog: www.davidanthonysam.com; https://www.facebook.com/DavidAnthonySamPoetry; & https://twitter.com/dasam

**Stephe Seton** teaches high school English and journalism near Portland, OR. His previous books are *Diary of a Scout* and *Four Years*

*in the Mitten.* The latter is a spoof on his four years teaching at a university in Michigan. His upcoming novel is a collection of flash for YA: *Fifty Reasons Not to Read* and *The Theater of the Absurd*, a theatrical reinvention of individuals he knew while a writer in residence.

**K. F. Shovlin** is originally from Beaver, PA, and currently lives in Lorton, VA, with his young family. He moved to the DC area in 2002 to study at American University and saw fit to stick around. After writing for various newspapers from high school through college, he endeavors to explore the imaginary and try his hand at writing fiction. His first novel, *Polk's Soliloquy*, was as much a labor of love as a grand experiment for him. His second book, *Life's Penance*, was the first in a series of novellas that remain in progress. Weblink: www.aois21.com/creative/shovlin; Twitter: @KFShovlin

**Elizabeth Spencer Spragins** is the author of three original poetry collections: Waltzing with Water and With No Bridle for the Breeze (Shanti Arts Publishing) and The Language of Bones (Kelsay Books). Updates are available on her website: www.elizabethspencerspragins.wordpress.com.

**Sofia M. Starnes**, Virginia Poet Laureate from 2012 to 2014, is currently working on her seventh poetry collection, a recasting of the *dizain*, a 15th-16th century poetic form. This form, now mostly in disuse, lends itself to concise thought and tightly focused experience, a discipline in succinctness that Sofia finds both demanding and attractive. The poems featured in this issue are from this manuscript in progress. Other *dizains*, as well as earlier poems, have appeared in numerous journals such as *First Things, Bellevue Literary Review, Notre Dame Review, Blackbird, Christianity & Literature*, and *Modern Age*. Further information about Sofia's work can be found by visiting www.sofiamstarnes.com.

**Charles Tabb** is an award-winning author of fiction whose work is enjoyed by thousands of readers worldwide. "We Need to Talk" was his first effort at flash fiction and chronicles the way people build their own prisons. His debut novel, a coming-of-age literary novel titled *Floating Twigs*, has been read by thousands worldwide and is in the process of being translated into Russian to be published in 2022 by

AST Publishers LTD in Moscow. His other fiction includes the Detective Tony Pantera Series about a flawed but caring Richmond detective who solves the most heinous crimes in the city. His latest literary novel, *Canaries' Song*, was published in January 2021, and his next, a sequel to *Floating Twigs* titled *Finding Twigs*, will be published in the summer, or fall of 2021. You can find Charles at his website, charlestabb.com, or on Facebook at Facebook.com/charlestabb919 and on Twitter, @CharlesTabb919.

**Cecilia Thomas** After "Celie" retired as an elementary school counselor, she opened a tropical café with a staff of kids and published her first book, *Active Meditation for Manifesting the Kingdom*. Her early education in Catholic school is reflected in many of the spiritually oriented stories and poems she began writing as early as second grade. In her second book, *You Can't Hide a Dead Fish* (2014), Celie shares her experiences as a counselor in the public school system and discusses many challenges, successes, and suggestions for change. She currently works as a Life Coach and Hypnotherapist in Mechanicsville, VA, while working on her next book.

**Stanley Trice** has over two dozen short stories published in online and print journals. This year he published his first book, a young adult science fiction High School Rocket Science (For Extraterrestrial Use Only). He grew up on a dairy farm in Spotsylvania, Virginia, and ended up commuting by train to the Pentagon to work on defense budgets. To keep his sanity, he wrote short stories. A few years ago, he escaped the long commute and politics to move to eastern North Carolina, where he belongs to several writing groups and volunteers to write grants. Find him at stanleybtrice.com.

**George Vercessi** was born and raised in New York City, and retired from the U.S. Navy with the grade of captain. At his final assignment, he held the post of Chief of Public Information for NATO's southern European command, headquartered in Naples, Italy. He is the author of several novels, a guide for authors wishing to self-publish, and a children's Christmas story. He developed and co-produced the MGM/Showtime drama *The Silver Strand*. He is a member of the Authors Guild and the National Press Club. Visit www.vercessi.com.

**Paula Weiss's** submission is a chapter from her sequel, currently in draft, to the recently published "The Antifan Girlfriend." "The Antifan Girlfriend" is a devastating social satire and spy thriller, published just as the dystopian anti-freedom politics and culture that it ruthlessly illuminates emerge in postmodern America. "The Antifan Girlfriend' is Ayn Rand...with no lectures," says one reviewer.

**Paulette Whitehurst** was a classroom teacher for more than 30 years, teaching grades 4 - 8. During retirement, she supervised student teachers for Virginia Commonwealth University, mentored and coached new teachers, and taught developmental reading and writing at John Tyler Community College. Visit this author's website at fairyfortbooks.com. She wrote *A Child Is a Poem You Learn by Heart: A Memoir in Verse*, and is now working on her second memoir, also written in free verse about her classroom experiences.

# Notes on Illustrations

Page 2, "A Preacher Cam",. Permission: https://www.alabamapioneers.com/baptism-roupes-creek & treatment of "The Good Old Way", an American slave spiritual

Page 16, "Bert & Joel". Contributed by the author.

Page 30, "Dear John" derivative, "Baa baa black sheep" by rkramer62 is licensed with CC BY 2.0. To view a copy of this license, visit https://creativecommons.org/licenses/by/2.0/; dog provided by author.

Page 33, "Nivana", "Ice Storm 2007" by Mona Loldwoman (Look for the good) is licensed with CC BY-NC-SA 2.0. To view a copy of this license, visit https://creativecommons.org/licenses/by-nc-sa/2.0/

Page 34. "Lady Evangeline", derivative, public domain elements

Page 39, "Like Sophia Loren", "Image is public domain, Wikimedia.com;

Page 50, "Old World Pedestal Dining Table and Shield Back Chairs with Fabric Seat." Courtesy https://shopfactorydirect.com/

Pages 69, 73, "Neurophile" Illustrations by Dave Powell

Page 64, "A Train to Somewhere, Images unattributed, public domain.

Page 74, "We need to talk", "Kipling watching television" by General Wesc is licensed with CC BY 2.0. To view a copy of this license, visit https://creativecommons.org/licenses/by/2.0/; "Sleeping Old Man at the Mall" by adamdachis is licensed with CC BY 2.0. To view a copy of this license, visit https://creativecommons.org/licenses/by/2.0/

Page 82, "Conversations", "Suddenly Sofa" by phooky is licensed with CC BY-SA 2.0. To view a copy of this license, visit https://creativecommons.org/licenses/by-sa/2.0/ with added elements

Page 91, "Grocery Central" derivative. Images unattributed, public domain.

Page 100, "The bonus", Images unattributed, public domain.

Page 101 ff, "A Mountain Trek" Mary Elizabeth Ames A Mountain Trek is an excerpt from the novel *Homo transformans: The Origin and Nature of the Species*. It has been adapted as a short story.

Page 115, "From the grave", see footnote. Fair Use.

Page 138, Julio Iglesias, *Vuelo Alto. Fair Use.* https://www.lyrics.com/lyric/25228774/Vuela+Amigo%2C+Vuela+Alto

Page 148, "We shall survive", "Two Friends, Bogor, Indonesia" by kentclark333 is licensed with CC BY-NC-ND 2.0. To view a copy of this license, visit https://creativecommons.org/licenses/by-nc-nd/2.0/

Page 151, "A mistake," Images unattributed, public domain.

# Notes on Illustrations

Page 158, "Acting out", James Cagney publicity photo https://commons.wikimedia.org/

Page 160, "Y POR ESO DICES", Images unattributed, public domain.

PAGE 163, "Valentine", Images unattributed, public domain.

Page 168, "Petrogylphs",Images unattributed, public domain.

Page 170, "Mrs. Creekmore's May Peas" Images unattributed, public domain.

Page 173, "A Prayer for less love",Images unattributed, public domain.

Page 174, Nonfiction, "High School Girls in Japan : 日本の女子高校生" by Dakiny is licensed with CC BY-NC-ND 2.0. To view a copy of this license, visit https://creativecommons.org/licenses/by-nc-nd/2.0/

Page 178, "Connected by strings," Images unattributed, public domain

Page 183, "Duty", provided by author

Page 186, "The upshot of courtship", provided by author

Page 193, "In Praise of Shame", provided by author

Page 202, "Hard Cider", provided by author

Page 213, "What does courage look like?"Images unattributed, public domain.

Page 228, "Life before Richvale", Images unattributed, public domain

Page 231, "Out in the cold", "Plow" by Stradablog is licensed with CC BY 2.0. To view a copy of this license, visit https://creativecommons.org/licenses/by/2.0/

Page 241, "The Cake", Images unattributed, public domain

Page 249, "Authors" Images unattributed, public domain

Made in the USA
Monee, IL
20 April 2021